N

W · · S

Hudson Bay

LABRADOR

NEWFOUNDLAND

ONTARIO

Lake Nipigon

ac des Mille Lacs

Prince Arthur's
Landing

Quebec

NEW
BRUNSWICK

P.E.I.

Halifax

NOVA SCOTIA

St. Lawrence River

Montreal

Toronto

New York

Atlantic Ocean

Chicago

# TRAVELLERS WEST

# TRAVELLERS WEST

*By*

Mary Quayle Innis

*Illustrated by*

Illingworth Kerr

Toronto
CLARKE, IRWIN & COMPANY LIMITED
1956

To H. A. I.

# A NOTE ABOUT BOOKS

In addition to the books mentioned in the text, a number of other personal and first-hand accounts fill in the outlines drawn by the travellers in the published accounts of their journeys. Aside from the full documentation of the fur trade and the general histories of western Canada, a few of these books may be referred to here.

Several cast light directly on the present narrative. Sandford Fleming's account of his journey with Grant by the Illecillewaet River in 1883 is airily entitled *England and Canada, a Summer Tour between Old and New Westminster*. He recalls that in their earlier journey in 1872 he and Grant crossed the plains from Fort Garry to the mountains in thirty-six days. Eleven years later they travelled by train from Winnipeg to Calgary in fifty-six hours.

The redoubtable John Macoun, botanist of Fleming's expedition, produced an omnibus of a book, *Manitoba and the Great North-West*, combining history, geography, travel, biography and practical advice to settlers. Paul

Kane's *Wanderings of an Artist* is, of course, a classic. James Hargrave's *Red River* contains a first-hand account of the colony, as well as of O'Byrne and other characters only slightly less colourful than that unlikely traveller.

*The Canadian Northwest, Its Early Development and Legislative Records*, compiled by E. H. Oliver sounds far less entertaining than it actually is. Small, bright pictures of the life of the whole region shine through its matter-of-fact lines.

Among secondary accounts, there is Lawrence Burpee's biography, *Sandford Fleming*. Margaret McNaughton, in *Overlanders*, tells the story of that intrepid company and George Bryce's *Mackenzie, Selkirk and Simpson* outlines the lives of three most influential travellers west.

It should be noted that throughout the text of the present narrative the spelling of words and of place-names is not always consistent, since the spelling of each author has been followed in quotations from his work.

# CONTENTS

# I. A MORE THAN PASSING INTEREST

# I

So UNIMPRESSIVE a term as "Northern Department" can never have covered so imposing an extent of territory. The Hudson Bay Company's Northern Department extended from Hudson Bay to the Rocky Mountains and from the United States boundary to the Arctic Ocean. This domain the Company held absolutely and administered at its discretion for almost fifty years from the time of its amalgamation with the North West Company in 1821, to 1869 when the area passed to the control of Canada.

Westward exploration, begun with the first landfall of John Cabot and Jacques Cartier, had been pressed forward with the optimism of ignorance. Enchanted with the facility of Indian canoemen, Champlain had written, "in the canoes of the savages one can go without restraint and quickly everywhere, in the small as well as large rivers. So that, by using canoes as the savages do, it would be possible to see all there is, good and bad, in a year or two." It had taken longer than a year or two to see what there was, good and bad, but the canoe, sure enough, had been in the main the medium of travel.

On his great journey westward Alexander Mackenzie had seen in 1792 "vast herds of elks and buffaloes", grazing with their young on the plains and uplands. Since he had reached the Pacific, in his lapidary phrase, "from Canada by land", the great west had become common ground to fur traders of both the North West and Hudson's Bay Companies. The traders had in some measure adapted the Indians of the region to contribute to the trade as fur hunters, middlemen, or provision gatherers. They had learned to live on the wandering buffalo herds, to travel with horses and with dogs as well as in canoes. The explorer-traders Simon Fraser and David Thompson had blazed new ways through the mountains and many had followed them over the portages, the foothills and the more southerly mountain passes.

In the 1850's, when the western prairies of what is now Canada were still in full possession of Indian, fur trader and buffalo, the prairies of the United States were threaded by trails leading westward and by westward-moving lines of prairie schooners. The white-topped wagons chained in a circle against Indian attack, which motion pictures have dulled to a cliché, had their reality, as had the down-streaming Indian bands and those other stock figures, the stage-coach and the pony express. By 1853 the railroad had reached Chicago and, on the Platte and the Missouri rivers, towns which provided emigrants with supplies were enjoying the prosperity which in another decade the railroad would destroy. Captain Butler, following a herd of buffalo on the banks of the Platte in 1867, saw a deserted town. It had been Kearney City,

4

he was told, "it had a good trade in the old wagon times, but it busted up when the railroad went on further west." It had only one man left and "he shoots everybody he sees."

Until the 1850's Canada had been occupied with her own rapid growth, with the taking up and cultivating of land, the trade in timber and flour. Nearly a million people had crowded into Canada West where towns doubled in population in a few years. Canals had been completed, railroads stretched from city to city—nearly two thousand miles of rails in a decade. Woollen mills took the place of the household loom and hides no longer went from the tannery to the itinerant cobbler but to the new boot and shoe factory. Iron ships began to push wooden ships from the chief lanes of commerce; indeed steamers now ran weekly, in the season, from Montreal to Liverpool.

The acreage of good land in Upper Canada had seemed boundless but already nearly all of it had been taken up and occupied. Little room remained in the east and the pioneer habit of moving on, moving west was strong. People began to wonder what there was farther west.

The west of Canada was never to know the prairie schooner and the old wagon times of the western United States. The west of British North America was without such wagon roads or trails as crossed the west of the United States but it was by no means a featureless waste. There were the vast drifting buffalo herds and the Indian bands that followed and preyed upon them. Voyageurs, here more often mounted than canoe-borne, passed singly or in expresses and brigades, and missionaries moved among the tribes and between the forts. It was commonplace to find a blaze on a tree with a message to say who had passed that way and on what date, perhaps that the river ahead was in flood or that here the previous traveller had made a raft and gone on by water. If there was no explicit message there would be an implicit one in the trampled camp site, the fresh-cut stumps. Whenever traders, missionaries or Indians met they had news to exchange of weather, game, the whereabouts of such-and-such a trader, the present status of peace or war among the tribes. All these routes rayed out from the Hudson's Bay Company forts so that by the tracks of snowshoes or horses' hoofs one could tell, long before it came in sight, that the fort was near. It was all a fur trade domain and the single settlement at Red River was a subsidiary of the fur trade.

The attention of Canadians turned now toward this great empty west. The Red River colony, people began to realize, with all its distresses, its floods and grasshoppers, had prospered. But its centre was St. Paul. Minnesota, with an amazingly large population, became a state in 1858 and in the same year the Hudson's Bay Company sent much of its traffic by the American route to Red River.

More important still there was gold beyond the mountains along the Columbia, the Fraser, in the Cariboo. Was this to fall into the hands of the west-reaching United

States which had already swallowed up the Oregon country?

It became clear that the west of British North America, if it was to be saved for the Empire, must be opened by Canadians over a Canadian route and in 1857 both Canadian and British governments were at last ready to move in a matter which suddenly began to appear urgent. The first need was for a map of the west and none could be found except David Thompson's map of 1813 which is still to be seen, its cracked brown surface rippled with marks of mountains, thrust across with the powerful drive of rivers, and neatly and soberly lettered.

The British government accordingly sent out the Palliser expedition which discovered the Kicking Horse Pass. West of the Qu'Appelle Lakes, the land, Palliser wrote, "I may say is unknown and the whole country in this latitude is untravelled by the white man."

The Canadian government sent out the Dawson-Hind expedition to explore a route from Lake Superior to the Selkirk Settlement and again in the next year to explore from Red River to the Assiniboine and Saskatchewan rivers. In view of the later value of the lands the expedition explored, Hind was more than temperate when he wrote, "the discovery of a Fertile Belt of Country extending from the Lake of the Woods to the Rocky Mountains, gives to this part of British America a more than passing interest."

## II

THE EARLY Victorian world was among many other things a world of travellers. Beside the merchant, the statesman, the bonneted and crinolined lady of that much-documented period the traveller, armed with gun and guide book, takes his place. His world was peaceful and prosperous and too much peace and prosperity could weary even the comfort-loving Victorians. What is more, the English cherished a tradition of travel. The Grand Tour of the eighteenth century, that necessary ingredient in the education of every young man of fashion, had become, at its height, almost an exodus. In 1785 it was said that 40,000 English were at one time living or travelling on the continent. The French Revolution and the wars of Napoleon had put an end to the Grand Tour but after the return of peace, travellers journeyed still farther than before. Travel became organized; Murray's first Handbook appeared in 1836 and in 1868 Thomas Cook conducted a party of people, including seven ladies, on a tour of Egypt and Palestine.

It was an age of exploration especially in Africa where

8

within a few years Livingstone descended the Zambesi and discovered Victoria Falls, Speke discovered the source of the Nile, Sir Richard Burton discovered Lake Tanganyika. Charles Darwin was coasting round South America in the *Beagle*, Alfred Russel Wallace collecting beetles along the Amazon. Layard had penetrated into Turkey and Persia, Burton had gone disguised on pilgrimage to Mecca. It was the age of the empire builders like Sir Stamford Raffles, the founder of Singapore, and Sir James Brooke, the rajah of Sarawak. Even women were not exempt from the attraction of far places and many of them travelled or lived abroad though few in positions of such authority as that of Lady Hester Stanhope at Mount Lebanon.

Most of these wrote books about their adventures, but no class of travellers either travelled or wrote books with greater energy than the hunters. Indeed among them William Oswell was a striking exception, for though he travelled with Livingstone, always hunted elephants on foot, and was twice tossed by a rhinoceros—the straight-horned rhinoceros since named Oswellii—he never wrote a book.

Charles Waterton collected birds and animals in Demerara and Brazil and not only wrote books on his travels and on natural history but once, while in Rome, climbed to the top of the lightning conductor on St. Peter's. Sir Samuel Baker, who discovered Albert Nyanza, travelled also in India, the Rocky Mountains and Japan in search of big game and published in 1853 his *The Rifle and the Hound in Ceylon*. The Scot, Gordon Cumming, found

9

too little sport in America and went to Africa, producing in 1850 his book, *Five Years of a Lion Hunter's Life in the Interior of South Africa*. The work was extremely popular and Cumming for the rest of his life lectured on his adventures and showed his lion skins.

Travel, then, and especially big game hunting were approved pursuits for a young man of wealth and leisure. But Africa and South America were not the only resorts for young hunters. There were those who preferred a temperate and healthy climate and an English-speaking community. Moreover, for very many the place held in the imagination at other times by the jungle, the Antarctic, by the islands of the South Seas, by the summits of the highest mountains, at present by the planets and the infinity of outer space, was in the early years of Good Queen Victoria's reign occupied by the western plains of North America. There, beyond walls and fences, under a sky unhemmed by chimney pots, in inconceivable freedom ran that fabulous creature the buffalo. Books by Fenimore Cooper, Washington Irving and others, and the writings and paintings of George Catlin, had spread over England the image of the Indian brave, his brown knees gripping the sides of his rearing pony, as, riding into the storming buffalo herd, in full career he aimed his bow and twanged the string. The lowering buffalo head with its powerful horns and great shaggy ruff—what a trophy to display at home! The tepee with its painted sun and symbols, the chief with his beaded moccasins and his towering crown of eagle feathers, all were part of a legend into which few young men could hope to enter but which many enjoyed in fantasy.

Those for whom the dream came true found many details very different from their expectations but many, too, were stranger, more remarkable, though a good deal less comfortable. Chiefly there was the wonder of realization. One young man wrote in awed delight, "I had read of these things; now I was among them."

For young Englishmen, the west was in the sixties an enchanted land. The western plains of the United States, traversed by emigrant bands, where buffalo herds were beginning to dwindle and iron rails were already being laid, had lost their tang of excitement. Eastern Canada was well enough for serious settlers; it had towns, railroads, mills, all the dusty appurtenances of civilization. But the western plains of British America, beginning to emerge from the long sequestration of the fur trade, bright with the fur trade legend and gilded, moreover, on their western margin with newly-found western gold were all but irresistible to young men too well off to emigrate and too adventurous to be ready, just yet, to settle down at home.

The young men the accounts of whose journeys make up this book were not explorers in the full sense though they broke among the mountains into tracts of undiscovered wildness. But neither were they simply sightseers for they followed close on the trail-marks of the men who first penetrated the mountain barrier and they were often in danger from privation, from Indians and from hazards of river and precipice. They were travellers in the exploring tradition of their time, eager to examine the places they had read of, and preparing, in turn, to write about them.

## II. GOOD SPORT IN A HEALTHY CLIMATE

# I

In 1859, James Carnegie, Earl of Southesk, was thirty-two years old, a good-tempered, serious-minded young man; "fine-looking, tall, a gentleman", Father Lacombe called him. His tastes were literary but he was active too, very fond of deer-stalking on his Scottish estate. His right knee, as though to remind him of past adventures, was still tender from a balloon accident some years earlier. He had been educated at Sandhurst and in 1849 he had succeeded to his father's baronetcy. Six years later he had obtained by an Act of Parliament the reversal of the attainder of his great-grandfather, the fifth Earl of Southesk, who had been implicated in the Jacobite rebellion of 1715, and had become sixth Earl of Southesk.

In the autumn of 1858 he was visiting the home of his friend Lord Panmure. Southesk had been ill, he felt restless, and to the other gentlemen he spoke of his wish "to travel in some part of the world where good sport could be met with among the larger animals, and where, at the same time, I might recruit my health by an active open-air life in a healthy climate." The vast territories of the Hudson's Bay Company were at once recommended. "The country is full of large game such as buffalo, bears and deer," said one of the gentlemen present who was influential in the affairs of that Company, and he offered to write to Sir George Simpson for advice and assistance. No time was lost; six months later Southesk's steamer entered New York harbour.

The year 1859 was the year, in the United States, of John Brown's execution and of Lincoln's presidential campaign. That year also, the *Great Eastern*, the great iron ship, visited New York. The captain of the ship on which Southesk travelled was that James Anderson who soon afterwards was made captain of the ill-omened *Great Eastern*, and who took part in the laying of the Atlantic cable.

The Earl of Southesk went at once to see Niagara Falls. Perhaps no natural phenomenon has been so doggedly visited ever since the day when its roar arrested Father Hennepin and his Indians. Southesk wrote that he was neither astonished nor disappointed for drawings and descriptions had led him to form a mental image not unlike the reality. On the whole he disliked it—"it is too huge"—and he was shocked by "the disgustingly obtrusive civilisation that crawls over its sides".

At Lachine he joined the party of Sir George Simpson and immediately realized his good fortune for no young man, whether an Earl or not, could have launched on his travels under more august and powerful patronage. For forty years a firm administrator of the great Company, Sir George had been generous in encouraging exploration of the lands which even the Company saw it could not hold forever. He had ruled the Company by his intimate knowledge of its smallest details and he had gained that knowledge by constant travel on inspection trips to even the farthest and most isolated posts. His short figure in the tall hat with a piper behind him dominated the canoe-load of voyageurs, and his canoe travelled so fast that he was said by a Company secretary to be "in league with the Prince of the Power of the air." At every post he was received with gun-fire and flutter of flags, with shouts and songs and the skirl of his attendant piper, and his departure, after a keen appraisal of every detail of post management, was sped with the same flourish for, with his vigour and acumen, he loved colour and pageantry.

In his later years from his home at Lachine his famous voyageurs paddled him swiftly up the Ottawa, across Georgian Bay, down Lake Superior to Fort William and by the Kaministiquia, Rainy Lake, Lake of the Woods and Red River to Fort Garry and on to Norway House to preside at meetings of the Council.

But, in 1859 Sir George was seventy-one, in bad health and nearly blind. It was not, however, for such reasons as these that this year he gave up his famous and exhilarating canoe journey. A new route had been opened which might bring supplies more cheaply to the Company stores at Fort Garry and Sir George had determined to try it.

At Toronto where the party stopped overnight Southesk met the artist Paul Kane. Thirteen years before, Kane, eager to see and paint the Indians of the great west,

17

had appealed to Sir George Simpson who held the key to all that region. Sir George had agreed that Kane might accompany him but his pressing business concerns and the alarming speed of his journeys had kept him constantly ahead of Paul Kane's earnest pursuit. Kane's book, *Wanderings of an Artist*, was then in the press in London, to be published later that summer.

Dr. Rae, the Hudson's Bay Company surgeon, who had made voyages of exploration and of search for the lost expedition of Sir John Franklin, also met Sir George's party in Toronto and later joined them for the journey to Fort Garry.

The railroad had just reached St. Paul and Sir George had decided to try that route to Fort Garry, but the way was new to him and he did not trust it. When the party reached St. Paul by train they found the river in flood, the green willows along its banks almost submerged, and rumour said that beyond Crow Wing, a hundred and thirty miles north, the country was inundated. Sir George expected men with carts and horses to come down from Fort Garry to meet him; if they could not get through, he was determined to take the old route by canoe through Lake Superior, the route he had travelled on so many previous journeys. Old and ill as he was, still he was not the man to wait patiently till rumour evaporated or hardened into fact. Summoning his surprised company, he set out at once in a covered wagon to see the flooded country for himself. "There was no help for it," wrote Southesk, who had as yet bought none of his supplies, "we were all bound to obey our leader, even if we thought his decisions doubtful or mistaken."

They did not have to go far. At St. Anthony they found the party who had come down from Fort Garry to meet them. Streams were high, they reported, but roads passable and no delay need be feared. The leader of this party, James McKay, in his blue cloth capote and red flannel shirt wore the first moccasins Southesk had ever seen. "It amused me to watch this grand and massive man pacing the hotel corridors with noiseless footfall, while excitable little Yankees in shiny boots creaked and stamped about like so many busy steam-engines."

In the midst of buying horses, a saddle, wagon and harness, Southesk paused to go with Sir George to see, "the Minnehaha Falls, which had become so celebrated through Longfellow's poem." Again, as at Niagara, he was disappointed. It was pretty, no more, and would be of little interest, he said, were it not for Hiawatha.

And so they were off, Sir George in a covered and curtained cart, the rest on horseback, the spare horses running alongside. This first day of the actual journey was a day of wonders for Southesk. He saw for the first time a portage made—saw it only, for he was travelling with Sir George and there were plenty of guides to do the work. He was "astonished at the strength and hardiness of our practised voyageurs," McKay especially, "up to his waist or chest in the clinging mud or the sluggish black water of the creek, now passing heavy packages across, now dragging reluctant animals through the mire", never flagging in energy or cheerfulness. Along the way frogs croaked, cranes uttered "their doleful, throat-gargling cry, a sound only surpassed in wretchedness by the shrieks of the

19

ungreased cart-wheels, which moaned and screamed like a discontented panther." Then at night supper was prepared, tents pitched, and in the same tent with Dr. Rae, Southesk wrapped himself in his blankets. Dr. Rae slept at once. "For my own part, this first night under canvas was far from agreeable to one so lately somewhat of an invalid. A keen frost struck upwards and downwards through the blankets, making sleep difficult and troops of Whip-poor-wills and other nightbirds shrieked with a maddening persistency that made it nearly impossible. After many hours some broken slumber came at last and, thanks to the pureness of the air, I rose up tolerably fresh and ready for action."

A position such as Sir George's made travelling expeditious but laid his party open also to some of the disadvantages that attend upon power. They had not gone far on that second day when, a long way off across the prairie, they saw a band of armed Indians watching them from a mound. One of these ran at once to the first riders and tried to stop them, "loudly clamouring for presents." An Indian clutched the guide's bridle rein but McKay grasped his hand and flung him out of the way.

"Go on," Sir George called, "go on," and they went on though another Indian seized the wheel of the cart in which Sir George was riding. The Indians let them go at last but fired a bullet over their heads and sent after them a volley of shouted insults. They must not stop or go back, Sir George ordered, for any injury they inflicted would be revenged on the next travellers. These

Indians were Ojibways; their tribe had robbed a trader near that place about 1770 and had ever since been called the Pillagers, and the stream where the crime was committed, Pillage Creek.

The prairie seemed determined to present Southesk, at the beginning of his adventure, with as much excitement as possible. An hour or two after the attack of the Pillagers, he happened to light his meerschaum and throw away the match. "In an instant the prairie was in a blaze. The wind speedily bore the flames away from us, and ere long the conflagration raged far and wide. I never heard to what extent it spread, but for hours afterwards we could see its lurid glow illuminating the darkness of the distant horizon."

Coming to a higher level, they saw before them an immense plain on which the windings of the Red River and smaller streams were indicated by the narrow tracery of trees along their margins. It was so hot they could scarcely breathe; thunder rolled, lightning flashed now here, now there. And all at once on the south-west horizon they saw "a waterspout of gigantic size and singular appearance. Its thin and lofty stem was surmounted by a far-spreading cloud of inky blackness; at the base of the column torrents dashed upon the earth, rebounding in fountain-like masses of silvery spray." This spectacle, "grand and uncommon", after a quarter of an hour began to dissolve away.

They crossed a river on their horses and saw the indefatigable McKay made a scow by lashing two cart-wheels together and covering them with oilskin to carry over the luggage. McKay killed a bear, a thin and poor creature, which yielded very tough steaks for their supper. During a hard, uninterrupted ride of twenty-six miles they were surprised to meet, in contrast to their large and well-mounted party, a white man walking toward them alone. He was a Yankee pedlar—no one else would brave alone the dangers of hunger, bears and hostile Indians— with no weapon but a pocket-knife and no luggage but a small food-bag on his back. He had sold his entire stock at Fort Garry and having walked by himself the hundreds of miles from St. Paul, he was walking back, apparently unconcerned, and would wait at the rivers for a party which might help him to cross.

At Pembina, close to the international boundary at the Company post, Sir George ordered a calf to be killed for their dinner and the unique local fish, goldeyes, served. Two days later, on June 1, they reached Fort Garry.

Here the party separated so that Sir George could push on to Norway House to preside at the annual meeting of the Company's chief factors. He gave Southesk, before they parted, much advice and also the services of Toma, one of his best canoemen. Outfitting was made easy for Southesk and his social life at Fort Garry all but overpowering, not only because he was an Earl, for titled travellers were not uncommon there, but because he had arrived as Sir George's companion. He did not see the great man again. This was Sir George's last visit to Fort Garry. The next summer, though he had had a stroke of apoplexy, Sir George appeared at the entertainment for the Prince of Wales at Montreal and directed the display of canoe paddling and the singing of voyageur songs which had so often enlivened his own all-but-royal progress through the wilderness. A few weeks later he was dead.

The two Fort Garrys were a straggling and complex community, so straggling and complex as hardly to constitute a community at all except as they were united in the service of the Hudson's Bay Company. The original fort built after the union of the two fur companies and partially destroyed by floods was rebuilt with a strong stone wall and bastions at the four corners. This was called Upper Fort Garry after Lower Fort Garry was built about twenty miles below it. Lower Fort Garry, called the Stone Fort, had massive stone walls and bastions and was the strongest Hudson Bay fort after Fort Prince of Wales. Between the two, on a well-beaten road, carts and, later, American buggies plied back and forth, for the Hudson's Bay Company carried on operations in both places.

From the upper fort with its busy fur warehouses and offices, with houses clustered along the river and an outlying fringe of Indian lodges, one drove to Lower Fort Garry through a cross-section of the settlement. The French portion of the population was largely migratory, whole families joining in the spring and fall buffalo hunts, the men driving Company carts and propelling Company boats. English and Scottish half-breeds were more likely to be farmers and to live in the well-cultivated and relatively settled region between the two forts. Some Indians lived at St. Peter, farming a little, boating, hunting and fishing.

Frog Plain, a Scottish settlement, came first, then St. Paul with an Anglican church and school, then St. Andrew's church with its settlement. Houses hugged the river; there were not many along the road. At Lower Fort Garry was the large Company farm and its boat-freighting centre.

Until very recent years Fort Garry had had postal service twice a year, one packet by way of York Factory in summer and one overland from Canada in winter. There was at the time of Southesk's visit a monthly service. The population of about 10,000 was principally half-breeds. Minutes of the Council of Assiniboia were arranged under such headings as Horse Taking, Hay, Fires, Animals at Large, Intoxicating of Indians. The Council was concerned with the building of faggot roads and bridges, probably related to the corduroy roads and bridges in the more heavily forested backwoods of Canada West, with the enclosure of pigs, and with the need to improve the steam mill now out of commission "on account of the dilapidated state of the boiler, caused by the incompetency of the first engineers."

The punishment of crime, in the settlement, was tempered by due regard to the circumstances. A prisoner in the jail at Fort Garry had served three months of a ten-month term for manslaughter. He appealed because his wife and large family of children were destitute and because the crime had been committed in "the heat of fury and passion which he would have given worlds a moment after to recall." In view of these circumstances his sentence was shortened to six months in all.

In the settlement at the edge of the great prairie the Earl of Southesk found himself involved in a round of visits. The Protestant bishop and the Roman bishop called upon him and he returned their calls. He saw the Catholic nunnery where the nuns wore long fawn-coloured gowns with over-skirts of dark blue, black poke bonnets and moccasins. The bishops themselves, he noted, wore moccasins. The pupils of the convent sang for him and two dark young girls played on a pianoforte which it "surprised me to see in this remote and inaccessible land." He and Dr. Rae walked one day to St. James to call upon the rector there. In the parsonage he saw hanging on the wall a framed picture of Queen Victoria from the *Illustrated London News*. This was an object of pilgrimage to the Indians; "one old chief especially, a recent visitor there, had insisted on being allowed to kiss her Majesty's portrait in token of his loving homage."

On June 10 a great event occurred in Fort Garry, one of the great events in the history of Canada. On that day the first steamer ever to navigate the Red River arrived at Fort Garry. The winter before, Anson Northrup, a resourceful Minnesotan, had brought a boat up the Crow Wing River and taken it to pieces. He had packed its timbers, its cabin and engine on sleighs which horses and oxen had dragged to the mouth of the Cheyenne River, a tributary of the Red. There his money gave out but the St. Paul Chamber of Commerce advanced funds with which he put the boat together again and launched it on May 19. The first voyage of the *Anson Northrup* was not easy. The boat had to be tied up along the shore at night, and the crew cut timber for firewood all the way down to Fort Garry. The *Anson Northrup* was a shabby little stern-wheeler showing, probably, the operations it had undergone, but every member of the community turned out to look at it, including the Indians who crowded the shore to watch the first steamer they had ever seen.

Its coming had many meanings obvious to the watchers, among them the opening of a market for their produce, and access for new settlers. It would destroy the buffalo herds, it would push back the Indian and the fur trader, it would transfer, within a very few years, the fur trade traffic from York Factory, which had been for two hundred years the port of entry to Rupert's Land, to Fort Garry where the York boats would be supplanted by American trains, steamers and Red River carts. It would draw the attention of Canada to the west. Further still within the future it would become an important factor in dictating the route of the first transcontinental railway by strengthening bonds with the United States which later Canadian policy would be at pains to weaken. The clank of its paddle-wheel heralded the end of the old west, the beginning of the new.

# II

ON JUNE 15 Southesk was at last ready to launch out from Fort Garry on his own expedition. He had John McKay, a brother of the redoubtable James, for his head guide and five or six other men including Duncan, one of his gamekeepers whom he had brought with him from his estate in Scotland. His was a lavishly equipped and provisioned party. They had a four-wheeled wagon, three carts, and two large tents. They had an almost unheard of luxury, a portable table, tools and utensils of all kinds and presents for the Indians. The usual supplies of flour, tea, tobacco and dried meat had been provided in large quantities and such delicacies as sugar, jam, biscuits, even eggs as well. No wine or spirits were taken, an omission which the leader felt, and rightly, would save a great deal of trouble.

There were fifteen horses called, most of them, for their colours or markings, by names such as Gris, Mouldy, Spot, Bleu, Great Black; and an elaborate armament of rifles and shot-guns. In the late afternoon they set out; Southesk had already learned the importance of getting away from a fort by evening "to shake off that spirit of lingering which impedes the traveller when within the sphere of settlements."

The region was swarming with hunters, with carts and horses and whole families, making ready to start on the Great Spring Buffalo Hunt. For days as they travelled, Southesk and his party could not escape from the sound and sight of the Great Hunt, bound as they were themselves, toward Fort Ellice. Everywhere they saw trees barked or slashed or trimmed bare of branches to the very topmost boughs to make a lobstick in honour of some hunter.

The hunt on the march was a wonderfully colourful sight. "Their long moving columns sparkled with life and gaiety. Cart-tilts of every hue flashed brightly in the sun, hosts of wild wolfish dogs ran in and out among the vehicles, troops of loose horses pranced and galloped alongside. The smartly-dressed men were riding their showiest steeds, their wives and daughters were travelling in the carts, enthroned on high heaps of baggage." Southesk admired the hunters in their brass-buttoned blue capotes and moleskin trousers, their brightly embroidered and beaded saddle cloths and belts. He was disappointed in the appearance of the women, with their straight-hanging hair and "blue and white cotton gowns, shapeless, stayless, uncrinolined," which "displayed the flatness of their unprojecting figures."

Thirteen years before, Paul Kane had accompanied the Spring Hunt, and his book, which Southesk read later with intense interest, described the carts full of women and children, each cart with a flag or other emblem on a pole above it so that the hunter could recognize it from a distance. He went on to tell how the hunter, galloping recklessly into the storming herd, would, when his buffalo fell, throw upon its body some article of his clothing. This was intended to establish ownership later on and a hunter who killed many animals might soon have stripped himself completely naked. Next morning the carts were brought up and the women fell to work to dismember perhaps five hundred buffalo and cut their flesh into slices to be dried on racks in the sun and wind. All night the camp was kept awake by the howling and fighting of the dogs and wolves which had followed the hunt.

Southesk, like every other traveller, recorded the constant torture from insects with bitter eloquence. "The venomous, eye-blinding, hard-skinned little sand-flies," the "bulldog" which gives "one short bite with his scissory clippers,—then off like a flash, leaving a poisoned and bleeding wound." Mosquitoes, of course, were unresting and everywhere. Other travellers seem not to have resorted to the device used by Paul Kane in the woods near Lake Winnipeg. "I found it indispensably necessary to wear a veil all the way, as protection from the mosquitoes which I have never before seen so numerous."

"Mosquitoes on the wet ground," Southesk wrote, "sand-flies on the dry, bulldogs in the sunshine, bugs in the oakwoods, ants everywhere—it is maddening."

Rumours floated as freely on the prairies as in any town, indeed far more freely for there was no other means of gaining news of the country beyond, the tribes beyond,

29

what streams were in flood, which trader had travelled in which direction and most important of all, what war parties were on foot. For there were always, at least in rumour, war parties afoot and word blew before and after them like the smoke of their fires, the dust of their horses' hoofs.

Rumours such as these had been exploited from the beginning of exploration for the purposes of those who carried them. Indians had told Jacques Cartier as Indians had told La Vérendrye and other explorers that there were bad Indians farther on who would kill and eat them. Go no farther. If you do you will never come back alive. Sometimes such warnings were authentic; more often they were a ruse to get the trade goods or the trader's good will. Farther west, farther west, right across the continent from sea to sea, there were always dangerous Indians farther west.

So the rumour reached Southesk and his party that Crees and Blackfeet were on the point of going to war. There had been an unusual peace between them for four years which made the tidings all the more credible. This would bar the travellers from the route to the elbow of the Saskatchewan which they intended to follow. But they decided, wisely, to get further news at Fort Ellice before making a change of plan.

About this time Southesk began to write every evening in his journal. At first during the excitement of the early buffalo hunts and during frequent visits to Hudson's Bay Company forts, he wrote only the bare events of the day. Later, in the gloom of mountain valleys and on

the long cold return journey, he wrote a great deal—
descriptions of scenery, animals and birds, weather,
accounts of his guides and his hunting, stories heard by
the camp-fire and, conspicuously, analyses of books he
was reading. Years later he prepared his book, *Saskatchewan and the Rocky Mountains*, by elaborating these journal notes and interlarding them with later information.
But the journal entries are distinguished in the book
from later additions, and quotations here are from this
running record written, as he says, evening by evening over
the camp-fire.

At Fort Ellice the trader feasted the party on fresh
buffalo tongues—"excellent, as juicy and tender as possible"—brought from the Great Hunt which was still
going on. With the tongues came cart-loads of fresh
buffalo robes and four small buffalo calves, to be tamed
and herded among the cows belonging to the fort.

From the trader at Fort Ellice, Southesk bought two
more carts and hired extra horses while his guide went
to the oak grove to cut spare axle-trees. In the long
evening the Earl set up a target and practiced shooting,
to be beaten in some of his shots by McKay. McKay,
valuable as he was, at this point lost his position as chief
guide, for he knew nothing of the country along the
Qu'Appelle River which it was now proposed to follow.
Several acceptable guides refused Southesk's offers for fear
of the often-rumoured Blackfoot war parties, but at last
a half-breed named Pierre Nummé was chosen, an elderly
man in leather trousers as stiff as wood, and a pair of
goggles made of wire and glass to protect his eyes. He

31

demanded an enormous wage but at once began to prove himself a useful fellow. When the Earl shot a prong-horned antelope, "Pierre cut her up like a juggler doing a conjuring trick. One moment, an antelope stretched along the turf—the next, Pierre in his saddle enshrined amidst nicely-cut joints and limbs and strips of flesh, hung round him in the tidiest fashion; no London butcher's shop more severely trim."

While they were camped a mile from Fort Qu'Appelle to be out of reach of Indian visitors, Southesk discovered that there was no such thing as being out of reach of Indian visitors while one was anywhere in the vicinity of a fort. Indians thronged into his camp, twenty-four of them, Ojibways and Crees. They were particularly attentive because the store at the fort had run out of tobacco some weeks before and Southesk at once gave some to each man and a double quantity to the two chiefs who had accompanied them, whom he called Spots and Pointed Cap. Pointed Cap stepped forward to express thanks on behalf of the rest and offered a dressed buffalo skin to the Earl. His speech of thanks closed with a request for more tobacco and McKay, who as interpreter acted as a kind of public relations officer, told him that the Earl was not a trader and handed back the skin. The Indians stayed very late, Southesk wrote; it was his first experience of Indian visiting. The women sat a short distance away with their babies, in "little painted cradles," and "watched with unwearying interest." When at last they went to their camp not far off they began a dance which with its monotonous drumming continued most of the night.

Next day Southesk paid his ceremonial return visit to the camp. He had learned in the meantime that his guests were ashamed of the action of Pointed Cap in taking back the buffalo robe, not so much for his discourtesy as in fear that the Earl would not make his promised visit with its accompanying gifts. His only retaliation was to go first to the tent of Spots where he found a number of women and children, none of them pretty, he noted. In a corner a young man sat busily uniting two disparate cultures by fixing triangular arrow heads of sheet iron onto wooden shafts.

Spots invited his guest to sit beside him on the buffalo robe and made a long speech with "rather suggestive acknowledgments of my former liberality and reproaches against the other head-man for his shabby and unseemly conduct." Southesk replied briefly and McKay gave powder and ball to the men and some tobacco to the women. They then went to the tent of Pointed Cap who far from repenting his incivility, plainly "exhibited his discontent with my present of ammunition, though the supply was the same as that which had been so well received in the other tent."

Thickly scattered buffalo skulls across the plain marked former hunts and nearly always there was a wolf somewhere in sight. The prairie, covered with hills and bluffs and little lakes, was lovely with flowers, small tiger lilies, wild roses, wild strawberry blossoms, bluebells like "a vast oriental carpet thrown upon the plain." These flowers were the special fancy of Bichon, the Earl's favourite buffalo runner. The only one of the horses to prefer flowers, Bichon would wander off on purpose to eat a

33

tuft of bluebells or lilies. He was a good buffalo pony but too gregarious. If he found himself even a little way from the other horses he would neigh loudly and continue to neigh till he could join them again. Means were taken—the journal does not say what means—to break him of this habit which often frightened off game the hunters were trying to stalk. "At length he has learnt that this is a forbidden practice, so he takes great pains to check himself, and at any moment of forgetfulness or strong tension, changes his incipient neigh into the funniest little muffled squeaks, ending in a sort of low appealing sigh."

They crossed the South Saskatchewan just below the elbow, that landmark which had been seen by very few white men because the area was a danger zone between Cree and Blackfoot country. The march went on. At evening sometimes beside the fire the men told stories of Indian magic—how an Indian conjuror bound from head to foot with cords and straps and left for a few minutes in his tiny medicine tent would throw out the fastenings, every knot still tied, and walk out free himself; how the swiftest runner at Edmonton had had his legs rubbed by an enemy with some magic stuff while he slept and had never been able to run again.

In the main Southesk kept to his own tent. "Having no companions," as he said, he turned to his two favourite resources. One was watching the animals about him, especially the horses—Wawpooss the Rabbit, "who looks such a weak, poor wretch and is really one of the fastest and most enduring of buffalo runners", and Bichon who ate flowers. Then when the wind fell and the sun

34

floated gorgeous in orange and gold against pale grey clouds, he read *Troilus and Cressida*—"ah! with what different scenes did my memory come to link the most noble passages of that drama."

On another day when steady rain began in the afternoon, he read *Two Gentlemen of Verona* for a time and then tried to assess the values of his journey which, indeed, had scarcely well begun. "This open-air life suits me well, though, when one considers it bit by bit, it does not seem so charming. Long wearisome riding, indifferent monotonous eating, no sport to speak of, hard bed upon the ground, hot sun, wet, no companion of my own class; nevertheless I am happier than I have been for years."

His complaint that there was "no sport to speak of," was promptly remedied. "This morning," he wrote on July 16, "brought us the good news that a vast herd of buffalo was close at hand."

The buffalo herd covered the whole face of the prairie and the sound of its trampling advance reminded him of the booming of the ocean. He and McKay mounted and dashed forward; the herd quickened but kept in close order. Then as the horses came nearer, the buffalo separated and the Earl and McKay galloped furiously close together to cut out a small herd of cows. These ran fast, faster than the bulls; riding their hardest the men could not overtake them. McKay's horse fell back, Southesk's yellow horse Bichon would soon tire. "I sailed away after the cows—the heat intense, the dust perfectly blinding." Bichon began to flag, it was now or never. "I stood in the stirrups and leant over his head, held my gun forward at arm's length, took the level of the cows, and fired into the heaving mass where the best ones seemed to be. To my joy one of them instantly stopped; the others rushed madly on their course but she crawled slowly along."

Southesk gave her a finishing shot and halted for a moment. He had come out with two objects; a young man who always had objects and knew with precision what they were, he had wanted to kill a cow for food and that he had done. Also he had wanted "a large and perfectly unblemished head to carry home as a trophy."

"All this time bands of buffalo were streaming past me; the plains were alive as far as the eye could reach." Suddenly he saw gallop past him the very thing he looked for, a fine bull, "with very long perfect horns and most luxuriant mane and beard." Instantly he remounted and galloped after his trophy. The bull gave him a hard race. "It was interesting," he wrote that evening, "to ride in the midst of that vast black mass of buffaloes, for, as I went on, the scattered bands seemed more and more to unite, and I sometimes found myself moving in a sort of tri-angled enclosure with living walls around me, as the nearer animals strove to edge away on either hand, while the ranks were closed in front, and ever-increasing numbers came thundering in the rear. As long as Bichon kept his footing there was little risk."

Suddenly, as though he realized that he was the marked animal and could no longer hide himself among the herd, the bull rushed off at an angle and seemed to run even faster. Then he checked, whirled, lowered his head and charged. Southesk cantered aside, the bull galloped on. A mile or two farther on, he stopped and charged again. With only a few yards between them, Southesk fired and to the heart. His prize fell. "I got off the panting pony and took a long look at my bull . . . then remounting, I began to make my way slowly homewards, thirsty in the extreme after all the heat and dust of the gallop." One of the guides had laid his saddle on the body of the cow Southesk had killed to keep the wolves away till they could come back for the meat. They had a long search later to find the bull, for the chase had gone farther than seemed possible. Southesk was surprised at the weight of the head as they lifted it into the cart, McKay marvelled at the perfection of the horns. Perfect ones with sharp and un-nicked points are very rarely seen. The wallows in which the buffalo liked to roll in hot weather were made by digging up the earth with their horns which were thus worn down or broken against stones. The guide congratulated Southesk on killing at his first attempt a cow and a very fine bull but the young man was not satisfied.

"I find myself awkward," he wrote, "in managing a gun on a galloping horse. I do not succeed well in urging my horse close to a buffalo, and shooting it at the gallop." Later he added, "No one, till he tries it, can fancy how hard it is to shoot a galloping buffalo from a galloping horse."

So persistent had been the talk of Blackfoot war parties that when suddenly upon the camp at dinner time broke the noise of invasion, the word "Blackfeet!" sent every hand toward its gun. "In an instant without the slightest warning, a storm of noise burst upon us— bells jingled, whips cracked—the tramp of galloping horses resounded close at hand." No gun was within reach. It was Sunday and rifles had been laid aside. "In a semicircle which completely hemmed us in, a number of armed and mostly naked warriors were rushing down the slope, urging their horses to furious speed with whip and heel." When they were only a few feet away, the invaders suddenly checked, stared and then trotted up with friendly smiles.

They were Crees from Fort Carlton who had noticed some grazing horses and supposed the camp to be that of the expected Blackfeet. "They planned to surprise us—and so indeed they did." Every man's mouth was full of bullets for rapid loading, every move had been planned. Some were to attack the tents, some to drive off the horses. When the excitement died down a little, the Crees gave their news. There was little food at either Fort Pitt or Fort Edmonton, for the Blackfeet, in view of their impending war with the Crees, had brought in no meat. These posts would therefore have none of the stores of pemmican on which Southesk had been counting to support his journey into the mountains. At once he decided to hunt buffalo on the plain and employ women of the Cree party to dry meat for him.

At a place called Cherry Bush, accordingly, the guides went buffalo hunting but Southesk himself was drawn to a hill, called Bad Hill, known to be the haunt of grizzly bears. The men told how an Indian had been killed there only last year by a single slap of a grizzly's paw. To kill a grizzly bear was the highest ambition of nearly every traveller through the west, stories of the size and ferocity of the breed losing no emphasis in repetition. Now, early in the morning, Southesk and Pierre approached Bad Hill and saw almost at once a large grizzly and her cub. The men galloped forward to cut them off from the dense thicket before which they stood but the bears retreated and disappeared. The men dismounted to cross the stream that ran at the foot of the slope and were starting up the opposite side when Pierre cried, "Shoot!" The bear sat on its haunches in plain view about a hundred and fifty yards off. Before either could fire the grizzly again disappeared.

As they watched, a buffalo bull ran close to the thicket and Pierre was sure he saw the bear strike at it. The bear appeared, reared on its hind legs, swaying slowly and staring at the two men as it sniffed the wind. The first shot missed, the second struck. The bear almost fell, recovered and blundered into the bushes. Just then Pierre who was a little way off thought he saw a bear run past him and fired twice at it. "We were now on a steep bank, with thick underwood beneath us, and could see the bushes moving to and fro as the wounded bear writhed and raged in his pain; we could also hear its heavy panting, but the beast itself was quite concealed. Presently we heard it splashing in the water just below; then it lay still, and neither shots nor stones could move it."

39

A long anxious vigil followed outside the thicket. Pierre felt sure that the bear was crouching inside ready to clutch with those fearful claws anyone who came within reach. It was a female with a cub, he reminded his master, therefore doubly savage, and Southesk prudently agreed that to try to push a way into the thicket would be madness.

During the rest of the day they killed buffalo and early next morning they went to look for the wounded bear. The other guides were stationed around the thicket to prevent its escape, and Southesk and Pierre began to crawl on hands and knees into the dense brush, their guns at full cock. They found a narrow path which led to "a small pool of water overarched with thick brushwood, and beside it we saw the grizzly bear lying dead on its back, with its legs outstretched." Pierre cried out. It was a male, about three years old. "The tracks of a cub were stamped in the mud all round," Southesk wrote, "most singularly like a child's footmarks. This brought such thoughts to my mind that I felt almost glad the little bear and its mother had escaped. She had probably slipped away in the bush, while the male, already there, showed himself and got shot."

The Earl carried home to Scotland the skin and the skull along with the buffalo head, a beautiful antelope head and others which he collected later. The grizzly skin was not, he recorded rather wistfully, of the largest size, being only about six feet long. At Fort Carlton, a few days later, he saw a grizzly bear skin "immense, larger than I could have thought possible," which Captain

Palliser the year before had bought from an Indian.

The buffalo hunting continued good, in fact so good that they soon had enough. They might have killed hundreds but confined themselves to killing for food and for a good specimen. The horses were fagged, for "buffalo-running under a July sun comes hard upon grass-fed animals already wearied by a long and toilsome journey." Southesk noticed with interest how the men made a set of harness by carving it out on the skin of the dead buffalo and then lifting it in a single piece, quickly dried and toughened by the sun. They made long rawhide lines in the same way by carving a spiral on the hide and then straightening the line by tying it between two pegs to dry.

The women on the margin of the field of action were constantly busy. One of them prepared the grizzly skin for packing, the others dressed buffalo skins and heads, dried meat, made clothing. Southesk, in providing presents expressly intended to please them, had chosen large oval beads which, he had been assured, were very popular with Indian women. But those had been their choice a year or two before. Now the fashion had changed. The women were eager for tiny white beads which he had regarded as trash and with these they felt themselves well rewarded.

Five or six weeks from Fort Garry they came to Fort Carlton. At Carlton, stores and houses crowded inside a high palisade with bastions at its corners, and buffalo-skin Indian lodges scattered outside. This like the other forts was a transfer depot where both guides and horses were changed. Pierre, handsomely paid off, at once bought a horse from a Cree who had stolen it and who knew that the owner was in close pursuit. In these circumstances he sold it very cheap and Pierre mounted and rode off at once.

The party's horses, thin and tired, were turned out to graze and Southesk went with Mr. Hardisty, the factor, to the horse-guard to choose horses for the next leg of the journey. The rich and beautiful country through which they rode, with its lakes and poplar groves, looked to him almost like an English park. From the seventy horses grazing in the guard he chose a number for riding and drawing wagon and carts, and in the tidily arranged store where blankets and pots and pans were stowed beside furs and skins he bought beads and other presents while Mr. Hardisty took his animal heads and skins for safe keeping. Women at the fort were busy making moccasins for the Earl and his guides and when he took a morning walk Southesk saw Indian women washing clothes at the river's edge.

Mr. Hardisty, the factor at Carlton, was to become an increasingly important figure in the Company. He was one of six brothers, all in the employ of the Company and all sons of a Company factor and brothers-in-law of Donald A. Smith who was to become Lord Strathcona. Chief Factor Richard Hardisty of the Labrador district had been succeeded by Donald Smith who had married his daughter Isabella Hardisty in 1853, and his sons and his son-in-law had spread over the Company's great domain in its service.

The Southesk party got quickly under way again; Fort Edmonton was its immediate goal, the fitting-out place

for the dreamed-of Rocky Mountains. The short journey
to Fort Pitt had no greater event than the breaking of a
cart axle. While it was being repaired, Southesk sat on a
sunny slope covered with wild strawberries and finished
*The Winter's Tale*. At Fort Pitt they stayed only one
night. Pitt "enclosed by high palisades with bastioned
corners, forms a square rather more than half the size of
Carlton"; it stood on the south bank of the North Saskatchewan near the site of the present town of Lloydminster.
It was the buffalo fort of the Saskatchewan district, where
in most years herds came close enough for convenient
hunting and it was, as well, a famous horse-breeding post.
Both buffalo and horses thrived on the excellent grass of
the region and horse-trading was always done there.

From Fort Pitt Southesk's party pressed on into more
wooded country with swampy land lying between the
hills. The mosquitoes were here even worse than before
and particularly painful to the horses. The guides made
them a smoke fire every night by covering burning logs
with turf and the frantic horses, struggling for places in
the smoke, often pushed one another into the hot embers.
Cendré went lame from stepping with one hind foot into
the fire. While the men ate dinner one evening they
laughed loudly to see a young horse, called Rowland after
his former owner, come jumping along with his forefeet together as though they were still in hobbles, though
he was perfectly free.

Here Southesk ate prairie chicken for the first time
and thought it delicious. The evening before they reached
Fort Edmonton, he "sat up late reading *Much Ado About
Nothing*. The wolves howled, the night was very cold."

## III

FORT EDMONTON, the largest post in the west after Fort Garry, had at this time a population of about one hundred and fifty and the only farm in the Saskatchewan region. Its buildings sheltered behind a strong wooden palisade with bastions; in addition to Company officers and clerks there were interpreters, boat builders, blacksmiths, carpenters and hunters. To Fort Edmonton came thirteen different Indian peoples speaking eight languages, many of the tribes implacable enemies, and the Hudson's Bay Company needed all its tact and experience to keep, as it usually succeeded in doing, a working peace among them. The fort, first built in 1795, stood on the bluff above the river, the ground sloping sharply from its walls to level land at the water's edge where wheat was being cut on the Company's thirty-acre farm.

In its long history the fort had been the scene of many struggles, many ceremonies. In the course of his famous journey around the world in 1841 Sir George Simpson had been met at Fort Edmonton by nine Indian chiefs in full regalia, including scalp locks, who, along with their good wishes, had implored Sir George "to grant that their horses might always be swift, that the buffalo might instantly abound, and that their wives might live long and look young."

When a chief arrived to carry on business he was met at the gate by the officer in charge and as the two men shook hands a flag rose to the top of the pole in the palisaded square and the cannon boomed. However, as there was only one flag and one cannon, and chiefs often arrived in groups, a pause then ensued while the flag was lowered and the cannon reloaded. The Company had in stock some military coats said to be of the time of Henry VIII, each of which cost a good horse. A chief's ambition was to possess such a coat with a long embroidered vest, red trousers with gold stripes down the sides and a high beaver hat with a foxtail waving in front. Even when a chief managed to acquire the entire costume he rarely put it on but preferred to wear the beaver hat along with his breech clout and moccasins.

One feature dominated the approach to Edmonton and many travellers might have written as did John McDougall the Methodist missionary after "a long, dead hard run," behind his dog-team. "I looked up westward and saw in the waning light the wings or fans of the old windmill which stood on the hill back of Fort Edmonton."

Southesk's first impression was of multitudes of dogs, for Edmonton was well known to harbour more dogs than any other post. One night, in his bed at the fort, he was wakened by the fighting and howling of several dozen

45

dogs in the passage outside his room. Someone had left a door open and it was only by energetically whipping them down the stairs and out into the grounds that he could get a remnant of sleep. There were more dogs than he had ever seen before, dogs of every colour, brown, blue-grey, red, yellow, white with black spots, black with white paws like Russian setters, light gray with black spots like the dogs common in Blackfoot camps. Many were almost pure wolf, so vicious that they had to be stunned by a blow on the nose before they could be harnessed.

He had much to do in the matter of buying and exchanging horses; pack-saddles had to be made to replace the carts which had squealed their way across the open plain, a guide secured who knew the Blackfoot language and a hunter who knew the mountains.

In intervals of looking at horses, arguing the proper treatment of polygamy among the Indians, and listening to the usual terrifying stories of Blackfoot savagery, Southesk read the account of Lewis and Clarke's travels and the Journal of Daniel Harmon, who had journeyed over this same region fifty years before. For hours he talked with Mr. Woolsey, the Wesleyan missionary, who showed him the characters which had been invented to reduce the Cree language to writing and gave him a Cree hymn-book.

This reduction of the Cree language to writing was a remarkable accomplishment, the work of a remarkable man. James Evans, born in England in 1801, had come to Upper Canada at the age of twenty-two to teach an

Indian school at Rice Lake. Later he was ordained as a Methodist minister and sent to work among Indians on the St. Clair River and then on Lake Superior. In 1840 he went to Norway House as general superintendent of Northwest Indian Missions. He was struck by the need for a written form of the language so that religion might be presented to the Crees and so that members of that far-flung nation might communicate with one another. In his six years of labour at Norway House, he invented the syllabic form of writing, which made possible the Cree hymn-book and later text-books, and opened the possibility of education to the Crees. These syllabic books represented the first printing done in the North-West and James Evans' syllabic characters are still, more than a hundred years later, the form of writing used by the Crees.

As these lines are written, the name of James Evans has reappeared in the newspapers. He returned to his home in Lincolnshire in 1846 and died soon after. His grave there was disturbed this year, to make way for that typically modern enterprise, a housing project. According to the newspaper account, the Indians at Norway House requested that his ashes be sent to the post where his great work had been done. The Rev. James Evans was therefore buried at last at Norway House, 280 miles north of Winnipeg, in 1955.

One of his successors, the Reverend Thomas Woolsey, was well known to everyone who visited Fort Edmonton between 1855 and 1864. He was one of those genial misfits irresistibly drawn to a frontier. He had come straight

47

from London to the wilderness, an elderly man, "handicapped by physical infirmities, "as John McDougall wrote without indicating their nature. He had no sense of location whatever and was frequently lost. A party with which he travelled had to go very slowly and to answer cheerfully his frequent plaint, "we are lost, we may never find our friends again." He could never urge his horse forward and often lost his stirrups and his balance. As a dog-driver he was even more incompetent for he never got out of his cariole but lay comfortably wrapped up and often sound asleep while the dogs strayed or loitered and he was often wakened by the cariole rolling over and over to the foot of a slope. He was careless, impractical and helpless in many matters in which frontier life demanded vigour and skill.

Yet Mr. Woolsey was by no means a ludicrous or ineffective person. He was a good nurse and practical physician, patient and tireless in caring for the sick or injured. Year after year he travelled over the plains and through the forest to preach to the Indians. He had learned Cree, as Southesk found, and taught many young Indians to read the syllabic characters. He had great sweetness and goodness, and not a little courage. John McDougall who lived with him for a year tells two little stories which offset the many accounts of his incompetence in riding and dog-driving. When Mr. Woolsey discovered that his dog had eaten a carefully saved buffalo tongue, he grasped a whip, but while he held it aloft he exclaimed, "Poor fellow, it was my fault for not putting it away."

Then when a sharp quarrel had broken out at the

fort which engaged Mr. Woolsey's sympathy for the loser, he announced, drawing himself up, "I never yet struck a man, but if I did it would be a mighty blow."

After Fort Edmonton the easy going was over, the days of riding across grassy prairie and rolling park land where mosquitoes were the greatest evil to be met with and no more difficult transport problems presented themselves than the breaking of an axle-tree or the making of oilskin scows to cross a stream. Now began the days of all but impenetrable forest, of steep trails, lowering mountains, torrential rivers. It was past the middle of August and nights were severely cold. Southesk and his party had almost reached the mountains.

Southesk's intention was to go to Jasper House, from there "along the mountains" as far as the Kootenay Plain and back to Fort Carlton no later than October 1. But he had gone only one day's journey west of Edmonton when he met Mr. Moberley of the Company who gave a depressing account of Jasper House, from which he had just come. He had the summer before reopened the Jasper House trail, which had long been closed, but the prospect there was discouraging. No game was near, he said; the people were starving and preparing to leave. He advised Southesk to go up the McLeod River which gave a view of the highest peaks. From there south to the head of the South Saskatchewan "there extended about a ten days' march of country, which, as he believed, no European had ever seen (one half-breed hunter perhaps had long ago been there but it was very doubtful) where bears and wild sheep were certain to be abundant." Following this route would make it impossible to reach Carlton by October 1; nevertheless Southesk decided to attempt it. He had reached the last margin of civilization, the mission at St. Ann, where he received from the fathers a supply of fish and potatoes and bought still more horses, two of them from Father Lacombe.

Father Lacombe represented the Roman Catholic church in the Edmonton region as Mr. Woolsey and the McDougalls, father and son, did the Wesleyan. He had served the mission at Pembina and had been for the last seven years at Lake St. Ann where, like Mr. Woolsey, he learned Cree. Like the McDougalls he was to devote his life to the Indians and half-breeds of the North-West.

Southesk, as all travellers were who passed through the mission settlement at Lake St. Ann, was entertained at dinner by the priests, "agreeable men and perfect gentlemen," he noted. He was even persuaded to spend the night, "everything wonderfully neat and flourishing . . . meals served up as in a gentlemen's dining-room. Excellent preserves of service-berries and wild raspberries."

The very day they left St. Ann "our road was extremely bad, running through dense woods, chiefly of poplar brush with a few firs, and often through deep morasses filled with fallen timber. It was one incessant struggle. There was no longer a road wide enough for carts, only a narrow foot track, and the horses had to force their way through the brush, which tore everything to pieces. One's gun had to be carried under the arm instead of across the saddle, which was very tiring at first, especially with a strong double-barrelled rifle like mine. Bichon is not good in mire, and rolled over on his side in one deep place, after sticking on the concealed trunk of a fallen tree."

The going, indeed, was now bad every day. "We had hard fighting to get through the brush." He was glad of the present Mr. Hardisty had given him at Carlton, a leather hunting shirt, for "no woollen clothes but the stoutest can stand against these horrible thickets." "All the men had come out in leather since we entered the wood country, and looked infinitely more picturesque and sportsmanlike than when dressed in their blue cloth capotes." Thickets, as Southesk called them, were so dense that when one of the horses strayed, though a guide followed him till the track disappeared, he was never found.

"This," he wrote on August 24, not far from the McLeod River, "has been a most fatiguing day. In many parts the track was barely wide enough for a loaded animal to pass between the trees, and it was generally so soft and deep, from the effects of former traffic on such wet and sponge-like soil, that the horses were forever trying to escape from the treacherous boggy ditch in which they found themselves. Leaping to one or other side of the trench, they endeavoured to make their way along the firmer margin; but there was seldom much room there, so after a struggle that displaced or scattered their packs, down they inevitably plunged, and continued their floundering in the mire. . . . By the end of the day my knees were one mass of bruises, from cannoning off the fir stems, when Rowland made sudden dashes for the bank, or attempted to rush into some opening where the trees grew wide enough apart to allow a passage for himself,

51

though none for his rider's limbs. . . . If ever I get home I shall know how to appreciate comfort. Still, health is better than comfort. That evening I read with particular pleasure some articles in the *North British Review*, of which I had lately got a few numbers at one of the forts. I believe intellectual reading, in moderation, to be a rest for the body after hard labour: it seems to act as a counter-irritant, drawing off fatigue from the muscles to the brain."

Three days later, the going even worse, "one solitary gleam of consolation enlivened this weary day." Very far off and obscured by the dark shadow of thunder clouds Southesk had his first glimpse of the Rocky Mountains. "It was but an imperfect view, but so marvellous was the contrast between the damp, confined darkness of our track through the dripping fir-trees, and the sudden freedom of an open sky bounded only by the magnificent mountain-forms, that for a moment I was quite overwhelmed. . . . All weariness vanished. . . ."

Later the same day after the McLeod River had been crossed for the second time, suddenly the clouds were gone, the Rocky Mountain range stood before him. "Below us rolled the river among dark pines; hills, also covered with pines—some black and scorched with fire, some green and flourishing,—filled up the prospect for many miles; then came flat bare eminences, the footstools of the loftier range, and then uprose the mountains themselves, rugged in form, peaked and tabled, and scored with gashes . . . in certain ravines, and on some of the high shoulders of the greater peaks, spots and masses of snow glittered in the sun, or looked cold as death where no rays were able to reach them."

"With feelings almost too deep for utterance," he turned to Antoine for some sympathetic response and found the hunter's eyes gleaming, his arm outstretched toward the mountains. "Monsieur Milord," he said earnestly, "moutons ici."

On a piece of paper Southesk sketched the principal peaks before him, then they went down again and crossed for a second time the Embarras, a tributary of the McLeod.

Nights were very cold now—water froze in the basin—but at noon the sun poured into the valleys through which they travelled. They ate new dishes: moose, excellent but tough; roast skunk, white and tender but attended by "painful suspicions"; porcupine, too rich and fat when roasted but like delicate mutton when boiled. Beaver tasted like sucking-pig but better, and beaver-tail, that famous delicacy, he thought was "like pork fat sandwiched between layers of Finnan haddock."

But pemmican was the staple and Southesk regarded pemmican very darkly. To make it, he said, one must "take scrapings from the driest outside corner of a very stale piece of cold roast beef, add to it lumps of tallowy rancid fat, then garnish with long human hairs and short hairs of oxen, dogs, or both—and you have a fair imitation of common pemmican, though I should rather suppose it to be less nasty."

A year or two later young John McDougall found his first introduction to pemmican a considerable shock. He was taken to the Hudson's Bay Company storehouse "and here, sure enough, was pemmican in quantity. Cords of black and hairy bags were piled along the walls of the store. These bags were hard and solid and heavy. One

53

which had been cut into was lying on the floor. Someone had taken an axe and chopped right through hair and hide and pemmican, and here it was spread before me. My friend stooped and took some and began to eat, and said to me—help yourself, but though I had not eaten since supper yesterday, still the dirty floor, the hairy bag, the mixture of the whole almost turned my stomach."

At this time Southesk and his party had companions, an Iroquois family, consisting of father, mother, a young girl and two small children, and the parties camped near each other. A few Iroquois were to be found so far from their native region along the St. Lawrence because Sir George Simpson had employed Iroquois as his canoemen on his western journeys and some of these had remained behind near the western forts. The wife rode a grey and white mare with bells tied around its neck to scare away the wolves. At night how odd it sounded, Southesk wrote, to hear a child's cry in the heart of the wilderness.

One night the father came hurrying to ask the Earl's help because the baby was very ill. He went to their camp and found the mother crying over the baby who lay nearly naked on her lap. Southesk looked at the feverish little creature, caught in the dilemma which has puzzled so many travellers before the appeals of so many suffering natives. "I dared not give medicine, knowing that pills and powders fit for men might kill a ten-month baby—fearing, besides, lest if the child died I should be held by these untaught people the cause of its death, according to a prevalent Indian fancy."

54

He considered and then, putting on "an air of decision", he sent McKay to his own camp for a pot of weak tea, asked to have the fire made up and wrapped the baby in blankets. Then he directed the mother to hold the baby close to the fire and spoon tea down its throat. "With perfect confidence in my skill" she fed tea to the shrieking, struggling child and soon saw the fever relax and perspiration appear on the little brown forehead. Next morning he was glad to learn that the baby was almost well.

That day they crossed the Embarras ten times, the next day no less than thirty-seven times, the next day four times and were happy to leave it behind. The hills grew steeper and more rugged. The horses sank in muskeg, though Southesk's own horse, Jasper, a relaxed animal, even while sinking would snatch a bite of grass when his nose came near the surface. Again the horses had to cross fallen trees on the steep hillsides, some jumping over, others forced to labour and scramble.

Southesk maintained strict discipline among the men. One day "McKay hurried over breakfast and started the men before I was ready. He took my reproof admirably, and has been doubly attentive ever since. I believe it was a fault of inadvertency."

The Earl had not lost hope of stirring aesthetic appreciation in Antoine who was often his only companion on shooting and climbing expeditions. "As we were riding past a deep pool as clear as crystal, at the foot of a low but rugged crag, old Antoine paused and eyed it attentively, admiring its beauty, I hoped. . . . He has some sense of the beautiful after all, said I to myself. 'Milord!' said he, 'les petits poissons':—and immediately began to make a rough fishing rod."

Then during the dinner halt, "in the midst of noble scenery, while the horses grazed among the scattered rocks and fir-trees, and the men smoked and chatted good-humouredly together, I passed a very pleasant hour in reading *Macbeth*."

It was so cold in the nights that no matter how many blankets he burrowed into Southesk could not sleep. The temperature in that high thin air varied sharply between burning noon sun, from which one had to seek shadow, and icy wind and penetrating cold, but one evil had temporarily vanished. "There are no mosquitoes, so welcome cold, heat, wind, rain, fog, anything, if only these tormentors are cut off!"

The farthest point of the journey, both in distance and in importance as exploration, had now been reached. On September 3 they entered the valley of a river which Antoine called Medicine Tent River and saw splendid mountains one of which, "this wild and beautiful mountain", Southesk named Mount Lindsay after his friend Sir Coutts Lindsay of Balcarres. His rapid sketching of this mountain was cut short by the closing in of clouds about its summit. These sketches of the Earl's, retouched and completed by another hand, are reproduced in his book, as are two maps, that of the Rocky Mountain portion of the journey being based on a sketch made by Southesk soon after his return.

Across the end of the valley stood a mountain which

Southesk and four of the guides set out, next day, to climb. "It was hard work, the excessively steep slopes being covered with loose shingle which yielded to our feet." Even when at last they reached the top, thick-gathering mist obscured the view though they could see in a valley far below a number of wild sheep, females with their lambs. The men set to work "piling up big stones, and built a sort of rough tower or cairn, some six feet high, on the highest and most commanding point, as a memorial of our visit; then we descended more quickly than was altogether agreeable."

Before leaving Medicine Tent valley Southesk sketched the opposite peak and blazed his name on a fir-tree. The place was called, he said, the Height of Land, for head-waters of the Athabasca flowed northward from the snows of a mountain before him and the so-called North River (probably the Brazeau), from a point not far off, flowed south to the north branch of the Saskatchewan. "This country," he wrote, "is very little known," and added, "I am the first European who has visited this valley, and if I might have the geographical honour of giving my name to some spot of earth, I should choose the mountain near which the two rivers rise," the mountain, that is, on which he had erected his cairn. He added that even the Indians had no names for these mountains which "is the less surprising, as the whole district is only inhabited by a few families of wandering hunters, and they are rapidly decreasing in number."

The route of the mountain portion of Southesk's journey has proved very hard to trace. When he was later asked about it he replied in a letter to the *Geographical Journal* in 1899 that he could throw no light except that he thought he had gone close to what was later called Jonas Pass. This proved to be wrong. The country was totally unmapped in 1859; indeed between 1857 and 1880 narratives of only three journeys into the mountains had appeared, those of Palliser, Milton and Cheadle, and Southesk himself.

When Southesk's party left the Embarras River they entered a territory beyond names and maps and one that is still very little known. An article by J. N. Wallace called "Southesk's Journey Through the West", published in the *Geographical Journal* in 1925, stated that the mountains described by Southesk had up to that time never been recorded. In that year a man was said to have climbed Southesk's mountain and to have seen the cairn on its summit. He was spoken of as the first white man to climb it since Southesk and his party but another may have intervened. In his letter of 1899 Southesk wrote that his son, visiting Banff "a few years ago", had met there a man who had seen Southesk's cairn.

Thirty-three years after Southesk's expedition, in 1892, Prof. A. P. Coleman of the department of geology of the University of Toronto followed Job Creek and Coral Creek which lie between the Brazeau River and the Saskatchewan but his account does not mention Southesk. Certainly no one has ever contradicted the claim of Southesk that he was the first European to visit the valley of the Medicine Tent, now called the Rocky River.

Southesk was very modest in the matter of naming

mountains. He gave no names to the highest peaks he saw, thinking that they might have been discovered and named from the western side and he named only three mountains, all of lower altitude.

The course of his mountain journey described a large triangle with its apex at Edmonton. He turned south at Mount Lindsay where he encountered the Medicine Tent valley and followed that, the North River and the Bow to Old Fort Bow where he turned east again and returned to Edmonton.

Now that they were in the mountains and grizzly bears, always the first consideration with western travellers, were, alas, not numerous, they set out to hunt Rocky Mountain sheep, called in the United States big-horn. "I went to stalk a herd we had perceived some little way off, while Antoine remained to watch the ravine. It took me a long round to get to the place I was trying for—an isolated hillock about sixty yards from the sheep, —and when I arrived there I shot badly, being dreadfully out of breath. However, after missing with both barrels, I had still time to load and fire again, the animals being confused, and looking about them instead of attempting to escape, and with these shots I wounded one ewe severely, and mortally wounded the only ram in the herd—a good-sized two-year-old, which, running down the ravine, was met by Antoine, who finished it, and shot another ewe besides." Fresh meat was needed in camp so Antoine at once began to "arrange" the animals, his word for cutting them up.

As Southesk rode back with Antoine toward the camp

59

he heard the rest of the party returning from their own hunt and waited to see them come up. He was greatly struck with their picturesque appearance. All wore leather hunting shirts ranging from new almost-white to deep blood-stained brown. McKay, heavily bearded, wore a wide-brimmed black hat like a Spaniard; Matheson a blue Saskatchewan cap with bright ribbons and broad bands of scarlet across his chest; McBeath wore a military belt and sword and a red blanket as a saddle cloth; Kline a white hat with blue streamers and red and silver belts across his chest. There was Munroe in an embroidered black cross-belt, Short wearing a leather pouch beaded in blue and white and that oddly contrasting pair, Duncan, the gamekeeper who had come out from Scotland with his master, wearing a grey shooting-suit and looking "every inch the worthy Scotsman that he is", and Toma, Sir George Simpson's Indian canoeman, dressed in leather. Then Le Grace in a purple shirt and a white cap with scarlet streamers and a battered eagle's feather and Antoine, in leather, an old man but active and strong, carrying his hatchet and the old flint rifle, "bound up and mended with leather and brass-headed tacks", which looked "like some curious antique toy" yet with which he made remarkable shots.

Southesk himself wore a cream-coloured fringed hunting shirt, trousers fastened under the knee with green braid, a wide-brimmed white Yankee hat with green ribbons, from his shoulder hung a telescope and from his belt a hunting knife and tobacco pouch both in mooseskin cases embroidered with black and white beads.

"As this gallant party topped the crest of a low hill fair in my view, ribbons streaming, guns swaying, whips flashing, gay colours sparkling in the sun, some approaching at a quick trot, others dashing after vagrant steeds, or urging the heavy-laden pack-horses, who jogged along like elephants with castles on their backs—all life, dash, rattle, and glitter, they formed a bright picture, so gaily fore-grounded by the crisp green sward, that I could not refrain from attempting to describe it, though the ablest pen or pencil would fail to do justice to the scene."

## IV

HUNTING WAS very good as far as mountain sheep were
concerned and Southesk secured a number of fine heads
with "very handsome large horns, more twisted than
usual, and entirely perfect in their points." One day he
went off alone and, firing at some rams on the face of the
precipice far below, he was surprised to see through his
telescope that he had wounded one of them. He
attempted to go down and "suddenly found myself in a
very dangerous place, where a wide and steeply-descend-
ing trench-like hollow, between two firm hard ridges,
was filled up and hidden by an accumulation of pebbles
and small fragments of rock. Wherever I stepped, the
stones and shingle gave way in masses, carrying me along
with them as they went sliding on their downward course,
hurrying towards depths I tried not to think about; and,
to add to my trouble, Whisky appeared just above me—
whining with fright, and struggling desperately to keep
his footing on the treacherous surface—and sent the
stones in showers past my head. I hardly expected ever to
get to the top,—to descend or stand still would have been

death—but with great care and exertion, using my rifle
as a support by laying it flat on any firmer ledges, and
leaning on it as I dragged myself upwards, I at length
reached solid ground—feeling very grateful to a kind
Providence for bringing me safely through."

Whisky, the dog he had brought from Edmonton,
was a constant liability in mountain climbing for he
insisted on following the Earl, and being old and very
fat was always getting underfoot or falling behind and
squeaking loudly for help. Now, with Whisky at his
heels, he decided to try to reach the wounded ram by
another route. "He was standing by the edge of a cliff
about thirty feet high. I was exactly beneath him, on a
narrow and sloping grass-covered shelf of rock, which
overhung a tremendous precipice that dropped sheer to
the very base of the mountain itself. I stepped back as
far as I could and fired at his heart; it was a miss apparently, for he only moved higher up; then he turned and
came to his former position, and looked at me over the
verge of the height. I instantly gave him the second
barrel; the ball struck home; he made one spring off the
cliff into empty air, and came crashing down on the
turf at my feet,—nearly falling on poor Whisky, who
must have entered this day in his journal as one of hor-
rors."

Southesk caught the creature by the hind leg and
propped the body with stones to keep it from rolling off
the ledge. Just then he heard Antoine calling and learned
that McKay had killed several more rams, all of which
had to be "arranged", the meat covered with the skin

and a handkerchief hung on a stick close by so that the guides with the horses could find the place. It was now almost dark and the men had a long and difficult ride home, lit by flashes of lightning. They had scarcely finished supper by the camp-fire when a violent storm of wind and rain swept down the valley upon them.

For a day or two the men dried meat, prepared the heads and skins for transportation and turned their hands to blacksmithing. On rocky ground it was necessary to shoe the horses' forefeet to keep the hoofs from breaking, while on the plains it was the hind feet which had to be shod because the hoofs slipped on the grass as if on ice unless stayed with shoes.

Almost every day a wave of excitement went through the camp because someone had seen or heard or thought he had seen or heard a grizzly. Indeed they sometimes found footprints or patches of earth ploughed up by a bear digging for roots but the rumours were either faulty or too late for no bears were actually killed. However, one was seen by the guide, Short, who "reported that he had come close upon a large grizzly bear, in the valley below the ridge where I had been shooting the rams. It looked at him, and he at it, but neither cared to begin the fight, so each went his own way. At the time, Short's behaviour seemed to me rather over-cautious; with a good double-barrelled gun in his hand, I thought he ought not to have declined the combat. But on reflection, I believe he acted rightly, having no sufficient inducement for such a hazardous venture. . . . A failure at close quarters leaves a solitary hunter small chance indeed of escape."

Talk around the camp-fire naturally dwelt much on grizzlies and one of the men, a grizzly authority, told the others how to kill the animal. If a bear, he said, sees a man in open country it will advance toward him and at about one hundred yards will raise itself upright to look at him. It may then go away but if it continues to advance, it will stop again about thirty yards from the presumably stationary hunter and again rear itself upright. It then comes on till it is ten yards away from the hunter. "For the third time he rises in all his gigantic height, prepared to hurl himself forth in the last terrible spring. Now is the hunter's moment: quick as thought his bullet passes into the chest of the bear, sped at that short range with such precision that it carries with it instantaneous death—woe to the hunter if it does not!"

For two days the party was storm-stayed, the men singing songs around the fire in their large tent, Southesk reading in his smaller one. "To be storm-staid for an indefinitely long time in the heart of the Rocky Mountains, with winter stealing on apace, and a long and difficult journey before one, is not an encouraging prospect. Nor, disguise it as one may, is it very enlivening to sit, with wet feet, under a thin canvas covering that does not quite exclude the keen north wind." Nevertheless, he went on to reflect, anything was better than a life of indolent luxury and he bent to the consideration of *Titus Andronicus*, "a most disagreeable play", not, he felt sure, written by Shakespeare at all. "How inferior the commonplace fiend Aaron to that splendid villain Iago!"

The next morning broke clear and he rode out with two guides to look again for grizzlies. Finding none, he left the men to prepare to move camp and set out alone to climb to the top of the ridge and perhaps get a view beyond the valley through which they had been travelling. "I had a long and hard climb to begin with, and then a succession of difficult climbs over the numerous rocky walls that obstructed me as I slowly made my way along the ridge. . . . At length I got close to the foot of the great principal cliff at the top of the mountain; but there found myself stopped by a small but excessively steep and difficult rock, which stood right in the path, where the sharply-cut ridge was at its narrowest, flanked also on either side by a tremendous precipice coated with layers of sheet ice. Twice I tried this rocky barricade, but it was quite impassable, unless by scrambling round it, where, though less steep, it partly overhung the precipice; but even there it was very difficult, and a fall involved certain death." When he had lowered himself a little way he found that he had left his rifle behind having laid it down near the top where he had to hold on with both hands. By the time he had struggled up again to get it, night had fallen and he had still four or five miles to go, mostly uphill.

"There were rocks to descend and streams to cross; the woods were much obstructed with fallen timber and deep rough water-courses, and the opener spaces were filled with thick brush. There was no path, and though the moon had risen, the spruces cast such a shade as to cause almost total darkness; added to this I was very tired, for the day had been hot and my toils severe; besides, at every moment I expected to stumble upon the grizzly bear, whose very domain I was traversing, and against whom I should have had no chance, as the light was not sufficient for shooting." He fired his rifle to attract the attention of the guides but echoes flung back the sound and he was near camp before McKay met him with his horse. On horseback, and "no easy chair is so good a rest for the man tired out with walking", he was soon in camp and revived by a good supper and plenty of strong tea.

Next day, September 11, they broke camp and halted on the North River, opposite a mountain covered with small pines which he named Mount Dalhousie, in memory of his friend Lord Panmure, the eleventh Earl of Dalhousie, "at whose house my journey to America was first suggested." It was on this day also that they saw in a little glen through which a stream trickled a flight of thousands of butterflies, Painted Ladies, hovering thickly in the air, covering the stones of the stream and the dark branches of the fir-trees with their tawny wings spotted with black and white. The men were not so much absorbed in this lovely sight as to fail to notice with wistful or wary glances the tracks of a bear.

Antoine led the party confidently for two days of very bad going through burnt and fallen timber. Then suddenly it appeared that he did not know the route and that they had taken the wrong valley. The guides at once held anxious council and their doubts and the long discussions in Cree he had overheard convinced Southesk that the men were trying to lead him out of the mountains by the quickest and easiest road "instead of exploring the finer and less-traversed routes, according to my frequently expressed desire." Thoroughly angry, he at once turned his horse and rode back alone to the place where they had crossed the river. The men followed, abashed, and after some confused argument, pushed on again. These were bad days. "The river was so flooded that we were obliged to keep a high line, over a succession of steep ridges with deep hollows between, the whole of which was covered with burnt and fallen pines lying about in the most obstructive manner. Nothing can exceed the discomfort of passing over such a country, especially when the ground is soft and miry." The dry sharp branches of the prostrate pines tore hands and knees. "I often felt as if in one of the tournaments of old as these lances of the forest splintered against my buff jerkin" and sometimes lifted his hat from his head, "well-nigh treating me to Absalom's fate." The horses' legs were cut and one horse, severely stabbed, dropped suddenly and died in his tracks.

Nights were fiercely cold, tents and blankets sheeted with ice, and again and again they found themselves fronting an impassable rock wall or at the edge of a dizzying precipice, "none of the men knowing this part of the country". They faced at last a slope "not only exceedingly steep but composed of very sharp, many-cornered blocks much the size of a cart", and above this a nearly perpendicular wall of frozen snow about twenty feet high. McKay here organized an almost incredible ascent. Steps were cut for the men and the horses were dragged up with ropes. Blond slipped, just as he reached the top, and crashed to the bottom flattening the pots and kettles but saved, by falling on them, from damage to himself.

68

After this feat the going was still so bad that Southesk no longer wrote that no European had ever passed that way but that he felt certain that no human being could ever have done so.

Traces of bears continued but no bears appeared and nights were too intensely cold for sleep. The men were constantly hungry as well as tired; at supper "I astonished myself consuming at least three pounds of fried sheep." The horses too were exhausted so that the party rested for a day and Southesk and Antoine looked for mountain sheep and killed five while the men mended their moc-casins, the soles of which in climbing were sometimes worn through in a few hours. After supper Southesk, finishing *The Merchant of Venice*, wrote in his journal that Shylock had by no means had a fair trial. "Are we to understand that Shylock, Judas-like, committed suicide when he left the court? There is something peculiar in his exclamation, 'I am not well.' A man of his stern character would have scorned to acknowledge any feeling of illness at such a time, unless he intended to end illness and health alike by ending his life. Besides, he would never really have consented to become a Christian."

At Kootenay Plain "a space of some fifty acres, bare of trees and covered with short prairie grasses", perhaps part of what is now Kootenay National Park, they crossed the North Saskatchewan, there forty yards wide, on rafts. In these last weeks in the mountains the party, for the first time, ran out of food and Southesk, through simple good-ness of heart, made a mistake which drew after it a train of embarrassing circumstances.

It was the candles, indispensable for the Earl's reading, which failed first. Toma quickly improvised, by hardening sheep fat in a mould made of cartridge paper, a candle which burned almost as clearly as wax. The flour was gone, the dried sheep meat was mouldy, there remained only a little pemmican and tea. A horse failed and had to be abandoned.

Southesk hunted mountain sheep with Antoine and even wounded one but could not get it. The Earl turned back exhausted but stout old Antoine climbed to the spot where the sheep lay and carried it down for more than a mile on his back, to his master's great admiration. "Never," Southesk wrote despondingly, "did I feel more utterly prostrated. From various causes—my long journey on horseback, bad sleep owing to the cold at night, indifferent food of late, no drink stronger than tea, sudden hard work on foot since we came to the mountains, perhaps also owing to the height above sea-level of the valleys among which we were;—I am now very weak, and only able to climb steep places slowly, and with constant rests."

He was eager to secure some specimens of Rocky Mountain goat, a species which he described as smaller and whiter than the sheep, but after several days' hunting, he had caught none. While he hunted, the guides who remained in camp occupied themselves in eating pemmican all day. They were still several weeks away from Edmonton with no likelihood of any game except ducks along the road. In this dispiriting situation, Southesk "read *Romeo and Juliet*."

The next day they passed a camp site with a tree on which was written "Exploring Expedition, Aug. 23, 1859. Dr. Hector." About a month before, Dr. Hector, the geologist who accompanied the Palliser expedition, had taken that route and it was heartening to receive this message from the world of men.

That very evening they came upon the first human beings they had met for weeks when they heard Indians singing hymns; and it was as a consequence of meeting them that Southesk made his well-intentioned blunder. These Indians—they were Stonies—gave the most practical help. They had just killed three moose, one of which they sold to Southesk. Another horse had fallen the day before and a deal was at once under way to exchange some of their worn-out horses for the Indians' fresh ones. One of the Stonies, settling the matter of horses with Southesk, "talked very religiously" and said, through McKay as interpreter, that what his people most wanted was to hear more about religion. At McKay's suggestion, the Earl wrote out the Lord's Prayer, the Apostle's Creed and some sentences from the New Testament, "of a simple and encouraging character." McKay then read them to the Indians in Cree. They said that they had heard the Lord's Prayer and the Creed before but that the rest was new to them. None of them could read but they asked to be allowed to keep the paper to remind them, they said, "of the good things it contained."

Southesk gave the men a gun, blankets, ammunition and tobacco and to the women trinkets and a fine-tooth comb, "certainly it seemed needed." The Stonies were delighted and Southesk and his party no less so for they had secured meat for a week and two strong horses in place of tired ones.

To complete the story of this episode, some days later the Stony Indians caught up with Southesk's party. By this time the Indians themselves had no fresh meat or provisions of any kind and Southesk supplied them with ammunition so that the hunters could bring in geese. Every evening the Stonies joined in singing hymns, led by an old man, one of their number, who seemed to have a natural gift for preaching.

Considering what he could do to help these poor and worthy people, the Earl offered to take two of their young men with his party to Edmonton and to give them supplies to carry back to their tribe. This plan was carried out; at the fort Southesk gave them blankets, remembering to include a green one for the man who had specified that colour, ammunition, tobacco, shirts and other clothing. So far the encounter had been very satisfactory on both sides. But at Fort Edmonton the Earl told the story of the pious Stony families and of their longing for religious instruction. Almost exactly a year later, he received a clipping from the newly launched paper, the *Nor'Wester*. It stated that the Earl of Southesk on his recent hunting expedition in the Rocky Mountains had encountered Stony or Assiniboine Indians who professed Christianity and appeared to live up to their profession. "These families were far from any mission station, and had not even seen a missionary for many years." Their knowledge of religion, they had told the

Earl, had been gained from the Reverend Rundle, the first Wesleyan missionary in the Edmonton area, who had left the country because of illness in 1847 and they had seen no missionary since.

This clipping was accompanied by a long letter from the Reverend Thomas Woolsey, whom Southesk had met at Fort Edmonton on his outward journey and who had given him the Cree hymn-book. The letter was kindly but firm. His Lordship had been misinformed. The Reverend Woolsey himself had visited the Stony families frequently, seeing them indeed only the winter before. Either His Lordship or his interpreters must have misunderstood the Indians.

The missionary went on to relate a few of the difficulties under which he laboured—a harrowing enough picture of work on the frontier. All his letters in the fall of 1859 had been lost when the carrier threw the entire mail into the Saskatchewan River. Then the Sarcees stole two of his horses and one was eaten by wolves. Bloody skirmishes had occurred between the Blackfeet, Sarcees and Crees, "a Cree deliberately shooting a Blackfoot chief and scalping him near the very spot where your Lordship and I took leave of each other. . . . Just as I am finishing this letter a messenger has arrived from Fort Pitt with tidings of a war party of Blackfeet having fallen upon the Crees, and killed twenty of them, and that four Blackfeet fell in the struggle. . . . It is well that your Lordship went through the country last year, as it would have been unsafe this season."

Distressed by his mistake, Southesk blamed the misunderstanding on McKay's imperfect knowledge of the Cree tongue which had perhaps caused him to exaggerate "some remark about their distance from teachers and desire for further instruction." This had led him to "underrate the extent of Mr. Woolsey's ministrations among these people." In any case he made generous amends by printing the clipping from the *Nor'Wester*, the Reverend Woolsey's letter and his own apology in his book. He also printed a note relating how these very Stonies had all died of smallpox in 1870, ten years after his visit.

Now the party was approaching Old Fort Bow, the Hudson's Bay Company post on the Bow River which had been abandoned twenty-five years earlier for Rocky Mountain House. They were passing through dense poplar bush, the bright yellow leaves shining out against the wall of dark pine and fir. Most of the trees seemed to Southesk to bear the marks of fire "the curse of this region", ruining magnificent forests and "leaving in their stead endless tracts of charred and decaying remains. . . . It grieves the heart of a lover of trees to travel through America. . . . Fire everywhere, the axe everywhere, the barking-knife and bill-hook—joint ravagers with the storm, the lightning and the flood—all busy in pulling down nature's forest handiwork—and who builds up anything in its stead?"

They had left the mountains at last and looking back, Southesk summed up the experience. The worst features of the mountain adventure had been the loss of three horses and the fact that they had eaten all their provisions and endured severe cold. Beyond these rather inconsiderable discomforts, the Earl had been disappointed. Grand as the scenery had been, he had looked in vain for "sky-piercing peaks and heights towering above the clouds." He realized, he said, that the general elevation of the whole region made the mountains appear less high than they really were. The valleys they had passed through were 5000 feet above sea level and their present camp at Old Fort Bow was nearly as high above the sea as Ben Nevis, the highest point in Great Britain.

Besides seeing no astounding peaks he had seen almost no grizzlies. "Instead of the hundreds of grizzly bears I had been led to expect, I have only seen one and that at a distance." True he had killed many mountain sheep but at the cost of great labour.

Then there had been "something appalling in the gloom of the deep mountain valleys which had so long been our home, confined within tremendous barriers of unmitigated rock. The very mass and vastness of the mountains depress and daunt the soul." "On the first of September," he summed it all up, "I entered the mountains with joy, on the first of October I leave them with greater joy."

Here again they overlooked the prairies bounded by low hills where clumps of trees showed the ripe colours of autumn, gold, yellow and crimson, and the plains were thickly scattered with buffalo skulls but not with buffalo which once had been common in the foothills. "They are now rapidly disappearing everywhere; what will be the fate of the Indians when this their chief support fails, it is painful to imagine." He had seen large herds in July but like the grizzly bears, "they were nothing to what I have heard and read of." The winter before there had been no buffalo near Edmonton, Pitt or Carlton so that the inhabitants had almost starved and the Blackfeet had been obliged to leave their usual hunting grounds and go south in search of the herds.

Glad as they were to reach the plains again, their first night there was far from peaceful. In a violent storm, the poles of Southesk's tent broke and he spent the rest of the night lying, in furious wind and rain, under a flapping heap of canvas. In the morning the guides made a lucky find. Previous travellers, about to enter the mountains, had abandoned their carts and McKay now collected all the best portions and proceeded to construct three carts from them and to put together three sets of harness. Meanwhile Kline mended one of the Earl's shooting boots "as firmly as any professional cobbler", for Southesk could never accustom himself to moccasins in the mountains, and patched his telescope case with the same skill.

As they proceeded with the carts, one day was remarkable for encountering "certainly the prettiest Indian woman I had yet had a chance of seeing. Instead of being lean, flat and bony, she was plump and well-proportioned in figure." As the Indians rode on with them, they saw a large party coming across the plain and at once supposed them to be Blackfeet. They loaded their guns and the pretty Indian woman rode rapidly forward to keep close to her husband's side. Soon they found "the enemy to be nothing but a company of Americans" bound for the Fraser River. The Americans supplied Southesk with salt, flour, rice and dried apples and received in return tobacco, fresh meat and a shoeing-hammer, with which Matheson quickly set to work and shod several of their horses.

Fording and then following the Red Deer River they went on in intense cold, killing ducks and prairie fowl for food. Another horse had to be abandoned and in spite of all their shooting by the way they approached Fort Edmonton at last with only a little mouldy pemmican. One day before reaching the fort, some of the men, starting very early, went ahead to find game. What they killed they hung on trees so that as the main party advanced they found "ducks and rabbits they had killed and left hanging on conspicuous branches for our benefit." This welcome provision was eaten at White Mud River where they paused to make themselves as tidy as possible before they came to the fort where flying colours and cannon salutes gave them a hearty greeting.

## V

EDMONTON AT last. Coffee, vegetables, cream tarts. News
from Europe—not very recent—of a battle impending
between the Austrians and the French and Sardinian
armies. The two mountain guides were paid off and
presented with gifts; the complicated horse-account was
settled—eleven to be left behind, nine to be taken on.
These were sent to Fort Carlton under the care of two of
the guides, for Southesk planned to travel by river in one
of the Company's large boats, to go from Fort Carlton to
Fort Pelly with the horses and from there by dog-team.
Days were precious now; there was barely time to reach
Fort Carlton before freeze-up.

The brief stay at Edmonton ended on a note of com-
edy. While Southesk was bathing in his rubber tub, suddenly the door was flung open and "two splendidly
dressed Indians walked into the room as if the place
belonged to them, but on seeing me they stopped, and
stared with all their might. We stared at one another for
a moment, and there was a general laugh, after which I
continued my sponging, to their evident wonder and
amazement."

78

These men with whom he laughed were Blackfeet, apparently the only ones he saw in the course of his journey. They were envoys sent to announce the approach of the tribe for their fall visit, and Southesk regretted that he must hurry away before this ceremonious invasion. The next day, October 17, he was on board the factor's own boat *The Golden Era* and off on the broad breast of the Saskatchewan.

The sun shone but the air was intensely cold and overhead enormous flights of wild ducks moved steadily southward. Guides who were not at the oars seized their guns and blazed away but few ducks fell, for the flocks were flying very high. At night the men landed, lit a fire on the sand and ate supper around it, a party of six guides beside the Earl; the dog Whisky had chosen to remain in the comfort of the fort. It snowed all night and next day the cold was so intense that Southesk to warm himself took a turn at rowing and found it "pretty hard work tugging at these eighteen-foot poles called oars." And he added the ominous words "river beginning to freeze." The distance to Carlton by the river was still a long one; they had taken a narrow chance in setting out so late by water and the odds were quickly decided. The journal entries are sharp with apprehension. "October 19th. Cold intense, ground covered with snow. . . . The river is very nearly frozen over; unless a change come tonight we shall be ice-bound, and have to walk a hundred miles or more to Fort Pitt, where the horses ought to be. October 20th. Snow in the night, frost in the day. River blocked with great masses of ice; boat closed in."

Plans were quickly made. Two of the guides set off to bring horses from Fort Pitt; the rest, deciding to stay where they were, tidied the camp and cut logs for the fire. "We shall probably have to stay more than a week in this wretched place," wrote the Earl but then he reflected that he had been fortunate so far, especially in escaping a Blackfoot rising of which he had heard rumours. The next day he was ill with influenza but in a day or two he felt much better and the severe cold relaxed. McKay remarked and his master agreed with him that such an illness disappears more quickly when the sufferer is living in the open air than when he is closed in a house.

Southesk was reading *My Novel* by Bulwer Lytton and writing, in the chill of his tent beside the frozen Saskatchewan, pages of analysis of the motives of the principal characters. Whence is Randal Leslie supposed to derive his evil genius? Why is Riccabocca's grotesqueness so dwelt upon and why is Leonard made such a milksop? While wind shook the canvas and snow sifted through the flap the Earl went on to consider how Shakespeare gives faults even to his heroines and good qualities to his villains. On the other hand the weaknesses of Sir Walter Scott's heroes, he thought, robbed them of much of the reader's sympathy.

So the long week passed. The Earl walked out with his gun to look for game and found none. At noon the ice cracked and melted a little so that McKay walked a long way down the river and made the annoying discovery that about three miles below the camp the ice, at a bend between steep banks, had packed itself into a dam and the stream from there on was open as far as he could see. If only they had gone on a little farther on the day of the freeze-up, if only they could break the dam or get the boat around it. McKay philosophically put away such speculations and made a draught board and a set of men for it.

No game, no fresh tracks in the deep snow. "Never have I passed such a wearisome time. Each day is like the other. I rise soon after the sun, then breakfast on cold ham, then read or think till mid-day, then dine on beef either fresh or dried, then read or think till dusk; then the lovely star Capella appears, and I look at it and think of many things; then Cassiopeia begins to shine, and soon all the stars are in their places, each reminding me of some dear friend with whom I associate it. Then comes supper—cold ham and tea; then a long time of restless thinking, till Aldebaran and the Pleiades have passed the large tent, and the Pointers lean from east to west, and Arcturus is below the horizon; and then to bed, per-chance to toss wearily from side to side for many a tedious hour."

On November 1 "deliverance at last." A shot in the distance, another, and the men came riding in from Fort Pitt with sixteen horses. The two messengers had had a hard struggle to reach the fort, six days of floundering through knee-deep snow, the last three days without food. They had kept from freezing at night by letting their fire burn for an hour or two and then moving it and lying down in the warm ashes.

They broke camp and set off next morning, riding in a blizzard. The open water they had seen below the camp was fast frozen now. "Agonizing cold, our beards hung with icicles." "During the height of the cold," Southesk wrote in his tent that night, "the thought occurred to me—Why am I enduring this? For pleasure—was the only reply, and the idea seemed so absurd that I laughed myself warm. Then as circulation returned, I remembered that I was taking a lesson in that most valuable of human studies—the art of Endurance; an art the poor learn perforce, and the rich do well to teach themselves—though they have their own trials, in a different fashion. I often think of the story of an officer who was so anxious to harden himself before a campaign against the Kaffirs, that he used to leave his comfortable quarters, and sleep uncovered in the open air during the worst of weather. The end was that when marching orders came he was too rheumatic to go with his regiment."

After a week of this they reached Fort Pitt. They had felt the cold so keenly because they were still in their autumn clothing, though Southesk had buffalo robes between which to sleep. At Pitt they outfitted in winter clothing—white flannel leggings drawn over their trousers, blanket-cloth moccasins, blue capotes over the leather shirts, fur caps of fox or otter or marten, and leather mittens lined with flannel. Southesk invented for himself a luxurious pair of huge buffalo-hide boots with the wool inside; he "thought them masterpieces" at first, but scorchings by the camp-fire soon made them too small and stiff for comfort. Instead of pack-saddles or carts, horse-sleds hauled the baggage and slid easily over the frozen surface of the river which was sometimes their road. When they had to travel through the snow, two men went forward on snowshoes to make a path for the horses and sleds.

When they camped, after leaving the fort, at the Red Deer Hills, Mr. Isbister, the factor at Pitt, joined them for the night, travelling in his own dog-sleigh with his own handsome dog-team. Seeing him dash off over the ice next morning, Southesk, beard and moustaches frozen, felt depressed. "It is melancholy to think that more than a month of this hardship lies before us, between this and Fort Garry. Then a fortnight more of it to St. Paul—frail nature shrinks—"

There was something ominous, almost terrifying, to Southesk in the featureless, unbounded waste of snow through which they travelled, no landmarks, all the lovely colour and variety of summer obliterated, only in the white expanse "brown spots where naked clumps of poplar brush uplift their heads, and the lakes are only distinguishable by . . . the greater smoothness of their surface."

On a day when it was thirty degrees below zero they camped near the lake beside which they had camped in July, in the place where Southesk had sat on a sunny slope covered with wild strawberries. While he thought of this he saw a party coming from Fort Carlton bringing the mail and the green hands, the newly-engaged men for the back-country forts. He regarded with sympathy these five or six young Scottish lads, dazed with cold and the strangeness of this world of snow, and looking, he thought, "not half strong enough for the work in store for them." Thereafter his party travelled in the tracks of the party from Carlton at some saving of time and effort, till the path was snowed up again. On November 15 they reached Carlton, Southesk doubtless recalling that his original plan had called for reaching there on the first of October.

Again horses must be examined for exchange or purchase and Mr. Hardisty, the factor, ordered a large drove to be gathered in an enclosure for Southesk's inspection. As each horse was selected, it was lassoed until fifteen had been chosen. Again they were off with five sleds through country rich in rivers and lakes and handsomely wooded: country, Southesk thought, which would be good for settlement. "Had I the power," he wrote, "I should be inclined to make a strong colony along the Saskatchewan, of Englishmen and Scotchmen, *with their wives*, and introduce the system of stock-feeding as in Australia. The Company should retain their privileges in the district so long as necessary to establish such a colony, which ought to be free or nearly so, and perhaps, in recompense, might have their charter renewed and made more stringent as to the other districts."

Commissary troubles arose almost at once, for a little Indian dog which had attached itself to the party ate all the fresh meat during the first night and for dinner the men had to eat pemmican, to which Southesk had not become reconciled. "Pemmican is most endurable," he wrote, "when uncooked. My men used to fry it with grease, sometimes stirring in flour, and making a flabby

84

mess, called 'rubaboo', which I found almost uneatable. Carefully-made pemmican, such as that flavoured with saskatoon berries, or some that we got from the mission at St. Ann, or the sheep pemmican given us by the Rocky Mountain hunters, is nearly good—but in two senses, a little goes a long way."

The horses seemed more than ordinarily annoying in their painful contrast to the well-fed and carefully trained horses Southesk was accustomed to ride at home. Now, tired and impatient, with a long cold journey still before him he felt more sharply than ever the "misery of riding a half-wild, half-broke, obstinate, underbred, grass-fed beast. . . . They treat their rider as a mere encumbrance, to be jogged about as it pleases them, like any other pack, not as the master whose will is their proper guide." Moreover, the sole desire of the horses was to keep together in as close a group as possible. "If you choose to ride in front, farewell to ease; . . . if you turn in the saddle or slack your rein, or make any sort of movement, he instantly stops and begins to graze; and if you urge him on, he neighs to his companions till your head aches from the horrible noise. Very different is it if you wish to stop behind; the dull slug wakens into a fury, and rears and pulls and fights till you allow him to rejoin the band."

Snow fell constantly, any track had long ago disappeared and since they had no guide they often went astray in the blinding snowfall and had to make short marches and camp early to be sure of finding firewood. On November 27 they set off across a bare plain with blue woods at its farthest edge. All day they pushed on hoping to reach the trees before nightfall for the plain furnished a cold and wind-raked camping place with no fuel in sight. But as they went on the trees drew no nearer, they seemed rather to draw away, and the horses floundered into an unfrozen saline swamp and soon threshed deep into the mud. It was long after dark and they were at last forced to camp where they were, eating cold pemmican and melting snow for drinking water by burning wisps of straw.

Again next morning they plunged on with the wind in their faces, hoping soon to reach the shelter of the woods but distance across the snow-covered level was deceptive and it was noon before they reached the first poplars and could make a fire and breakfast. Going on again till sunset they were all tired and would have stopped but before them lay a criss-cross of fresh snowshoe tracks. In gathering darkness they followed the tracks for a long way and were about to make camp when they heard dogs bark. Southesk rode to the top of a slope and saw sparks rising from a chimney, which led them to the door of Touchwood Hills Fort. There he found not only comfort and warmth but also newspapers only five months old with news of the armistice after the battle of Solferino.

Touchwood Hills Fort was small and rough but its huge log fire offered welcome shelter during the heavy snowstorm which raged all that night and the next day. Its comfort was made even pleasanter by the factor's account of the perils which had dogged Southesk's party as they travelled toward the mountains in July and of which they now heard for the first time. It seemed that both a party of Crees and a party of Blackfeet had followed them, attracted by the lavish provisioning of the expedition and planning at the very least to rob them of food and goods and of all their horses. This had only been prevented by the fact that the two Indian parties had encountered one another and indulged in one of those ambiguous actions, too evasive to be considered an attack, too furtive to be an action at all, in which each side tried to elude the other and yet drive off a horse or two, and in which one man, a Blackfoot, was actually killed and portions of his body brought to the fort as trophies. A few weeks before, the factor who told them this story had been informed "by Mr. S.—an English gentleman travelling in the country, that it was believed that I and all my men had been killed by the Blackfeet. I trust," added the Earl in his journal, "this report will not reach home."

## VI

On the last day of November they were off again in terrible cold. Here Southesk wrote a sentence which, however closely one may have followed his day-by-day account, strikes the reader with astonishment. The cold was so intense, he wrote, that "the tea-cup kept freezing to the saucer when any tea ran over, requiring some little force to remove it." The words tea-cup and saucer suggest chinaware and though the reader has been accustomed to Southesk's books and his love of as much comfort as a wilderness journey could afford, the idea of a tea-cup and saucer still seems incongruous. Had they been carried all through the mountain journey or acquired at one of the forts with the slow approach to civilization?

Southesk had invited John McKay to have tea with him which was unusual for the Earl always ate alone. "Breakfast, dinner, tea or supper," he wrote, "whatever the name of the repast—it consists much of the same materials—tea, flour-cakes and such meat as happens to be available." He had at this time slices cut from huge frozen joints brought from one of the forts. Sometimes

88

he ate dried meat but never pemmican if he could avoid it. When currants or raisins were among the stores, Toma boiled them with rice to make a pudding and once in the summer he had made "a delicious jelly with saskatoon berries—much to my astonishment."

That day, half-way to Fort Pelly, they covered eighteen miles across the bare prairie, the wind for once at their backs, the sun shining. That night the Earl re-read *Troilus and Cressida.* Certain lines in Agamemnon's speech followed him. "When the frost bit keenest, and the icy winds congealed one's blood, and the men were cheerless and silent, and the skeleton horses slaved wearily along,—hour following hour in miserable monotony, till life was almost too grievous to endure—" he seemed to hear:

> *And call them shames? which are indeed nought else*
> *But the protractive trials of great Jove*
> *To find persistive constancy in man:*
> *The fineness of which metal is not found*
> *In fortune's love.*

Trying snowshoes for the first time the Earl thought them at the beginning much easier than wading through deep snow but later found his muscles aching and his feet cut by the frozen straps. The horses were failing rapidly for their only food was such dry grass as they could find after scraping away the snow and their legs were badly cut by the hard icy crust. Southesk's favourite horse, Cendré, had to be abandoned and the others could hardly drag themselves the last cold miles toward Fort

Pelly. A dog-team waited to carry Southesk to the fort
and after the painful crawl of the last few days the dogs
seemed to fly. Horses were no longer practicable for
winter travel and dogs, which were scarce, were sent for
to various places to make up teams to carry the party to
Fort Garry.

Fort Pelly, since it stood in the region of the peaceable
Saulteaux Indians, had not even a stockade. From the
new, white-washed house, surrounded by storehouses,
Southesk looked far across a level country of swamp and
willows, plain and poplar. The remains of the old fort
had been made into cattle barns. Here, in the weeks of
waiting, the Earl read an old copy of *Blackwood's Maga-
zine*, keeping indoors when the temperature, since the
mercury was frozen in the thermometer, was judged to be
about forty degrees below zero. He looked at the horses
and cattle, at his own horses, improving with rest and
food, and at the small farm where they told him potatoes,
barley and turnips were grown. He went hunting with
a young Company clerk, recently out from Inverness-shire,
but they found no game. He was shown through the
Company store where few furs had yet come in. He and
the factor went for a drive in the horse cariole which upset,
throwing them both into a snow-drift. In the little bury-
ing ground near the fort they saw above a new-made
grave a pole bearing a string of buttons, a beaded bag, a
piece of tobacco and a dried human hand. It was the
grave of an Indian's beautiful young wife who had died
suddenly of a heart attack. Her husband had been drunk
when she died and when he sobered and realized his loss

he had begged harder than ever for rum "because his heart was heavy and he wanted to make it light." And every evening there were the usual stories—of the rivalries of the free fur traders, of how wolverines could rob any cache, and always of Indian raids and Blackfoot cruelties.

News came of an expedition to mark out the boundary between Canada and the United States. Southesk deplored "the new-fashioned custom of running boundary lines on parallels of latitude or longitude . . . it seems far better to put rivers, lakes and mountains, to their natural use of dividing territories, so that a real instead of a fictitious boundary is obtained."

Britain, he reflected, "possesses two powerful colonies on the eastern and western oceans, and retains that vast fur-bearing territory of the north, which, being unfit for settlement, will require no greater facilities than at present belong to it in its water communication with Hudson's Bay."

"Along the North Saskatchewan might be formed a chain of settlements sufficiently strong to protect the frontier, maintain communication between Columbia and Canada, and provide means for carrying on such government as the thinly populated northern districts might require. If a Pacific railway were deemed necessary, this appears to me to be the best, perhaps the only feasible, line, as one more southern must pass through hundreds of miles of barren prairie, incapable of growing crops or timber, and scarcely suitable even for grazing purposes." A few weeks after writing these lines Southesk saw a map made by Mr. Dawson who conducted the survey of the

Dawson-Hind expedition for Canada and "I find it to be his opinion also that Lake Winnipeg and the North Saskatchewan are the true lines for Pacific communication, the route he lays down being identical with that which suggested itself to me."

On Christmas Day Southesk attended a communion service at Fort Pelly. "Two Indians were present, and Mr. Settee addressed them in their own language when giving them the bread and wine." Two days later he was ready to leave the fort.

Enough dogs had been collected to draw Southesk's own cariole and three sleds loaded with baggage, but as more goods remained, two of the guides were directed to stay at Pelly till more dogs could be secured. Four of his old guides on snowshoes made up the party with two or three men from the fort. Almost at once McBeath dropped a ninety-pound bag of hard-frozen pemmican on his foot and was unable to walk. Southesk put him in the cariole and walked himself. It was so cold at night that as Southesk sat in his tent reading, so close to a huge fire that holes were scorched in his leggings, at the same time tears of cold fell from his eyes and froze on the page before him. It seemed to him, long afterward, that he could see the marks of those frozen drops on the pages of *Othello*.

As he crossed the ice of Swan River his nose was frosted and had to be rubbed by his driver. On New Year's eve "tall pine trees encompassed us with their rugged stems, and canopied the whole ground, save the small space that held us, with their vast spreading branches, all

thickly covered with masses of the softest, purest snow. Our camp-fire, once more built up with fragrant pine instead of the dull poplar logs, blazed gloriously and sparkled, and threw out a delicious odour, while its light illumined the stately trees around." On New Year's day, 1860, they reached Lake Winnipegosis.

Southesk was disturbed by the cruelty with which the drivers treated their dogs. His own driver ran for miles after the galloping dogs shouting a constant stream of abuse in English, French and Indian. With a burst of shouting, now and then, "he rushes past the cariole, shaking his whip, while the wretched dogs dart from side to side in agonies of fear, whining, squealing, and shrieking, like a drove of distracted pigs." From the team that followed his came "a fearful cracking and thumping, and the poor beasts set off with their heavy load, howling as if their hearts would break." He saw such furious beatings and cudgellings that he gave orders to Kline to forbid such cruelty. "Not to beat our dogs?" he heard the men ask in astonishment. "Beat them— yes," replied Kline, "you may do that, but you are not to *hammer them about the head*."

On January 5 they got up and breakfasted at two a.m. and set off at four on the ice of Lake Manitoba. The snowstorm was so violent that the tracking party who set out an hour before the sledges could scarcely make its way. Southesk hated travel in his cariole, feeling it a humiliation to be hauled while the men walked, but he could not go on snowshoes for more than a few hours. On this day he found the cariole for all its wrappings extremely cold and was glad to spend the night at Manitoba Fort.

Now every day they came upon houses where in a confusion of men, women, children and dogs they could spend the night or at least stop to rest and drink hot tea. On Sunday they passed the Roman Catholic church at White Horse Plains and saw the congregation coming out, the men in their dark blue capotes and striped or crimson sashes, the women in dark shawls or blankets with only a bright kerchief here and there.

Along the banks of the Assiniboine "for twenty miles, almost without a break, small farms run outwards from the river-side into the uncultivated but grass-clad prairies. The soil seems rich, the ground undulates considerably in many parts, and altogether this settlement looks warmer and more home-like than that on the Red River near Fort Garry." The settlers' houses, square wooden boxes, had no fences or gardens, "the cottages stand all raw and bare-faced, as boulders are strewn by a flood, or meteor-stones dropped from the sky."

Drawing near Fort Garry at last, the party met James McKay driving in a horse cariole. He insisted that South-esk should get in beside him and stirred up his horse. Seven months after leaving it, the Earl was in Fort Garry again.

It was January 8, 1860 and the first number of a news-paper, *The Nor'Wester* had just come out; in an early issue was to appear an account of Southesk's meeting with the Christian Indians of the Stony tribe. Within seven months, Southesk wrote, "thus it was my fortune to wit-ness the appearance of the first steamboat and the first newspaper in this remote part of the world. . . . There is a good deal to fill a newspaper in this settlement, for besides other things, there are many ecclesiastical and judicial matters to record, in a place possessed of two bishops and a numerous clergy, a governor and various courts in continual employ."

In the period of waiting for the rest of his baggage to be brought from Fort Pelly, Southesk paid his respects to both bishops and attended the funeral of Mr. Mackenzie who had had charge of the station at Buffalo River. Provisions had run short there a few days before and Mr. Mackenzie had volunteered to go alone to Pembina for help. He expected to reach there the same day and so took with him no blankets or axe, only a little pemmican and some matches. It began to snow heavily, he lost his way and wandered in the woods for three days. Men coming from Fort Garry had found him, frozen to death. He had lain down quite calmly at the end, with his head on a fallen pine bough. "Thus died a man experienced in travelling, one born and bred in the settlement;—a sad proof of the danger of a solitary journey during winter in this terribly rigorous climate."

Southesk studied the agricultural possibilities of the region and found that wheat grew well though hurt by late frosts and that barley grew very well. Wood was scarce, labour very scarce, as young men preferred the fur trade to farm work. Scottish settlers at the west side of Red River appeared to be thriving. There were not many Englishmen in the settlement partly, he was told, because their wives were not strong enough for heavy outdoor work. Yet settlers with wives and families were, it seemed to him, what Red River needed.

After his goods from Fort Pelly had arrived, came the farewell visits. On January 25 he left Fort Garry by dog-team, covering the last fifty-eight miles to Pembina in one day which began at three a.m. and ended at eight-thirty at night. With a new dog-team they went on and reached Crow Wing on February 7. The rest of the journey was a breathless and exhausting series of short laps—Crow Wing to Sauk Rapids in eighteen hours and on by stage to St. Anthony. From St. Paul he went on to Wabasha and travelled the last thirty-five miles to La Crosse on the frozen surface of the Mississippi River. At La Crosse he reached the railway and proceeded with several changes of train for three nights and two days to New York and the Cunard steamer *Etna*. And at last "right glad was I once more to set foot on my native land, after so long an absence and such distant wanderings."

Fifteen years passed before Southesk's book was published in a single small edition under the title *Saskatchewan and the Rocky Mountains, A Diary and Narrative of Travel, Sport and Adventure, during a journey through the Hudson's Bay Company's Territories, in 1859 and 1860*. The book's appendix contains a long essay on *Hamlet* and "remarks" on *The Winter's Tale, Macbeth, The Merchant of Venice*, and *Othello*. These as well as the body of the narrative had in part been written in the mountains or on the prairie beside the camp-fire with guides quarrelling or singing, dogs fighting, wolves howling outside. "Hamlet was more mad that he himself supposed—it was not all feigning," he had written on July 31, after shooting a white wolf beside Jackfish Lake; and of *Othello* he had written on December 30, the night when tear-drops froze on the page, "there is some similarity in the first part of the plot of *Cymbeline*. Why is it that one is inclined to have more sympathy for Imogen than for Desdemona?"

He added to his book, beside these literary excursions, footnotes from Sir John Richardson's *Fauna Boreali-Americana* and from other sources, identifying the animals and plants he had seen on his journey. But though he was interested in natural history, his deepest devotion was to literature and the rest of his long life was occupied with the writing of poetry and with antiquarian research.

# III.  A PARTY OF PLEASURE

# I

ON THE second day of July in the year 1862 two young men landed from a steamer at Quebec. Eighty years earlier they would have been landing at Calais after a choppy channel crossing to begin the Grand Tour. Precise specimens of that classic pair the aristocratic young man and his tutor, they would have spent a year or two in travel and a modicum of study, in taking the waters, perhaps, and indulging in the fashionable dissipations of the moment.

But since the wars in France and the revolutions over all Europe, habits had changed. Hunting and exploring were now favoured pursuits for adventurous young men. Moreover, the younger of this pair had visited the prairies two years before and had even taken part in the Great Fall Hunt of that year from Fort Garry. To the end of his life he was to be convinced that the air of the prairies benefitted his frail health.

William Fitzwilliam, Viscount Milton, was pale, slight and only twenty-three, a spoiled, impulsive young man, in poor health and obstinate with a weak man's frightening tenacity.

One is tempted to call his companion a bear-leader, for if Lord Milton was not altogether a bear he was by no means easy to lead. Walter Butler Cheadle, a large, hearty young man with a full beard, looked older than his twenty-seven years. The recorder and backbone of the expedition, Dr. Cheadle was a former Cambridge oarsman and the tutor of Lord Milton, as well as his personal physician, protector, supporter and general manager.

As they stepped into the streets of Quebec and began their journey west there were indeed not two young men but three. With them was a shipboard acquaintance named Messiter. "Mr. Messiter, a tall fine young fellow, Etonian and Oxonian," wrote Dr. Cheadle, "has been suffering from prairie fever for the last five years and is now on his way to enjoy what he has so long looked forward to—hunting the buffalo and grizzly bear in the neighbourhood of the Rocky Mountains—a glorious life in the far West. We . . . agreed to travel in company as far as might be agreeable to the plans of each."

The three young men, of course, visited Niagara Falls which they found on first view disappointing, on further consideration very fine. They went on by train to Chicago and to La Crosse, by steamer up the Mississippi and by train to St. Anthony. So far their journey was much like that of the Earl of Southesk three years before. But here the difference between the two expeditions begins to appear. Southesk, travelling with the great Sir George Simpson, found guides, wagons, and horses prepared and waiting at every turn. Milton and Cheadle and their temporary companion Messiter travelled by public conveyance.

From St. Anthony the Great Pacific Railroad was to be built westward across the plains to California and the line had been begun. To go north, however, the young men had to take a stage to Georgetown on the Red River. The stage was a covered wagon crowded with "German women jabbering and slapping squalling babies, Yankee women chattering like magpies" and two Yankee men with whom Cheadle discussed the Prince of Wales's visit to the United States two years before where he had made a very favourable impression. "All spoke in terms of great admiration for Queen and Prince Consort. Could not understand why England favoured South. Insisted . . . that the real question the North was fighting for was abolition. Told them we didn't swallow that in England. Awfully tiresome ride."

A seventy-mile drive brought them to St. Cloud where they spent the night. Next day the stage went on with its tired, mosquito-bitten passengers through open prairie land dotted with clumps of poplar and scrub oak. Two dogs tied on top of the baggage which was piled on the roof often lost their footing and fell to the length of their chains where they hung strangling till passengers could haul them up again. The second night the party spent at Sauk Centre.

There the travellers, after an attempt at duck shooting, realized that they needed a dog of their own. The man at whose house they spent the night offered them his dog, Rover, and they agreed to buy him. But when they held out their money the man drew back. He must, he said, consult his wife and sister who were very fond of the dog. He went out to speak to them and almost at once they came running into the room. Both were crying and one of them clasped Rover in her arms. The young men hastily apologized for having suggested buying their pet.

But next morning as they were going off, their host came to the stage leading Rover by a string. He needed money badly, he said, and had talked the women round. "Be kind to the little fellow," he added wistfully, as the stage got under way.

During the next few weeks the travellers heard rumours that the Sioux were about. A few people looked anxious, but most merely shrugged their shoulders for rumours of hostile Indians flew on every wind. The Sioux occupied in the west of the United States the place held by the Blackfeet in the west of British America; rumours of hostile Sioux, however, often had a good deal of substance behind them. Several weeks later when the young men were camped far away on the prairie they heard of the fate of Rover's former owner and of the two women who had cried over him and of many others. They had all been massacred by a Sioux war party. The stage wagon to Georgetown on which they themselves had ridden a few days before had been attacked, the passengers and driver scalped and the wagon overturned into the river. The Sioux party had come to Fort Garry after the massacre carrying swords and revolvers, some of them driving buggies, and wearing women's finery, with twenty dollar gold pieces hung round their necks.

But now, scoffing at talk of war parties, the young men arrived in Georgetown and found the river so low that the steamer *International* might not come for a long time. At once they decided to paddle the five hundred miles to Fort Garry. They bought two canoes, one of them full of bullet holes because it had belonged to an Indian who had been ambushed the previous summer, and both very leaky. They caulked the canoes, and bought flour, pemmican, salt pork, matches, tea, salt, tobacco and ammunition. The Red River had made itself a deep channel across the plain, its banks covered with trees and bushes to the water's edge. On they went in the monotony of chopping wood, loading and unloading, paddling, shooting and patching the canoes. Very soon they found that they had run out of food.

We have two accounts of the remarkable journey of Viscount Milton and Dr. Cheadle thus prosaically begun. Both were written by Dr. Cheadle. Every day or evening he wrote up his journal in lively phrases and half sentences, brusque, exciting, funny and grim. He was a practical man and he had little time to read Shakespeare or anything else for, unlike the Earl of Southesk, he had not only the whole responsibility for the expedition upon his shoulders but he had to do most of the work as well.

After their return to England, he wrote, based on his journal, the staid account resoundingly entitled *The North-West Passage by Land, being the Narrative of an Expedition from the Atlantic to the Pacific, undertaken with the view of Exploring a route across the Continent to British Columbia through British Territory, by one of the Northern Passes in the Rocky Mountains.* Relating the events of their almost incredible journey Cheadle adduced impressive reasons for having embarked upon it.

"The Authors had in view . . . to draw attention to the vast importance of establishing a highway from the Atlantic to the Pacific through the British possessions; not only as establishing a connection between the different English colonies in North America, but also as affording a means of more rapid and direct communication with China and Japan." They wished, he said, to discover a direct route through British territory to the gold-fields of the Cariboo and to open up for settlement the fertile regions of the Red River and the Saskatchewan. It is apparent, however, that they were moved by a natural desire "for hunting the buffalo and grizzly bear" and for "a glorious life in the far west;" in a word by prairie fever.

The book came out in 1865 with two maps and twenty-three full-page illustrations. It was extremely successful and ran through nine editions.

The existence of Cheadle's original journal was known, and extracts from it were published and compared with the text of the written-up account. In 1931 the journal itself was published. The editors, A. G. Doughty and Gustave Lanctot, conjectured, probably rightly, that the *North-West Passage by Land* may well have served to interest Britain in the British American west and to draw attention to the route by the Yellow Head Pass which the Grand Trunk Pacific was later to follow.

The respective styles of the finished account and the journal cry out for comparison. According to the *North-West Passage* the travellers went by canoe on the Red

River, "a few days' slow and monotonous voyaging". Here is the journal account for one of those "monotonous voyaging" days.

"Get up at sunrise after very wakeful night. Bitten to death, hands and face much swollen. Messiter much disfigured. Lord M's arms very red & sore. Messiter's back, hair gone to grief. Lord M. with red handkerchief over head set out again about 8, very hot, kill 3 or 4 ducks & a goose, canoe leaks, have to stop in about an hour to pitch, put her in, still leaks, take her out, & do it over again, still leaks, find the place and tar for the third time, effectual cure, go on for another hour & then stay for dinner. Pemmican utterly condemned by Messiter & self as chips & tallow, start again about 4, camp at 6 not liking our late hours of yesterday. Bitten again. Hear a shot, expect our Yankee friends. Fried goose and ducks. Pleasant camping ground with plenty of shade & wood, break axe handle, turn in, done 7 or 8 miles only."

As Lord Milton paddled ahead one day to try to pick up a wounded bird, he came suddenly on the steamer *International* working her way up a shallow rapid. He was hungry and so he paddled toward the steamer as fast as he could. When he felt the strength of the current he let it carry his canoe along but it swept him with perilous speed toward the churning rear paddle-wheel. He and the canoe were saved by members of the crew who caught hold of both and dragged them on board.

Cheadle and Messiter in their larger canoe now hailed the steamer and the captain waved them to come aboard and ordered the paddle-wheel stopped. But as they reached the side of the steamer, suddenly the paddle-wheel churned again and drew the canoe into its stream. The two men saved themselves by frantic exertions from being drawn under the wheel but they were carried, before they could stop, down a quarter of a mile of rapids. Blaming the captain and each other, paddling with all their strength they were able to reach a point about a hundred yards from the steamer. Here the force of the current tumbling through a turn in the narrow channel swept the canoe round again and back they went down the rapids. Three times they struggled to the head of the rapids and three times they were flung back.

They were tired out and in despair when they saw a canoe coming from the steamer with two strangers paddling expertly. They changed places in order to have one experienced man in each canoe and "by holding on the bank, bumping the bottom against the stones and the most frantic paddling," they at last succeeded in reaching the steamer, "but only just."

After their exertions the captain could only agree to hold the steamer while they ate their first good dinner in several days and bought a supply of flour and salt pork. Then, refreshed, they launched their canoes and were off again. That night in the words of Cheadle, "Messiter constructs such a luxurious tent of our two sheets that we sleep like tops and do not wake till 10."

Three violent thunderstorms in rapid succession drenched everything in the canoes. "Again we set to work to wring out trousers, shirts and blankets and clean our guns, sulkily enough." They saw great trees blown down or splintered by the last of these storms which must have been a tornado for Cheadle described it as a "riband storm which passes over only a narrow line but within these limits is exceedingly violent and destructive."

They lived for several days on ducks and geese and then game failed altogether. Their last fish hook broke and they contrived a hook out of two needles tied together which served to catch two goldeyes for supper. Then at last they saw some geese. "On—on—on—paddle —paddle—paddle—awfully empty, especially Messiter who ate his allowance first. A yell of delight and furious chase, although before pulling very languidly and hardly speaking a word. . . . Set to work plucking geese and ducks; make a roaring fire and roast them on sticks. Lord M. and Messiter eat a goose apiece and I three ducks. Nothing to them but Harvey sauce and salt—no bread or vegetables but manage to stay our stomachs."

Then at five in the morning the steamer caught up with them. "Such a breakfast—wonderful! ditto dinner, ditto tea. Good wash and luxury of clean clothes. Dress Lord M's foot with splinter in it."

Two days later they arrived at Fort Garry.

They had been travelling for sixteen days from George-town and over a month from Montreal and this with the advantage of the railroad to the Mississippi and steam-boat on the Red River, both innovations of the last three years. Red River had been a settlement for nearly fifty years but there was no other way of reaching it except by Hudson Bay and York Factory, the route which Selkirk's first band of settlers had taken.

Apart from its occasional difficulties with grasshoppers and floods, Fort Garry was prospering. The farmers raised splendid flocks and herds on the rich prairie grasses and crops of wheat too large for the colony or the Hudson's Bay Company to consume. Half-breeds continued to farm, fish and hunt as occasion or fancy dictated and to furnish voyageurs and hunters for the Company and for passing travellers. Their great concern was not the lack of a market of which the farmers complained but the Great Spring and Fall Buffalo Hunts. One of these the Earl of Southesk had watched as it started out in June three years before. At the time Milton and Cheadle arrived the Spring Hunt was over, the Fall Hunt at least a month off.

Indian visitors, Saulteaux, Crees, Assiniboines, Blackfeet, even sometimes the dreaded Sioux, were to be seen at Fort Garry. Everyone who entered the west visited there. It was the place, as the Earl of Southesk had found, to hire guides and buy horses and supplies, to hear advice and horrifying stories of encounters with Blackfeet and grizzlies, to organize oneself and take breath before launching on the ocean of grass. At the time of the visit of Milton and Cheadle, Lord Dunmore and his party were just leaving to hunt buffalo. They enjoyed their hunt and were ready to start through Minnesota for home when they heard of the terrible Sioux massacre and were obliged to take a very long and round-about route in order to avoid the disturbed area. A little earlier that summer two hundred Canadians, the famous Overlanders, had passed through Fort Garry on their legend-making way to the British Columbia gold-fields.

To Dr. Cheadle Fort Garry was neither a gateway nor a meeting place but a community with many ailments. From the moment of his arrival he was busy seeing patients. Word went round that a doctor had come and people crowded upon him or sent him urgent appeals—a man with chronic bronchitis, a boy in an epileptic fit, boils, even cholera. Lord Milton developed a bad leg with sunburn and small boils and had to be treated by means of rest and cold water bandages.

While he carried on an emergency medical practice, Dr. Cheadle had also in odd moments to examine, try out and buy horses, and to order supplies—flour, pemmican, tobacco, powder and shot, tea, a little rum. At night mosquitoes made sleep all but impossible. When Messiter slept in his own tent, taking his mosquito net with him, Lord Milton and the doctor spent an agonizing night. Only toward morning when the doctor wrapped his head in a flannel shirt was he able to sleep a little, to wake half smothered and swollen with hundreds of bites. The next night they made a small fire on the ground inside the tent and then placed sods over it which filled the tent with smoke and gave them a chance to be suffocated instead of bitten.

Their chief guide was La Ronde. He came on board the *International* at Fort Garry before Cheadle and Milton could disembark for he had been Lord Milton's guide on his earlier visit to the west. Two men who had met Cheadle's party at Georgetown had brought news of their approach and La Ronde had been alarmed at the lateness of their arrival. He showed intense joy at seeing

Lord Milton again, expressing his readiness "to go with him to the end of the world, if required."

In addition to his previous service with Lord Milton, La Ronde had accompanied Dr. Rae on one of his journeys. Another guide, Vital, boasted that he had gone with Captain Palliser on his expedition and also that he had killed a surprising number of grizzly bears. A few days after the start of the journey Vital was scolded for riding all day in a cart and that night he ran away and returned to the fort. Two other guides made no claims to superiority and were satisfactory enough.

Of the horses the party bought the most conspicuous was Cheadle's, which he named Bucephalus. It was an odd-looking animal with crooked legs and a large head but it proved the best horse of them all and the only one to cross the Rocky Mountains and complete the journey with its master.

The days were hectic as are all days of preparation and departure when business is mixed with social claims. Dr. Cheadle's journal grows breathless among the urban distractions of Fort Garry. Lord M's leg worse. Call at Post Office, Printing Office and office of *The Nor'Wester*. No letters. Chief Factor killed six grizzly bears. Grizzly jumps boat and carries off a man like a baby in arms. Drunken Indians. Tom-tom going all night. Mme. La Ronde makes the party twelve pairs moccasins, moose skin breeches and leggings. Have a fierce argument with Messiter as to salvation of savages; who ended by using very ungentlemanly language, for which he soon apologized and all right again. Drawing up agreements with the men. Messiter casts bullets. Saw two patients. Cleaned gun and pistols. Got up in last clean collar, black coat and waistcoat and clean shirt to call on Bishop. Stayed to tea. Fetched to view body of a man killed by kick of a horse. Messiter starts for church. Returns unshriven, having arrived two hours too soon and finding it too hot to wait. La Ronde gets screwed and tells me in confidence that Lord M. said, "Damn the Doctor's carts", which he thought it his duty to tell me. Very silly. English cholera. Lord M. all day packing. Finds he requires another cart. Shall we ever get off?

Even after they got off, on August 23, it seemed impossible to get clear of the tangled fringes of civilization. They stopped to see the wedding of a cousin of one of the guides, where with violent dancing to two fiddles and much corn whisky, the crowd of guests made them welcome. Viscount Milton danced with the bride and was with difficulty persuaded to come away. After a mile or two Rover was found to be missing, Messiter went to look for him and Lord Milton and La Ronde, under pretense of looking for the dog also, returned to the wedding dance.

A day or two later at an isolated house they stopped and asked for milk. An old Scotswoman lived there who had just come out from Canada. Pressing bread and milk upon her visitors, she promised that if they would stay all night she would spread for them linen sheets not used since she brought them from Scotland twenty-six years before. There were only seven white people, she said, in that part of the settlement, more than fifty miles from Fort Garry.

Since it was now "too late in the season to attempt crossing the mountains before winter, we therefore decided to travel westward to some convenient point on the river Saskatchewan and winter there, in readiness to go forward across the mountains the following summer." Their ultimate objective was the Cariboo gold-field which they had determined to see before they returned to England.

Pushing on, they dined on pemmican with Worcestershire sauce, shot some ducks and lost them, and hobbled the horses. For they were now in Indian territory and, the doctor wrote, "have seen the last of houses for many a long day."

## II

"More afraid of not killing than of any dangers," wrote
Dr. Cheadle of his first buffalo hunt. Riding out with
La Ronde he saw eight or nine buffalo a mile or two
away and other small herds farther off. Guns examined,
girths tightened, they rode forward slowly in tense excitement. At about a quarter of a mile from the largest
herd La Ronde imitated the lowing of a buffalo and
the animals looked up from their grazing and moved
closer together. La Ronde gave the word and the horses
broke into a canter. The herd only glanced round and
moved on slowly, then drew together and advanced at a
lumbering gallop.

"Allez! Allez!" La Ronde shouted and off they went,
as fast as they could ride, "whip, whip, both heels ham-
mering our horses' ribs, arms flying, guns brandishing,
yelling true half-breed fashion." The buffalo looked to
Cheadle "very comical, head and shoulders covered with
long hair and bare quarters, like shaved French poodles",
going forward in a rolling gallop which was really much
faster than it seemed. At ten yards Cheadle fired both

115

barrels and one or two separated from the herd. His horse managed to cut off one while he slowed down to reload and then fired gun and revolver. Suddenly up went the buffalo's tail and Cheadle had a flashing recollection of a piece of advice half heard at Fort Garry—if a buffalo's tail goes up and the tuft at the end wags, he's going to charge. The tail was up, the tuft wagging, the bull wheeled, head down, looking very menacing. Cheadle fired again, aiming at the shoulder as he had been told to do, the bull turned, walked three yards and fell dead. Excited during the run, "screaming and shouting like a madman," Cheadle rushed up, elated, to look at his first kill and to cut off the tongue and tail to hang on his saddle.

When he rejoined the others, Lord Milton and Messiter were, as usual, disputing angrily, this time over which had killed the animal before them. From such evidence as the position of the wound and a cartridge case lying close by, the honour was accorded to Milton. Cheadle took one of the guides back with him to get the marrow bones of his buffalo; they had no trouble in finding it for wolves were already tearing the carcass. "Wolves seemed to spring up out of the ground at the first shot." Rain and sleet were falling by this time and Messiter could not be found. Firing their guns at intervals as a signal the men worked their way back to camp and at last went to sleep, wet and exhausted.

They had been hunting for Messiter for some time the next morning when the missing man came up with four Crees. Wandering numb with cold the night before he had come upon a Cree camp and been taken to the

chief's lodge, a large one made of fifteen buffalo skins. The women had brought him meat and muskeg tea and a mug of warm water and grease to drink. They gave him a pile of robes to lie on but, though he was very tired, the activities of his hosts made sleep impossible. All night the men and squaws cooked meat, smoked, beat the dogs, quarrelled and turned out all the lodges to look for a missing surcingle. In the morning the chief and three other Crees brought Messiter directly to the camp.

Everyone shook hands, then sat on the floor of the tent and smoked in silence for a long time. The chief, "rather fine looking fellow, Roman nose, spangled shirt, cap with ribands, medicine bag," at last stood up and made an oration which La Ronde translated. "I and my brothers have been much troubled by the reports we have heard from the Company's men, who tell us that numbers of white men will shortly visit this country; and that we must beware of them. Tell me why you come here. In your own land you are, I know, great chiefs. You have abundance of blankets, tea and salt, tobacco and rum. You have splendid guns and powder and shot as much as you can desire. But there is one thing you lack—you have no buffalo, and you come here to seek them. I am a great chief also. But the Great Spirit has not dealt with us alike. You he has endowed with various riches, while to me he has given the buffalo alone. Why should you visit this country to destroy the only good thing I possess, simply for your own pleasure? Since, however, I feel sure that you are great, generous and good, I give you my

117

permission to go where you will, and hunt as much as you desire, and when you enter my lodge you shall be welcome."

All this was said "with much dignity, his gestures graceful and easy, his speech fluent." He put the case so simply and so well that his hearers felt ashamed of themselves. But with that instant descent from denunciation to importunity which so often impaired the dignity of the Indian's position, the Crees, in accepting a gift of knives, ammunition, tea, salt and tobacco, expressed themselves as not satisfied and asked for a gun, blankets and especially rum. The chief had told La Ronde no less than five times that he had once been drunk, an occasion which he obviously regarded as a climax in his career and one he was eager to repeat. The request was firmly refused. After dinner the Crees went away, not in anger, but remarking that these white men could not have been as great as they supposed since they had no rum.

When they were gone the little camp fluttered with anxiety. The Crees had admired the horses and asked questions about them; could they mean to come that night and steal them? La Ronde hobbled them all and brought them close to the camp, loaded all the guns and watched through the night but no Indians came.

A day or two later the party met a line of carts returning to Red River and one of the drivers handed Dr. Cheadle a note. It was from Lord Dunmore who wrote that he was lying sick at Fort Ellice and requested the doctor to come as quickly as possible. Dr. Cheadle and

Lord Milton made ready at once. They tied their blankets to their saddles and equipped only with tin cups and pieces of galette or unleavened bread they rode on rapidly to Fort Ellice, leaving the men to bring on the carts. On the third day after hard riding they reached the fort only to find that Lord Dunmore had recovered and gone off the day before.

Charles Murray, the seventh Earl of Dunmore, who travelled just ahead of them and whom that year they never actually saw, was another of the adventurous young noblemen whose enthusiasm or restlessness carried him far and wide across the earth. At this time only twenty-one years old he was to travel in Africa, the Arctic and Chinese Turkestan, to publish a novel, *Ormiston*, to serve as Lord-in-Waiting to Queen Victoria. He was even to intrude briefly into Canadian politics and finance when in 1880 he telegraphed to the prime minister, Sir John A. Macdonald, a sudden offer to build a railway to the Pacific, a suggestion which came to nothing but which takes its place in the winding negotiations that led in time to an actual Pacific railway.

At Fort Ellice where the Cheadle party stopped for two days to repair the carts, Lord Milton saw a new lodge occupied by an Indian family, "nicely painted on outside with number of men killed and seen killed by owner and brother." At the fort, Milton selected a plated calumet or Indian pipe to use in bargaining and the Indian agreed to sell him the lodge for that and a cart cover. The lodge proved useful at once for on a day of steady rain the party, including the guides, sat there talking. Cheadle "told them of the size of London, the *Great Eastern*, the pace of our railways, and the small time it takes to sail 2,000 miles to England, and excited intense astonishment. Milton writes up journal a month in arrears. Messiter and I play All Fours. Very long day."

"A most unlucky day," Cheadle wrote on September 22, "I commence by burning my boots and socks which were drying by the lodge fire. After starting with Messiter to walk ahead I find I have lost the top of the shot bag Milton lent me. I then miss 5 ducks in succession and fire 3 barrels at snipe without success. I give up shooting and rejoin the carts. See a badger running along the road in front of me. Milton and I give chase. I get within 30 yards and give him a charge of No. 3; it turns him over and he stops and grins at me; other barrel not loaded from losing shot bag. I run after him and turn him repeatedly, trying to cram in a charge of buckshot in gun. Voudrie comes up and hits him over nose with switch, but he succeeds in getting to earth to my chagrin, as I hoped to begin my hunt. Rain coming on, camp about 5:30 having made a short day."

When they reached the South Saskatchewan the men cut down trees, made a raft and transported their baggage across the eighty yards of muddy water. Next morning they took the carts to pieces and carried them across in sections while the horses had to be vigorously beaten to make them enter the water. A few miles farther on they reached Fort Carlton with its high palisade and square corner towers, where Mr. Lillie was now in charge.

Though it was only September 27, four inches of snow
fell during the night and all day snow continued to fall.

One day in that same year a boy of twenty arrived
at Fort Carlton and took his seat at the Company dinner
table. He had eaten pemmican before but never fresh
buffalo steak and with a boy's hunger, as he said, he
relished it very much. His host offered him more steak
but feeling that he had had enough meat, he casually
asked the man seated beside him, "Will you please pass
the bread?" To the boy's amazement everyone at the
table burst into laughter. "An old gentleman said to me,
'Young man, you are out of the latitude of bread.' And
so it was; for looking down the table I saw there was no
bread, no vegetables, only buffalo steak. This was an
entirely new experience to me; though born on the
frontier I had never till now got beyond bread. I was
sorry I had not taken some more steak, but determined
to be wiser next time."

The boy was John McDougall who came to know the
plains and describe their life as perhaps no other man
ever did. He had several advantages over other travellers
who saw the west for the first time. For one thing he was
of the clearest pioneer strain, born in a log cabin near
Owen Sound in 1842. His father, the stalwart George
McDougall was, in the words of his son, a first settler,
trapper, trader, sailor and local preacher. His mother
raised a large family of children and entertained a constant stream of passing travellers in the most primitive
conditions and with unfailing energy and patience. John

spoke Indian before he spoke English and when he was twelve years old, went to work in the woods getting out saw logs while his father studied for the ministry at Victoria College at Cobourg.

Like a real son of the frontier John was strong and hardy, delighting in riding over the plains and in dog-driving. He took an ingenious pride in his strength and speed and in his very real skill in fishing, hunting and all the strenuous activities of frontier life. Also he came to the west not as a traveller or sight-seer but engaged very literally in a mission which bound him to the life of the Indians and half-breeds he met and impelled him from the first to accept their life as his own.

He was enormously articulate; few autobiographies can extend to so many volumes and cover the writer's career in such full and zestful detail. In successive books he described his life on the plains up to 1875 when he was thirty-three years old. The titles show his intense preoccupation. *Forest, Lake and Prairie, Twenty Years of Frontier Life in Western Canada,* takes him to 1862, his twentieth year. There follow *Saddle, Sled and Snowshoe, Pioneering on the Saskatchewan in the Sixties,* then *Pathfinding on Plain and Prairie, Stirring Scenes of Life in the Canadian Northwest, In the Days of the Red River Rebellion,* and *On Western Trails in the Early Seventies,* and other books based on his experiences, as well as a biography of his father.

John himself spent two years at Victoria College and then in 1860 his father was sent to take charge of the mission at Norway House which had been the post of

James Evans, and the family travelled by the St. Paul route, by stage-coach and York boat to that distant fort. There John, eighteen himself, taught a school of eighty pupils, and learned to drive dogs. He went with his father once a week to conduct a religious service in English at the fort, skimming home behind his dog-team under the crackling glory of the Northern Lights, which the Indians called the Dancers.

Two years later he went with his father to visit the western portion of the elder McDougall's parish which included the missions on the Saskatchewan River. John had arrived at Carlton on the day when he discovered that he was out of the latitude of bread. In all his travels over the plains he never became quite reconciled to the absence from his diet of bread and salt.

He was a bumptious, conceited, strenuous young man, fascinated by the new world into which he had stepped. His eager eyes compared these strange Indians with the woods Indians among whom he had grown up. Canoe and dog-train he knew; this was horse country.

Carlton enchanted him. "Ah, those first gallops on the plains! I will never forget them. Our crews from the boats, hunters from the plains, parties of Indians in the trade, the air full of stories about the Southern Indians and the tribal wars to and fro, scalps taken and horses stolen, the herds of buffalo said to be within a hundred miles from the fort, or less than two days out. Buffalo-skin lodges and canvas tents dotted the plains in every direction. Horse-races and foot-races were common occurrences. I championed older Canada against

123

Indians, half-breeds and Hudson's Bay officials and employees, and in the foot-racing and jumping—high, long, and hop, step and jump—cleaned out the crowd and made a name for myself and country, and amid such doings spent fifteen days, when father and his party came up and we moved on."

From Carlton John McDougall went to Mr. Woolsey's mission near Edmonton where his father left him to work for a year and where he lived with a man who became an important member of the Cheadle expedition. We shall hear more of John McDougall in due course.

At Fort Carlton Cheadle heard that one of the men had "discovered two full grown enormous grizzlies tearing up roots; stated he dismounted, loaded his gun, and prepared to shoot at them when he suddenly remembered it was Sunday." The ensuing bear hunt was unpopular with everyone but Dr. Cheadle and Messiter; La Ronde refused to go, the man who had seen the bears was found to have left the fort, Milton started off with the hunters and turned back. Even Rover declined to go. Cheadle and Messiter follow the tracks "to the edge of some pines, find some fresh sign and the place where they had evidently breakfasted, the earth being torn up quite lately, grubbing for roots; lose the tracks near the pines and conclude they have gone on to cover for the day; ride round the pines but see nothing of the bears. Greatly disappointed. Excited while following the fresh tracks, larger than a man's foot, and the impress of their long claws very well marked in the snow."

A party of Crees came to dine with the travellers, one

of whom, "a boy of sixteen told us with great pride that he had already been ten times on the war-path and last summer stole six horses from the Blackfeet." The usual gifts were made to them but two days later Cheadle learned that the Crees had followed them on their hunt the day before, intending to take their horses. They had been displeased with treatment which had seemed to the young men very handsome.

Milton, in particular, suffered from a chronic inability to understand the Indians. "Yesterday," Cheadle wrote, "the old Cree . . . told Milton we had been so kind to him and his squaw that he wished to present Milton with a horse. Milton very pleased but La Ronde said it only meant rum, and he declined the gift."

It had been apparent for some time that Messiter was not a very congenial travelling companion. Argument was a conversational staple as many of the journal entries show. A long discussion whether it was Saturday or Sunday. Squabbled about cooking bread, each stating his own way was best. Messiter was excitable and hot-headed. Messiter thought he heard Indians and nearly fired at Rover. Arguments in which he took part quickly degenerated into quarrels. Milton and Messiter squabbling all day, became a common entry. Milton and Messiter had had a violent argument about nothing and nearly came to blows. Even Cheadle who usually acted as peacemaker was provoked to retaliation. "I contradict Messiter in the same manner he uses to others and he becomes very irate. Messiter loses temper and calls me a fool." Cheadle and Milton accordingly decided to tell Messiter that he must leave their party. Messiter, shocked, protested but the other two stood firm. A few days later, having engaged guides of his own, he went off to hunt in the region of the Thickwood Hills.

Not long after leaving Fort Carlton they passed a place called Belle Prairie "surrounded by woods and small hills and one or two lakes in the opening; a pretty promontory jutting into one lake, covered with pine and poplar. Strikes both Milton and me as a very beautiful site for a house." Two of their guides had gone back to Fort Garry with some of the horses and the other two, La Ronde and Bruneau, were to spend the winter with them. After crossing the Crochet River a little farther on, they saw two small wooden houses. One had been built by a free trader and the other by the Hudson's Bay Company in opposition to it. One was now empty and the other occupied by a family which was to make itself a conspicuous part of that prairie winter. When Milton and Cheadle went up to the house they saw an old Indian mending a net and his squaw smoking her pipe by the fire. This was Kekekooarsis or Child of the Hawk from his beak-like nose. Cheadle in his journal called him Old Boy. He and his wife and children lived in one room of the house and his son-in-law and his family in the other. La Ronde introduced his two masters as a great chief and a great medicine man, who had travelled far to make Old Boy's acquaintance. Old Boy at once asked for rum and Milton ("Alas! mistaken generosity!") promised it to him. The great white chiefs went back to their lodge, drew some rum from the little keg, watered it well and sent it off to Old Boy. They had scarcely replaced the keg on the cart when Old Boy came singing and shouting, empty bottle in hand, with his son-in-law, wife and son. They showed some marten skins and asked for more rum. "La Ronde explained that we had not come to trade and had only a little for our own use during the winter. Very pertinacious, however, and after two hours discussion and nearly midnight we gave them a small quantity more. How they chuckled over it and hugged the pot! Squaws, children and all. Turned in very uncomfortable, and foreseeing the trouble the possession of rum would cause us."

Their experience for the rest of that winter sharply outlines the wisdom of Southesk in deciding to carry no liquor with him. The very morning after their visit from Old Boy "both the men were back with skins to trade for rum. Explained that we did not want to trade and sent them off with the remainder of the little barrel. In about two hours they returned very drunk, accompanied by two others, relatives; and presently another, the Company's fisherman here, arrived on horseback accompanied by his squaw and kid. . . . Directly after another employee of the Company arrived, already screwed, having doubtless gone shares at the house with the rest. Kept offering a beaver skin first to Milton and then to me and crying out 'rum, my master, my master, rum, I want a dram, give me a dram.' The old man's son then came in very drunk and proceeded to take off his coat and then his shirt which he passed over to me. I shook my head, but he persisted in offering it, but presently lapsed

into insensibility and fell into the arms of his squaw.
La Ronde came in having been absent after the horses,
and explained that we had not come to trade but hunt, and
had only a small quantity left. They persisted in demanding and we in refusing and we spent nearly the whole day
sitting in the lodge amidst the most infernal clamour.
We were not quit of them till nearly dark. We then held
a grand council as to what should be done, and decided
that the barrels must be safely cached at some distance
that night."

At midnight, for secrecy, Bruneau and La Ronde
shouldered the two rum barrels and hid them on the
other side of the river. They decided also to return to
Belle Prairie and build a hut on the promontory of the
lake where they had noticed a pleasant spot.

The site at Belle Prairie lay between the Shell and
Beaver rivers, two or three days journey north-west of
Fort Carlton. On October 20, they began to cut down
trees to build their house but they had scarcely begun
when Old Boy appeared with his son-in-law whom
Cheadle called the Chasseur. La Ronde quickly threw
a blanket over the rum barrels when he saw the Indians
coming, and they agreed to cache them again at once but
had not had time to lift them from the cart when three
more Indians came galloping up holding out furs and
asking for rum. When they were steadily refused, one of
them demanded angrily, "what the devil we want in
their country if we would not trade. The others shook
our hands most affectionately and sang our praises."

Next day they built four feet of the walls, the next,

raised them to six feet. Cheadle was deeply mystified when he saw a house rising without doors or windows and with spaces between the logs through which he could slip his hand. La Ronde provided the solution. "House at full height. Doors and windows cut out." The roof was covered with straight, dry pine poles supporting a thatch of marsh grass weighted down with a scattering of loose earth. Boards from the carts made the door and pieces of parchment the windows. Next, "fetching clay and building the chimney. Light a fire in the embryo chimney and part tumbles down; consternation."

The lake near which the house stood was now completely frozen over so that there could be no delay in finishing the house. Cheadle set out with a cart to get stone for a broader chimney, while guides chinked the spaces between the logs with a mixture of clay and chopped reeds. That afternoon Milton helped Cheadle to lay a foundation for the new chimney. It was on this day that the Chasseur returned from Fort Carlton with news of the Sioux Massacre at Georgetown. He said also that buffalo were not far off so that meat and sport would be available. But food would be needed before a hunt could be got under way and Cheadle and Bruneau made a rapid trip to Carlton for a supply of dried meat and grease. When they returned everyone set to work to finish the house. "I and Milton engaged in putting up shelves and arranging things thereon. Bruneau and La Ronde finish the planking. In the afternoon I commence cutting out a chair wherein to smoke withal. Milton ennuyeed." The Old Boy came and offered his daughter for sale but was declined with thanks.

If "rum" was one of the theme-words of that winter at Fort Milton, as La Ronde called the cabin, another was "wolverine". For Cheadle planned a winter of trapping. Trapping was an important part of the Englishman's dream of the North American west. Less exciting than the buffalo chase, still, trapping had the mystery of far places and strange, colourful occupations. The half-breed dressed in leather and furs striding on his snow-shoes over a wilderness of snow, penetrating dark pine forests where grizzlies lurked in every tangle, following his trap line and bringing back in the rippling gleam of the northern lights sleigh-loads of the finest furs—it was an appealing picture and even the practical Dr. Cheadle was drawn by it into his winter's employment.

He began with his habitual gusto. Immediately after his return from Fort Carlton he began to prepare strychnine for wolves and wolverines and La Ronde went out to find a promising trapping ground. On the way he showed Cheadle how to distinguish between the tracks of fox, wolf and wildcat. After laying poisoned baits and inspecting them every day for a week, Cheadle had a victim. "Descried mine ancient enemy the great wolf lying dead. A monster with a fine skin. Detached my belt and dragged him thereby to the hut; heavy work."

Tracks were everywhere. Cheadle laid new poisoned baits. Next day all baits were gone but no dead animals could be found. "Placed more poison treble strength. Started after breakfast for the woods to commence trapping. I took up my bundle and placed it on my back with misgivings; it felt *very* heavy; 2 blankets, 20 lbs. pemmican, 5 or 6 grease, 2 pair extra moccasins. La Ronde, meat, tea, salt, tin pot and 2 cups, baits for traps. In addition I had my belt with axe, knife, bullet and tobacco pouch, tinder and flint and steel ditto; powder horn, shot belt, gun, mittens, 3 pair socks on, leather breeches, mittas jersey, flannel shirt, tweed waistcoat, leather shirt, duffle shirt! Oh, by Jove! I could hardly move, trudged along with stern resolution. La Ronde going a great pace in spite of a load heavier than mine, but I was too proud to request him to be more moderate. 2 miles across the lake, and then plunged into the thick woods, and I soon found it very heavy work, my back aching before the first mile, the 4 inches of snow hiding the obstacles in the path which didn't exist and making footing very slippery and uncertain. After 4 miles of this work, when I had begun to curse my folly in making such a beast of burden of myself, La Ronde very considerately proposed a pipe to which I acceded without protest, and I seated myself on a fallen tree perspiring at every pore, for the day was extremely warm for the time of year. On again some distance and dine; devilish glad of it. After dinner on to large lake for night. See a few marten tracks on the way; three traps with baits eaten by magpies and ermine. Thank my stars able to lighten my load by eating pemmican, and gorge myself with that view, utterly careless of food for future emergencies. Saw a fresh moose track; no wind."

"Wolverine had broken most of my traps," he wrote on December 17 and the next day, "I found all traps broken and the remnant of one marten. The wolverine again. Eaten of the Yankee strychnine and made him hungry! Confound the Yankees!" When La Ronde came in later that day "he had not arranged a single trap the wolverine having broken all and eaten nine martens of which he found the remains, perhaps more. In a great rage, vowing vengeance against the wolverines. Very unusual for a wolverine to touch a marten. La Ronde thinks him half devil."

When he departed for the Thickwood Hills, Messiter had not stepped out of Dr. Cheadle's journal for long. Early in December the men saw dog-teams coming from the direction of Fort Carlton and soon Messiter arrived, scarcely recognizable in white capote and fur cap, talking as tirelessly as ever. He was full of a new and exciting interest; he was trading for furs. "Had made seventy marten, besides deer, bear and other skins of his two gallons rum, knives, flour." In his breathless way he told of a recent experience.

"One occasion Atagakouph wanted rum as a present. Messiter refused, wanting a marten. Atagakouph went out, fetched the marten (being already pretty well screwed), crumpled it up and threw it in Messiter's face. Messiter enraged, hit him in the face with his fist. Atagakouph drew his knife and stabbed at him, held back by Badger. The Columbian coming at the time, got a cut across the face; knives chopping about in all directions. One Indian seized the candle, dashed it on the floor and then collared the rum cask. Messiter in the corner farthest from the door and unarmed, made a rush, got a cut on the hand, one through the hair at the back of his neck, and another gash in the breast; none severe; met a man on the way; bright thought struck him; stooped down, seized him by the legs and chucked him over his head with a crash; gained the door, having seized the barrel, snatched up his gun which was close to the door and loaded, and seating himself on the barrel outside the house, kept guard over it with both barrels on full cock, vowing to shoot the first man who interfered with him." In this situation he had been joined by an Indian to whom he had made presents and who was strong enough to "bang Atagakouph against the wall most unmercifully." As a result Atagakouph had been unable to walk for a week. In spite of all this, Messiter was prepared to continue rum trading with unclouded enthusiasm.

He had not only traded but he had raced the Hudson's Bay Company trader for several days to get furs which the latter had been sent out to collect. This he seemed to consider great sport and he could talk of nothing but his new hobby while in the cabin he and Milton played whist for marten skins.

Whether it had not occurred to Messiter that the Company had the gravest objection to free fur trading in its territory, or whether he was aware of the fact and did not take the matter seriously, Dr. Cheadle did not record, but measures were very soon taken to arrest his activities. The train of dogs Messiter had bought at Fort Carlton was seized and further supplies were refused. Messiter hastened "to explain that he was only purchasing a few furs for his lady friends; but that wouldn't wash." After further sorties and recriminations Messiter went off with his guide, Milton and Bruneau went to Fort Carlton and La Ronde and Cheadle settled down to spend Christmas by themselves. La Ronde sat smoking on Christmas eve, an Indian boy who spent much time at the cabin looked with absorption at Cheadle's medical book and Cheadle himself wrote in his journal, "No mince pies, no good things, no family meetings this year." The Christmas dinner next day "consisted of galette and hot pot! I made some rum punch which La Ronde and I discussed with gusto, and found it raised our spirits and we passed the evening merrily."

Supplies, as usual, were low and there was no flour to be had at Carlton. It was therefore decided to send the guides La Ronde and Bruneau all the way to Red River for supplies of flour, tea and sugar. They set off the day after Christmas, in good spirits, to call at Fort Carlton for a dog-team and provisions for the journey. "Only sending 600 miles for necessaries," Cheadle wrote, "to be back in two months!"

# III

"First thing Old Boy and the young one go outside with their guns and fire a salute of six shots in honour of the New Year. After that a general shaking of hands and good wishes. We omit kissing the women which was part of the ceremony properly."

The only supplies in the cabin were two pounds of flour and a few fish so that a buffalo hunt had to be undertaken at once. Before the hunters could leave they had to make another rapid trip to Carlton to get pemmican and they set out, three men and a boy with nine dogs and, for provisions, twelve fish and a handful of flour. Milton was left behind with a few fish and some desiccated vegetables. It was a hard trip. The second day they broke camp early determined to reach the Fort that night. "Off we went; snow deep and snowshoes— no stopping in middle of the day. I felt very faint and suggested a stop; but the Hunter reminded me that we had nothing to cook, and that if we stopped we should not reach the Fort that night. I therefore gave up the point, set my teeth and went at it again, lighting up a pipe occasionally to ease the gnawing of my stomach. Oh that weary walk! How many vows I made never to be short of food again if I could help it! And I came to the conclusion that all those poor wretches who commit crime from force of hunger were deserving of the utmost pity. I'm sure I should have stolen then without scruple. No one who has not been in the same circumstances has the least idea of the suffering of hunger. Well, at last we came to a clump of firs which I recognized as only 8 or 9 miles from the fort. There the Hunter pulled up and sat down for a moment to light a pipe; before I could get my tobacco cut and my pipe lit he set off again; after 3 or 4 miles he said he was thirsty and broke open a (musk)rat house to drink. Getting done now, thought I. I improving fast. Some 5 miles from the Fort we came upon a hard cart track, and Kinamontayoo taking off his snowshoes, I did the same, the dogs set off at a gallop, and after them we ran at a tremendous pace, right into the Fort, I leading for the last mile, in magnificent wind and feeling as fresh as possible after getting rid of my snowshoes. . . . I felt very comfortable and not at all ravenous until I began to eat; then I did wonders. Old bull went down like English beef. Bread, fresh butter and the potatoes went down deliciously; only not enough of them. Ordered the Indians and dogs as much as they could eat, and went to bed not the least tired."

He sent off a supply of food to Milton and decided to wait for the mail packet from Fort Garry which was daily expected. On the first day Cheadle enjoyed comfort and idleness at the fort where he talked to one of the Company men who had been at Cambridge. The Edmonton packet arrived in charge of Mr. Hardisty who had been factor at Carlton when he entertained the Earl of Southesk in 1859. "He came in a cariole with a very fine train of dogs, harness set out with bells and plumes, very jolly; a yellow-haired Scotchman he, by descent, a Red River man born and bred, very pleasant fellow indeed and very obliging. No snow at Edmonton!" At the sound of sleigh-bells everyone in the fort would rush out to see which packet had arrived now and to hear the news. The dog-sleighs came one after another from La Crosse, and Norway House, bringing letters to be sent on to England and the messengers settled down to wait for the mail to come by the express from Red River.

After the first day, in spite of the recurring excitement of arriving packets, Cheadle began to feel very bored and found nothing to record except a great treat at dinner—boiled rice with sugar and butter. Then an Indian brought a rumour of a terrible disease at Fort à la Corne, his description sounding like smallpox. Finding some vaccine at the fort, Dr. Cheadle "vaccinated all the unprotected ones I could lay hold of." The vaccine proved to be worthless and none of the vaccinations was successful; however, in a day or two when the packet arrived from à la Corne the smallpox story was shown to be a false rumour.

The express, when it came at last, brought no mail for Fort Milton and Dr. Cheadle looked about for some means of returning home. A half-breed named Jemmy

Isbister who had a good team of dogs at last agreed to take him, refusing payment because the doctor had prescribed for his child. The trip was agonizing. The dogs, with their sleigh loaded only with blankets and buffalo robes, went very fast over the hard snow and Isbister and Cheadle tore along on their snowshoes at a "frightful pace." Lying that night beside a roaring fire, fully clothed and piled with robes and blankets, the men could not sleep for cold and the dogs crawled shivering into their coverings. The temperature was thirty-eight below zero.

In winter trappers and travellers always slept in the open air because of the need to travel as lightly as possible. They shovelled away the snow with a snowshoe to make a camping place and laid pine branches on the ground. Then they quickly cut wood and started a fire, unharnessed the dogs and unpacked the sleds. The men squatted close to the fire, smoking and cooking their supper, while the hungry dogs sat as close as they dared. Before the men rolled in their blankets and robes and lay down near the fire to sleep, they had to hang high out of reach or otherwise securely hide the provisions, as well as the harness, snowshoes and every article made of leather. The dogs would quickly eat their own harness and the netting out of the snowshoes if these were left for a moment unprotected. As soon as the men seemed to be asleep the dogs would creep quietly forward and curl up between them or on their feet.

On this long-remembered trip, Cheadle, though he was wearing "a very great many flannel shirts, a leather shirt, duffel shirt and thick Inverness cape over all," froze his arms, legs and face and when they stopped at night he was too stiff to strike a match and Isbister could barely strike one. The second day they kept up the same racing speed and reached the hut that night, very fast time indeed. There was no one in the cabin for Milton had gone to stay with the Indians at White Fish Lake. Cheadle was completely exhausted, stiff and sore from head to foot. Isbister chopped wood and made a fire, fed his dogs, ate a hasty supper of raw pemmican and tea, wrapped himself in a robe on the sleigh and within two hours of his arrival had started back to the fort. Without stopping for rest or food he arrived there the next day about noon.

For a time after they had been firmly refused rum, Old Boy and his family resentfully agreed not to ask for it. But the knowledge that the Okey Mows, the Great Chiefs, had rum with them underlay every contact with Indian or half-breed and sprang to the surface to cause frequent difficulties. The way to get anything done most quickly and easily was to promise a quarter pint of rum but the transaction could never stop there. A wife, a son, a friend or all three always came along and must be treated too. And once the Indian had drunk his rum he forgot all agreements, all promises, and broke into passionate entreaty. Chasseur had been promised a quarter pint if he hurried back with supplies from the fort. "That necessitated giving the half-breed, his wife, and Nashquapa-mayoo a little. Then the half-breed wished to stand treat to his friend. We agreed to give them another half pint between them on condition that they did not ask for any more. They promised and presently began to get very drunk (Milton foolishly having given them a pint instead of half one) and sing uproariously. Telling us how they loved us and would do anything for us. . . . About 9 o'clock the Chasseur asked for a *little* drop more, *only* a little. He was very drunk but talked pretty well. The Canadian tried to interpret but could not get the words out. We reminded them both of their promise and the half-breed said he could not say another word for it was true. But Kinamontayoo was oblivious; nothing could make him understand; we continued firmly to refuse and he to ask. He explained that we were very fine fellows in some respects but our hearts were very hard; he sat down beside me, drew his knife, seized me by the arm and placed the point at my breast. I sat quite unmoved but prepared for the emergency. However he explained that if he had been a plains Indian he should have stabbed me if I said no; but that he did not behave in that way. In spite of this theatrical display we still said no, Chasseur again begged, and at last said that if we would not give it he would return at once, and forthwith ordered the young one to get the sled ready. He remonstrated strongly but without avail and after tumbling about for some time, Chasseur set out singing and leaving us to our fate. The night bitterly cold and snowing. The half-breed lay on the floor cursing and in the interval stammering out 'Excusez, excusez, Milor, aussi Docteur, pour l'amour de Dieu.'"

It appeared later that the Chasseur after he left the cabin had been too drunk to travel and had fallen insensible in the snow. If his fourteen-year-old son had not been with him he would have frozen to death. The boy had made a fire, dragged his father close to it and kept it burning all night. Two days later the Chasseur came to apologize for his behaviour.

Cheadle remained in camp while the Indians hunted, for meat and not sport was the object of the hunt. They were lucky enough to see five buffalo and Chasseur killed one. When the other four galloped off he was surprised to hear distant shots. Cheadle moved camp to a place close to the buffalo carcass where wood was available and while they were cutting up the meat a strange Indian appeared. He was a Saulteur; it was he who had fired at the four buffalo and, sure that he had wounded one of them, had followed a long way but had not come close enough for another shot. He had eaten nothing for two days, he said, and had left his wife and children a few miles away, also starving. As they cooked the meat for supper, the Saulteur said that he had hunted for days and had seen no buffalo except these five. They had that night what Cheadle called an enormous feed and another the next morning. Then the Saulteur started out to pursue the four bulls which had escaped him, while Chasseur went to hunt in another direction and Cheadle and the boy cut up meat. After dark the Saulteur arrived "covered with blood; he had killed the whole four bulls!"

Cheadle, with great presence of mind, at once bought two of them and the Saulteur went off to carry food to his family who had now fasted for four days. He came back next morning with his wife and family to camp close to the bulls he had killed. "Reported 5 lodges of Indians following, all starving. They soon came in with their dog-sleds (dogs literally skin and bone); men very wan." The appearance of the newcomers spoke well for the care that had been taken of the women and children, all of whom looked much stronger and better fleshed than the painfully gaunt and haggard men. It seemed that there were no buffalo to be found; the Indians were sure that the five which had just been killed were the only ones within a hundred miles.

"As this miserable company came, they were invited to sit down by the fire. Their cheerfulness belied their looks, and they smoked and chatted gaily, without appearing to covet the meat which lay around, or making any request for food at once. No time was lost in cooking some meat, and offering a good meal to all, which they ate with quietness and dignity; too well-bred to show any signs of greediness, although they proved equal to the consumption of any quantity that was put before them."

When they had finished Chasseur persuaded three young men to gamble with him. The players squatted opposite each other and put a blanket over their knees. "The game consisted in one of the players hiding in his hands two small articles, as a ramrod screw, or brass hair-wire, whilst the others endeavoured to guess what was contained in either hand. The holder did his best to deceive the others, by continually keeping his hands in motion, now under the blanket on his lap, now behind his back, or clasped together. Between each change the hands were held out for the choice of his opponent, who watched eagerly, in great excitement, and generally took a long time to make his guess." All this time the rest drummed on a frying pan with a stick and sang a monotonous "He he, hi, hi, hay, hay." "This went on for about two hours and then ended by Chasseur winning all. The others went away very contented, still singing and having now neither knife, shot nor mittens. Chasseur was greatly delighted at his good fortune and told me that if he had lost he should have gone on until he had nothing, not even coat or gun! I told him I thought that very reprehensible, but he only said it was good and told me to observe how much it had done for him." After another two days of hunting they started home with heavy sleigh-loads of meat.

There is the usual relation between theory and practice in comparing the Earl of Southesk's strictures on the cruelty of dog-drivers with the grilling experience of Dr. Cheadle, actually driving a team of dogs in heavy snow. "Much swearing; dogs obstinate; harness wrong; sleigh continually upsetting and getting off the track, which is like a line of single rail, and, the snow being deep, requires no small exertion to get it on again; when you have effected that with immense labour, perhaps the leading dog won't start, you scramble past to lick him, and then the others lie down and howl and you can't get them to move forward until you have turned round and got behind them again, in doing which you catch your snowshoes in the bushes and come on your nose in a yard of soft snow or so. Verily I believe driving a heavily laden

143

dog-sled in a hilly country would spoil the temper of a saint."

At a very steep slope Cheadle's sleigh went over the top of the hill before he could dig in his toes to act as a brake, the sleigh flew down the slope overriding the dogs and dragging them over and over in a succession of somersaults to the very bottom. There the dogs lay helpless, tangled in their harness, and with the sleigh on top of them, "which seemed as if it would have broken every bone in their bodies." However none was hurt though it took a long time to straighten out the harness and get the team on its way again.

In the course of the winter Lord Milton engaged an Indian woman to come and wash some clothing. "She came, and continuing to wash till midnight and the eternal scrub, scrub, splash, splash, poking the fire and rattling of pails preventing any possibility of sleep, he ventured to remonstrate mildly; without effect; it becoming unbearable towards morning, he jumped up, emptied the water and put out the fire, greatly to her disgust. She rested quietly until she thought he must be asleep and then again lighted the fire and resumed her washing. He was beaten and resigned himself to his fate with many maledictions."

When, a month or two later, the cabin seemed choked with chips and ashes, the two men set to work to clean it themselves but sweeping was difficult because they had no broom and the floor of the cabin was two feet lower than the ground outside. Milton made a besom of pine boughs, they used a tin plate for a dustpan and crawled energetically about poking dirt out of every corner. They were so much gratified with the tidy result that Milton decided to become more domestic still and to make a plum pudding. Messiter on his visit had brought them a gift of a few raisins and currants and when Cheadle discovered that these were rapidly disappearing he had locked them up with a little flour and sugar in his strong box. The box also contained shot, caps, tobacco and soap and when Cheadle opened it he found that the paper which held the fruit had broken and that all the contents of the box were well mixed together. These were carefully sorted out, the pudding made, tied in a bag and put in a pot to boil. "No one who has not been restricted to one species of food for a long time can form any idea of the greedy eyes with which we viewed that plum pudding." They looked at it, poked it with a fork, ate a pair of partridges while they waited—would it never be done? After boiling almost all day it was at last ready.

"As big as my head," wrote Cheadle ecstatically, "most delicious; not had such a treat since leaving Fort Garry; it really was good; would have held its head up in any company." Caps, buckshot and bits of tobacco found in the pudding had no effect on its delicious flavour. They could not eat it all that night but both jumped up next morning before it was light to finish the pudding for breakfast.

# IV

THE CONSTANT thought of the two men was now for
their guides, La Ronde and Bruneau. Why had they not
come back? Their long journey to Fort Garry for flour
and tea was to have taken them two months and the
two months were up. Every day they watched and lis-
tened for the guides' return and while they waited they
heard from passing travellers many stories of privation
among Indians and half-breeds. It had been a bad winter
for buffalo. People at Fort à la Corne were said to be
starving, at Egg Lake they had boiled a buffalo hide for
food. Carlton men on the way to a buffalo hunt had
been forced to eat one of their dogs. On the whole Dr.
Cheadle felt that they had been lucky in their hunting,
though they were now very tired of tough, dry buffalo
meat and greeted a gift of fresh moose meat from the
Chasseur with delight.

They asked each other every day what could have
happened to La Ronde. They smoked and chopped wood.
Cheadle soled his moccasins, read *Henry VIII* and practised his tracking, finding his skill much improved. It

was so cold sometimes that "a crust of ice formed on the tea in our tin mugs as we sat within a yard of a roaring fire." But this had not happened recently for they had been without tea for many weeks.

Then on March 11 La Ronde walked into the cabin. He was very thin and worn and coughing badly. They had made a quick trip to Fort Garry, he said, but on the trip back everything had gone wrong. "Two days from Fort Pelly obliged to give up one train from weakness of dogs. Short of provisions and have to feed dogs on flour. At Fort Pelly found them short of provisions and took all the pemmican they had, only ½ bag, leaving a bag of flour there, the snow being too deep and the sled over-laden; La Ronde frequently having to go twice over the track before the dogs could move. Had had his bronchitis 20 days and was very weak." Bruneau now arrived with the sled "20 lbs. tea, 5 gallons grog, half sack flour; . . . above all the letters at last! What a treat!" They read and laughed and compared notes; the news from home was good for both men and after hearing nothing for nine months, they found every word important.

News from Red River was, however, bad. A large body of Sioux had camped near by, burning hay and stealing horses, while at the settlement a watch was kept day and night. The horses Lord Milton had sent back had been lost. Even this report could not spoil the happiness of the evening. La Ronde was put to bed and dosed by Dr. Cheadle, while Milton made a "feast of pancakes and strong tea—ah! what a treat!" and the two men sat up late reading their letters over and over.

The return of the guides had not gone unnoticed. Cheadle and Milton had just gone to sleep that night when they were waked by dogs barking outside and someone opened the door. Old Boy, Chasseur, their wives and families had come for their pay for the winter's services and also, of course, for rum. Lord Milton smoked a pipe with the visitors and persuaded them to camp outside for the rest of the night. At the reckoning next morning it turned out that Chasseur had already drunk up nearly all his wages and that Old Boy actually owed forty skins. His wife at last after bitter argument went off "abusing us and saying we had come into the country to starve them and so on." That day half a dozen other Indians came on various pretexts. Old Boy was soon back again. "He wished to trade a silver fox and Milton was anxious to buy it, but next morning La Ronde discovered it was a red one, very ingeniously dyed. He recognized it by the smell and feel of the fur. . . . We said nothing but declined the purchase." Now that La Ronde was mending, Cheadle could go round his trap lines again. At night both men re-read their letters.

Trapping had brought very little in the way of furs and now it resulted in actual damage for the dogs picked up poisoned baits in the woods and two of them died. But it was time to give up trapping. On March 27 Cheadle wrote, "Very warm and thawing in the middle of the day," three days later "tremendous thaw." On this day he dismantled all his traps in order not to kill animals needlessly. The skunk skin lying on the snow near the door, which served as a thermometer, told him that a thaw was near. It gave out no scent when the cold was intense but as the air grew milder its odour, as Cheadle said, was perceptible. On April 1 an Indian boy saw three ducks fly overhead. Food was short, spring was coming, it was time to go.

The horses had been turned loose at the beginning of the winter. "We had seen them or their tracks from time to time, and knew in what direction they had wandered." La Ronde found them about ten miles away and Cheadle, when he saw them, was astonished at their splendid condition. They had been very thin when they were turned out but now they were "perfect balls of fat, and as wild and full of spirit as if fed on corn—a most unusual condition for Indian horses." The prairie grass seemed particularly nutritious, since animals could fatten so well even in winter when they had to scrape away the snow to reach it. Cheadle recalled that "the milch cows and draught oxen at Red River and in Minnesota, feeding on grass alone, were generally in nearly as fine condition as the stall-fed cattle of the Baker Street Show."

He reflected that farming at the Company posts, "although carried on in somewhat primitive fashion, is very productive. Potatoes are abundant and attain an immense size; carrots and turnips grow equally well, and wheat would no doubt flourish as luxuriantly here as at Edmonton or Red River, were there sufficient inducement to sow it."

All day on April 2 they packed; the next day at noon they set out, "feeling some regret at parting from our winter quarters, where we had certainly endured much

149

hardship, but however had some enjoyment and at least learnt much of Indian life." They had nothing to eat now except what they could kill on the way and La Ronde shot muskrats and prairie grouse. At Fort Carlton the ice on the river was still strong enough for the carts to cross. Cheadle and Milton stayed at the fort and began the business of settling accounts with La Ronde and Bruneau and hiring a man for the mountain journey.

Baptiste Supernat said that he knew the route as far as Tête Jaune Cache and under his guidance they set out for Fort Pitt. Ducks and geese could be killed every day now and the prairie was covered with blue anemones. Ice on the rivers was so weak that the utmost care had to be taken in crossing and the English River when they came to it was open water. At night by the camp-fire Baptiste proved to be a great talker. Gold was his theme. Indians had found, near the mountains, lumps of something which, when it had been sent to England, was pronounced to be pure gold. He himself had found gold in a creek near Fort Ellice. More wonderful still—"piece of iron found by Indian near Edmonton and placed many years ago on top of a hill, size of fist when placed there, now so large no one can raise it!" This was solemnly attested to as simple truth. Men at the fort frequently sidled up to Dr. Cheadle to show him specimens of mica, granite or schist, and were much disappointed to find that they were not gold.

At last the party reached Fort Pitt. "Fresh meat and potatoes, milk; latter upset me. Slept like a top." Dr. Cheadle had to renew his medical practice next day for everyone hurried to ask for treatment or advice. Word had spread, too, that the party had rum and Indians converged from all directions upon Milton and Baptiste, offering horses and demanding rum in exchange. Two Blackfeet came to the fort, heralds of others to follow, for peace had once more, in the continual alternation between peace and war, been concluded and they too had heard that Lord Milton's party had liquor. The horses they offered were thin and poor with very sore backs but they were locked up at night with all the horses at the fort, in fear of the Crees. "The Crees had already stolen some thirty from the Blackfeet since the peace, and the Blackfeet rather more in return; so that hostilities will probably recommence before very long." The very next day the fragile new peace was shaken when a runner announced that a Cree woman had been killed in the Blackfoot camp. "It appeared she went to be married to a Blackfoot, but others in the camp took a fancy to her, a quarrel arose, and one of them, to prevent the others from obtaining her put an end to the dispute by stabbing the woman. Off tomorrow, if 10,000 Blackfeet arrive, for we are all tired of slow life here."

At Fort Pitt they engaged another guide, Louis Battenotte, called the Assiniboine, because he had lived as a little boy with that tribe. Dr. Cheadle attended his youngest child who fell ill and died while they were at Pitt and the parents in their distress were anxious to leave the fort and to accompany Milton's party. But Milton and Cheadle hesitated to take the wife and thirteen-year-old son and Assiniboine would not go without them. Moreover, he had only one hand, the left one having been shattered by a bursting gun. He had, however, a pleasant voice and manner and a very high reputation as a hunter and guide. Assiniboine had a violent temper and Cheadle learned later that he had been dismissed by the Company for killing another half-breed in a drunken quarrel. "The murdered man was, however, a notorious bully, the dread and terror of all the half-breeds. Everyone agreed that the provocation had been excessive and the deed done in a moment of passion."

Edmonton in 1863, Cheadle wrote, "boasts of a windmill, a blacksmith's forge, and carpenter's shop. The boats required for the annual voyage to York Factory in Hudson's Bay are built and mended there; carts, sleighs and harness made, and all appliances required for the Company's traffic between the different posts. Wheat grows luxuriantly, and potatoes and other roots flourish as wonderfully here as everywhere else in Saskatchewan. There are about thirty families living in the fort."

It had grown a little since Southesk's day but the talk, as then, ran much on grizzly bears. Cheadle and his party had scarcely arrived when they heard that five grizzlies had attacked some horses at St. Albans, and that a bear hunt was planned. Though they rode at once to St. Albans the hunt was postponed and in the end, like so many bear hunts, it dwindled away into a day of riding through the bushes and seeing nothing in particular. "Vastly disappointed," Cheadle wrote.

Gold, near Edmonton, was a new sensation fanned by the talk of an American who had been washing for it in

White Mud Creek and who showed a small bag of very fine dust as a specimen. Cheadle and Milton, fired by these accounts, crossed the river one day to wash for gold on their own account. "Worked away at our tin pans obtaining a perceptible quantity each time. . . . After tried to collect our gold dust with mercury, but owing to stupidity in using tin dishes and bad manipulation we lost it all."

As usual Cheadle was called to treat many patients among whom was a little Cree girl. At the conclusion of peace between Crees and Blackfeet, a Blackfoot brave had playfully snapped his gun at the child. It had been loaded and the charge had shattered her thigh. Cheadle did his best for her but her parents were deeply disappointed in his efforts. From his reputation they had expected him to remove the shattered bone and provide a substitute so that the leg would be as good as ever.

Mr. Hardisty told them a story from Fort Benton, an American trading post on the Missouri River in the Blackfoot country. A lone Cree one day came to the fort on foot, followed by a band of Blackfeet who demanded that he should be surrendered to be scalped and tortured. The trader, not wishing to give up the Cree and afraid to refuse, suggested a compromise. The Blackfeet were to return in a month when the Cree, who would be kept at the fort, would be loosed with a hundred yard start, the Blackfeet to chase him on foot, armed only with knives. "The Blackfeet took their departure, and the Cree was immediately put into hard training. He was fed on fresh buffalo meat, as much as he could eat, and made to run around the fort enclosure at full speed for an hour twice a day." When the Blackfeet returned a month later, their horses were tied up and their guns taken from them. "The Cree was placed at his post, 100 yards ahead of his bloodthirsty enemies, who were eager as wolves for their prey. The word was given, and away darted the hunted Indian, the pursuers following with frantic yells. At first the pack of Blackfeet gained rapidly, for terror seemed to paralyze the limbs of the unfortunate Cree, and his escape seemed hopeless. But as his enemies came within a few yards of him, he recovered his presence of mind, shook himself together, his training and fine condition began to tell, and to their astonishment and chagrin, he left them with ease at every stride. In another mile he was far in advance . . . shook his fist triumphantly at his baffled pursuers, and then quickly ran out of sight."

Cheadle and his party bought horses and planned their route. Days passed slowly at the fort where they were obliged to wait while the horses rested and grazed; the hard conditions of the journey required them to be in the best possible condition. "We wandered from one window to another, or walked round the building, watching for the arrival of Indians, or the sight of some object of speculation or interest. At dusk the scores of sleigh dogs set up their dismal howling, and disturbed us in the same manner at daybreak, from slumbers we desired to prolong as much as possible, in order to shorten the wearisome day."

They talked to Father Lacombe and to Mr. Woolsey,

just as Southesk had done. John McDougall had been living for a year with Mr. Woolsey and his books give vivid glimpses of the old Wesleyan missionary. With Mr. Woolsey and John McDougall had lived also the far more famous Mr. O'Byrne.

When Cheadle's book, *The North-West Passage by Land*, later became popular in England, one objection frequently made to its claim to be a circumstantial account was that O'Byrne, as depicted there, could not possibly have existed. This was flattering to Dr. Cheadle's fictional powers for Dickens would have been proud to have created O'Byrne. The existence of O'Byrne is as well attested, in its way, as that of Napoleon or Dr. Johnson, for almost every person who knew the plains in the early sixties and wrote at all had at least one story to tell about O'Byrne, and some like James Hargraves and John McDougall devoted many pages to his peculiarities. Whoever encountered O'Byrne seemed impelled to record the experience.

O'Byrne was described as being fifty or sixty years of age with a long face and few teeth, dressed in a long clerical coat, wide black hat and fustian trousers. "His appearance showed a curious mixture of the clerical with the rustic." His talk was full of classical quotations and of the most unsparing flattery.

His life, an account of which he was always eager to give, had been an eventful one. He had studied for the bar, edited a paper at Lahore, returned to England, and at length gone out to Louisiana. There he had acted as secretary to a rich planter and lived very comfortably till the Civil War threatened. He had felt himself safe as a non-combatant but was "confounded by planter coming up and congratulating him upon being elected Captain of the home guard! As he is a tremendous coward," Cheadle wrote, "he was horror struck and decided that the only thing to be done was to escape at once." He had then taught the classics at a small college in the north but the Civil War pursued him, and the college was closed for lack of funds, leaving his salary unpaid. He had come to Red River to seek employment in a school and here James Hargraves of the Hudson's Bay Company met him.

He was notable then, as later, Hargraves wrote, in that he "apparently knew intimately all about the personalities of leading English public men," and he lived by borrowing money and by visiting as long as he was permitted to stay at as many houses as possible. At one time he was well paid to teach several children every morning in his hotel room, but very often he locked his door and went away for the day, leaving the children to shout and play about the hotel, to the indignation of both parents and hotel guests. Hargraves wrote of meeting him once when he was much distressed about a frozen ear and many times saw him in one house or another seated on the sofa after dinner, pipe in hand, haranguing those present upon politics and current happenings with many references to famous persons or places, all well known to him.

But people in Red River grew tired of having their money borrowed by O'Byrne and of being visited and lectured by him. They concocted a plan to send him as chaplain with the party bound for the Cariboo which passed through Red River in 1862. However the party grew tired of him even more quickly than Red River had done and abandoned O'Byrne at Fort Carlton. John McDougall saw him there and described him as "an old wandering-Jew kind of man." The Hudson's Bay Company brigade brought him on to Edmonton but he had very soon been ejected from the fort. Governor Dallas, the successor of Sir George Simpson, had made a rule that no stragglers should remain around the forts. Whoever brought such a person to the fort must pay a fine of ten shillings sterling a day. Naturally O'Byrne was at once cast out.

He could not be allowed to starve and someone suggested that he might live with Mr. Woolsey. An Indian who was going in that direction was accordingly persuaded to guide O'Byrne to Mr. Woolsey's house. As the two left the fort, neither knowing a word of the other's language, some humorist whispered to O'Byrne, "Watch that fellow. He is a murderer." "Poor Mr. O'Byrne," McDougall wrote, "had an awful time of watching his companion and guide, and was a very grateful man when he came to our home safe."

That winter spent in close quarters in a small cabin was too much even for the warm-hearted Mr. Woolsey. When John McDougall was about to start on a trip to Edmonton early in the spring of 1863 Mr. Woolsey suggested, "John, I am about tired of Mr. O'Byrne. Couldn't you take him to Edmonton and leave him there?" They started the same night travelling by dog-team on the ice of the river. Toward morning they found water running over the top of the ice and John turned his team hastily toward shore. The dogs had almost to swim and water soaked the sled and reached the well-wrapped O'Byrne, who accused John of wetting him on purpose and "began to curse me roundly. All this time I was wading in the water and keeping the sled from upsetting; but when he continued his profanity I couldn't stand it any longer so just dumped him right out into the over-flow and went on. However, when I looked back and saw the old fellow staggering through the water, I re-turned and helped him ashore, but told him I would not stand any more swearing."

They reached Edmonton that evening and as soon as he saw him the chief factor said to John, "So you brought O'Byrne to Edmonton. You will have to pay ten shillings for every day he remains in the fort."

"Excuse me sir," John answered, "I brought him to the foot of the hill, down at the landing and left him there. If he comes into the Fort I am not responsible."

O'Byrne found a shanty near the fort in which to live and the factor was obliged to give him food. It was at this point that Lord Milton and Dr. Cheadle arrived. O'Byrne, seeing his opportunity, introduced himself to them as a fellow member of Cambridge University. He had been, he said, at Clare, and "he astonished us by tell-ing us almost as much about our relations, friends and acquaintances as we knew ourselves," with many refer-ences to his grandfather the bishop and his other aristocratic connections. He told them the story of his life, showing no gratitude for any help he had received. Though the good old Wesleyan had kept him through the whole winter he only, as Cheadle wrote, "sneers at Woolsey's vulgarity."

He was intensely afraid of bears and even wolves, as Cheadle said, and the men to tease him pretended to see and hear bears close to his shanty. Terrified, he moved to a lodge near the fort but the wind blew it down on top of him and he threw the lodge cover across Cheadle's cart and now lived under it. This recital and his contact with the man should have warned Cheadle. Perhaps he was disarmed by the idea of a man of nearly sixty, a Cambridge man, in a clerical coat sleeping on the ground under one of his carts. For Mr. O'Byrne wanted to join Milton's party and cross the mountains with them.

In his journal Cheadle referred to O'Byrne as helpless, and he was helpless, but only as a small child is so. He pursued his plan without rest. "Intends to walk with us, carrying 30 lbs. of pemmican on his back! poor provision for 36 days! Poor fellow, I wish we were not so short of carts, or we would willingly give him a lift, although he is an ungrateful dog."

O'Byrne pretended to be attacked by a variety of ailments and every day requested Dr. Cheadle's advice. When at last he admitted that his ills were imaginary, Dr. Cheadle ruthlessly insisted on giving him a large dose of rhubarb. Constantly he pressed his plea. He must cross the mountains and he implied that it would be in some way to Cheadle's interest to take him. He had been at Edmonton nearly a year, unable to go either forward or back and completely destitute. He would find, he said, a much more congenial community on the Pacific coast and there he must go. Worn down at last, "we made Mr. O'Byrne happy by consenting to take him with us; he made a most pathetic appeal to me as a Cambridge man, and although we knew it was foolish to burden ourselves with an extra mouth, yet we could not find the heart to refuse him."

The residents of the fort, delighted no doubt to get rid of him, raised a subscription to buy O'Byrne a horse and saddle and presented him also with forty pounds of pemmican and some tea and tobacco. On the day before they started Cheadle wrote, with foreboding, that O'Byrne "tells the men to do little things for him, as if they were his servants and he an emperor. Does not even attempt to pack his own horse. I fear trouble with the men on his account. He is the greatest coward I ever saw. . . . The Assiniboine to-day stopped in the bush to light his pipe. O'Byrne who was behind passed him without seeing and when he had just gone by, the Assiniboine set up a most fearful growling. O'Byrne took to his heels and ran for it immediately."

They were now ready to start but as penniless as O'Byrne himself. "When we paid our bill at the fort (£23.3.4) we found that we possessed only £23 and therefore had to deduct 3.4 from what we had put down for the servants, not a sixpence left now! Starvation in Caribou!"

On June 6, about noon, for they never learned to start

like Southesk in the evening, the party at last set out. Stories of the mountain journey they were about to make had poured in on them and all were alarming. Officers at the fort had warned them of wild torrents, rugged hills, dense forest, the Fraser River, so full of rapids and whirlpools that the Company had abandoned it on account of the numerous casualties. A guide who said he had taken a party across the mountains on close questioning gave very vague and contradictory information. Dr. Hector, the geologist with Palliser's party, on his expedition had tried to go from the source of the North Saskatchewan to the North Thompson but had found the dense undergrowth and barriers of fallen timber quite impenetrable. It was a blaze of Dr. Hector's which Southesk's party had found when they emerged from the mountains near Old Fort Bow. Warnings against the most northerly of the mountain passes, the Leather or Tête Jaune Pass were especially impressive but Milton and Cheadle decided to attempt it nevertheless. Their fixed intention was to cross the mountains far enough north to reach the Cariboo gold-fields on the other side and no stories of suffering and starvation could dissuade them.

When they had left Fort Edmonton behind they learned from their guides the fears that underlay the kind farewell wishes of their friends there. Indeed a report later reached Edmonton "that we had all been murdered by Assiniboine who was returning rich in the possession of our horses and property." Apart from the danger of violence "public opinion at the Fort had decided that our expedition would certainly end most disastrously, for they considered that the party was too small, and comprised too many ineffectives, to succeed in overcoming the difficulties we must necessarily encounter." The telling word, ineffectives, applicable as it was to O'Byrne, could not have been less suitable for Assiniboine's wife and young son.

The next morning they stopped at Lake St. Ann, a place of about fifty houses, and were treated, as Southesk had been, to milk, potatoes and fresh fish. There the Company's officer, Mr. Colin Fraser, told them of the old days in that country twenty-five years before, "when game was so plentiful they never missed a meal of moose and big-horns." The Blackfeet, he said, were much maligned, for in his thirty-eight years in the country they had never injured an Englishman though they had killed several Americans.

During the afternoon of June 9 they left the last houses, the last friendly farewell, and turned their horses toward the mountains.

## V

THEY STARTED toward the mountains through dense woods, the horses sinking to their girths in the swamp, and Mr. O'Byrne announced that though he had visited many countries he had never known what travelling meant before. Since he was afraid to go near a horse he could not help with the loading or unloading and confined his assistance to good advice. While the rest struggled with horses and packs he sat among the bushes, smoking his pipe and reading the only book he had left from his library, Paley's *Evidences of Christianity*. The guides scolded because O'Byrne would not help, mosquitoes made sleep impossible, Milton refused to get up in the morning. The expedition was under way.

At every stream Lord Milton stopped to pan for gold, finding sometimes traces, again authentic colours. In the river banks they saw seams of coal "rather soft and dirty like engine coal." Every rustling in the bushes terrified O'Byrne as evidence of the presence of a bear and the Assiniboine continued to growl behind O'Byrne's back to frighten him. But one evening the guide himself rushed in pale and gasping. In looking for the horses "he found himself within ten yards of an enormous grizzly bear, who rose from his employment of tearing open rotten wood for the insects therein; the man stood still and the bear ran up to him growling horribly till within three or four yards; he pulled the trigger but the gun missed fire.... At the bear's growling, two other great big fellows came running up and they in turn walked up to him, growling and showing their teeth horribly.

"They retired again and he cautiously withdrew and made a tour, having recapped the gun. One of them, the largest, immediately came up growling again, the other two going off at speed. Again the gun missed fire. After some time, the biggest bear still perambulating backwards and forwards and showing great disposition to fight, the Assiniboine stole off and succeeded in regaining the camp in safety."

O'Byrne, though he was lying wrapped in his blanket close by, could not understand a word of the Assiniboine's mixed Cree and French and Lord Milton explained to him in English. "Doctor," O'Byrne cried, "we are in a very serious position—in very great danger. This is a most terrible journey; will you do me a great favour, and lend me your revolver, for I am resolved to sell my life dearly, and how can I defend myself if the bears attack us in the night? I am an unarmed man." Cheadle told him "very maliciously" that the revolver "was liable to go off unprovoked, which made him in as great a fright of that as a bear, and he eventually took the big axe as a bedfellow."

Next day a bear hunt discovered fresh bear tracks and a freshly opened bees' nest but no bears. Cheadle followed a moose for miles and then lost the track while Milton, panning for gold, saw in the bushes what he took to be a horse and whistled to him. A moose crashed away through the trees and Milton had not his gun with him "having as usual given it to someone else to carry."

Milton quarreled with the guide Baptiste. It was a prerogative of the head guide to chose the camping place each evening but Lord Milton refused to abide by his choice. Baptiste, very angry, began to pack his belongings and talk of leaving but was persuaded to remain. He ate supper cheerfully and the next morning packed the horses and saw the party off, Cheadle walking first as usual, the others following. Baptiste said to Assiniboine that he would stay behind to light his pipe. They never saw him again. He took one of the best horses, some pemmican and tea, nothing else that was not his own. The party grouped and considered what to do. The Assiniboine thought that he could find the way and was promoted on the spot to head guide. This meant a good deal of heavier work for Dr. Cheadle who had to learn to lift "180 lbs. over the back of a tall horse," and otherwise assume much of a guide's work since, as he said, their one man had only one hand.

They were about to enter the mountains with one one-handed man, his wife and a boy of thirteen besides the helpless O'Byrne. No party can have embarked on so arduous an adventure with so few and such ineffectual members. The Earl of Southesk entered at the same point, one remembers, with ten men, nine of them experienced guides, and with ample equipment and provisions, for a much shorter and less difficult journey.

But they went on in good spirits except for Lord Milton who longed for revenge on Baptiste. "The country ahead was hilly and full of streams. The McLeod rolling down a fine, narrow deep valley well wooded. In fact the whole country is covered with pine and poplar. We passed one or two beautiful little spots, tiny prairies, with clumps of pine, cypress and poplar most beautifully arranged, with rounded knolls and hills around, very park-like." Here, while fishing for trout, both Cheadle and the boy fell into the McLeod and Cheadle lost, to his distress, his fourth pipe since Edmonton.

Cheadle and his party were following in the track of a large company, but since they often lost the path and cast round to find it again, the way cannot have been very plainly marked. Just a year before, the famous Overlanders had been the first party of pioneers to cross from Canada to British Columbia by land. They were also for a good many years the last.

Companies, mostly of young men, eager to find gold in the heralded Cariboo, had come together from various parts of Canada, a few even from England. They travelled by way of St. Paul and had passed through Georgetown six weeks before the great Sioux massacre which had occurred two days after the passing of Cheadle and Milton. The company of a hundred and fifty boarded the newly-built steamer *International* for Fort Garry where they bought supplies of pemmican, Red River carts and horses or oxen to draw them. On June 2 they left Fort Garry with ninety-six carts in one of which rode a woman, Mrs. Schubert, who with her husband and three children had just joined the party.

Encountering the usual difficulties with mosquitoes, salt lakes, and sudden heavy rains, they reached Edmonton on July 21, still in such good spirits that some of the young men dressed in black face and gave a concert for the residents of the fort. A week later the Reverend Thomas Woolsey preached a sermon in their camp and the party started forward again. They had sold their carts, exchanged oxen for pack-horses and engaged a guide to take them through the Tête Jaune or Leather Pass. At St. Ann's, the last toe-hold of civilization, Colin Fraser, the factor, entertained them by playing the bagpipes for them in the evening.

After St. Ann's, six axe-men went ahead clearing a path and the horses sank deep in swampy places. The going was terribly bad but now and then they found encouraging prospects of gold. Even before the advanced party reached Tête Jaune Cache on August 27 many were hungry and horses and oxen were being killed for food. Their guide could take them no further and food was so scarce that speed became important. The unwieldy company then divided into three sections. A group of twenty decided to reach Cariboo overland. The largest group decided to take the animals and go down the Fraser River and the third party, including the Schuberts and their children, were to go down the Thompson River.

The overland party suffered principally from hunger,

and arrived at Fort George in a starving condition.

The Fraser River party made rafts and canoes and underwent harrowing dangers in the Grand Rapids and Canyon of the Fraser in which several men were drowned.

The Thompson River party, appalled at the sight of the river, tried to cut their way through the brush, but found this hopeless and decided to risk the river after all. They killed their animals at a place they called Slaughter Camp, made rafts and dug-outs and launched into the river which was in places so choked with driftwood that they had to cut a passage through the water. After a portage of eight miles they, like the others, almost starved to death before they reached Kamloops. In all the parties six men were drowned on the way. Mrs. Schubert and her three little children came safely through all these hardships and the day after her arrival at Kamloops she gave birth to a daughter, the first white child born in the settlement.

Many of the men who went through this amazing expedition became important in the life of the new province; some amassed a competency, as the contemporary accounts say, and returned to live in the east.

Fortunately knowing nothing of the experience of the party which had preceded them a year before, Cheadle searched for traces of their route. One evening an adventure occurred when they stopped for dinner. "The horses trampling some of the embers of the fire into a fallen pine tree which quickly set fire to some neighbouring standing trees, and I thought we could not save it. I seized an axe and cut down the nearest trees. But then the little black horse getting burnt a little, got frightened and rolled in the fire and I had to seize a great pole and beat him before he would get out again. I thought he was done for but he turned out to be little injured. Whilst this was going on, the fire had again got head, and I set to work with the axe, and shouted to the rest to bring water, and Milton's activity and presence of mind in helping me at once saved us, and we got the fire under by sundry pansful. Whilst I was energetically cutting down trees and crying for water, I observed O'Byrne sitting down, tugging away at a boot. I shouted to him very angrily, 'Mr. O'Byrne, what on earth are you doing? why the devil don't you bring some water?' 'I can't, I've only got one boot on.' "

At Cheadle's brisk assurance that he would burn as well with one boot on as with two, O'Byrne began to carry half-pints of water in his tin mug. When they had repacked and started on, clouds of smoke behind them showed that the fire had revived and was still spreading, but heavy rain that night quenched it.

A few days later they reached the Athabasca River and found it very much swollen by rain. Here they had that breath-taking view of the Rocky Mountains which, in another place, had affected Southesk so deeply. A beautiful prospect, Cheadle thought, softened with blue haze, the river rolling between high, tree-covered banks, beyond the tree-clothed hills, farther still the sun shining on the snow of the highest peaks. "A cleft in the range, cut clean as if with a knife, showed us what we supposed to be the position of Jasper's House and the opening of the gorge through which we are to pass across." They hoped to reach it by sundown but did not do so for a week.

Camp life was difficult. Milton would never get up in the morning and when Cheadle roused him and forced him to make a good start he was angry and they would have "one of our usual squabbles as to the advisability of starting early and doing fairly long journeys; to reach here we have already doubled the time usually taken." The Assiniboine and Cheadle did all the heavy work, loading and unloading horses, cutting wood. By the way, in spite of all, Cheadle noticed the flowers, wild roses, tiger lilies, red and white vetches, blue borage and the marsh violets which he had seen at home near Bolton Abbey. The flies and bulldogs were so bad that the horses stamped and trampled about all night and O'Byrne crept into the lodge to sleep, in not unreasonable fear of their hoofs. In the lodge Milton jumped up as he often did, shouting in his sleep, and O'Byrne, terrified, cried out each time, "What is it, my lord, what is it?" A very poor night's rest, Cheadle wrote.

They were now in the mountains in earnest and Cheadle and Assiniboine climbed among the loose stones up a steep narrow path to try to kill mountain sheep. They shot two and climbed down to where they had fallen. "And when I looked up at the face of the rock, I could not believe it possible that I had come down there; but in the excitement of the moment I thought nothing of it." Looking down, they saw that their moccasins had been torn to shreds and that they had been walking almost barefoot over the sharp rocks without noticing it.

They cut up the sheep and laboured to carry the meat up the steep mountain side again to be rewarded by a dinner of mutton, "rather strong-flavoured but we had not tasted fresh meat for two months."

While Cheadle and Assiniboine cut timber for a raft on which to cross the river, O'Byrne as usual read Paley's *Evidences* over a pipe. When the trees were cut "we apologized for interrupting his studies" and told him to come and help carry wood to the water's edge. Cheadle and Assiniboine carried the heavier logs, Milton and O'Byrne the lighter ones, the woman and boy small logs and branches. "After the first few steps O'Byrne began to utter the most awful groans, and cried out continually, 'Oh dear, oh dear, this is most painful—it's cutting my shoulder in two—not so fast, my lord. Gently, gently. Steady, my lord, steady; I *must* stop. I'm carrying all the weight myself. I shall drop with exhaustion directly—*triste lignum te caducum!*' And then, with a loud 'Oh!' and no further warning, he let his end of the tree down with a run, jarring his unhappy partner most dreadfully."

When this had happened several times Lord Milton preferred to drag his logs alone and expressed his annoyance with O'Byrne. He, overhearing, "said it was all very well for Cheadle with shoulders like the Durham ox, but he was not so strong." Cheadle pointed out that Lord Milton was not strong and yet had worked very well. "'Ah, yes,' replied Mr. O'Byrne, 'he is fired with emulation. I have been lost in admiration of his youthful ardour all the day! But you see I am older, and obliged to be cautious; look how I have suffered by my exertions to-

171

day!'—showing us a small scratch on his hand. We exhibited our palms, raw with blisters, which caused him to turn the conversation by dilating on his favourite topic —the hardships of the fearful journey we were making."

Yet when there was no work to be done, O'Byrne could sometimes entertain them with his talk. One evening "O'Byrne told me story of missionary preaching about crucifixion. Indians delighted and wished him to give diagram showing how it was done. Missionary fled in terror."

They saw Jasper House, closed now, a pretty little white building surrounded by wild flowers. On their way they found in several places messages from Mr. Macaulay, in charge of that post, who was out hunting in the region and early in July they met him and his party and camped near them. He feasted them on white-fish and fresh mutton and advised them to hire an Indian guide for a few days, an Iroquois, who said he had gone as far as Tête Jaune Cache. Since they had no money, they promised him one of the horses in payment.

At this point O'Byrne finished the last of his pemmican, the forty pounds which he had sworn would carry him through the journey. Now that it was by no means half over, he as well as the others had to be provided with food. The going was very bad, for the country had been burnt over and fallen timber lay in all directions. "Dismount, whack them (horses) and chivy them, they rushing and leaping and crashing about, I expecting they must break their legs."

On July 9 they passed the height of land and saw

streams flowing westward and the next day, a glorious morning, they named their mountains. "Milton chose a fine hill to the left as his mountain and I a still higher to the right. His cone-like and terraced, mine a long range of very rugged rocks, very high and snow clad with green slopes, and bright pines half way up." They did not name or even pass very close to another spot which bears the doctor's name on the map. Cheadle, Alberta is a flag stop on the railway line between Gleichen and Calgary, near the town of Strathmore.

In one morning they crossed the Miette River six times on horseback, at the last place finding it a boiling cataract, the water rolling over the horses' shoulders. The Iroquois led the way, his horse hardly able to keep a footing, and got safely across. The pack-horses were driven in next. O'Byrne, terrified of his horse, always preferred to walk but was now forced to mount. Milton and the woman rode on either side of him. "Clutching the mane with both hands, he did not attempt to guide his horse, but employed all his powers in sticking to the saddle, and exhorting his companions, 'Steady, my lord, please, or I shall be swept off. *Do* speak to Mrs. Assiniboine, my lord; she's leading me to destruction; what a reckless woman! *varium et mutabile semper femina!* Mrs. Assiniboine! *Mrs. Assiniboine!* Oh dear, oh dear! what an awful journey. I'm going! I'm going! Narrow escape that, my lord! very narrow escape, indeed, Doctor. We can't expect to be so lucky every time, you know.' And the moment he gained the shore, he scrambled off and left his horse to its own devices."

On these frequent fordings both pemmican and flour were wetted and had to be spread in the sun to dry. Sometimes two or three large trees lay piled on one another and the heavily-loaded horses, exhausted with constant jumping, left the path and tried to hide in the brush. "Some of them under the pressure of repeated blows took some extraordinary leaps, and placed themselves in most awkward situations, sometimes with fore-legs over a tree over which they could not get their hind ones; now jammed fast between two trees too close together to allow the packs to pass; or trying to pass under a tree arched over the path too low for the pack-saddle. Milton got quite wild and savage, O'Byrne very confused. All three perspired at every pore and quarrelled dreadfully."

They came just before sunset to a narrow path along the cliff which showed a clear drop into the Fraser River, boiling over its rocks a hundred feet below. The Iroquois guide went down to examine the path and found that a huge rock overhung it, so low that a pack-horse could not get past it. Cheadle and Assiniboine set to work "with pine poles for levers, loosened the rock and hurled it down with mighty bounds and crashes into the stream below." The horses were then led across and though the path was only a foot wide and it was rapidly growing dark all made the passage safely.

Next morning they came to the Grand Fork of the Fraser called Tête Jaune Cache for an Iroquois trapper, Tête Jaune, Yellow Hair, who had hidden there the furs he collected on the western side of the mountains. Cheadle wrote, "the finest scene I have ever viewed. To the right,

Robson Peak, a magnificent mountain, high, rugged, covered with deep snow, the top now clearly seen, although generally covered with clouds. Ranges of other mountains and pine-clad hills run along the Fraser on each side, and the blue haze was quite fairy-like."

After the exalting moment of beauty the struggle with horses in dense woods went on and came that day to a violent quarrel between Cheadle and Milton. Lord Milton "had neither the patience, activity nor constant attention necessary to drive horses in the woods," he lost his temper with the Iroquois guide and abused him for choosing bad camping places and was only angered by Cheadle's attempts at peacemaking.

It was a bad beginning to what Cheadle solemnly introduced in his journal as "a day to be remembered during the rest of my life, as eventful and crowded with misfortune. In the morning both Milton and I were very sulky and would hardly speak to one another, and the Assiniboine said he and family would leave us at the Cache if Milton was so discontented." Cheadle led the grey horse carrying the flour and after him came the boy with Cheadle's horse, Bucephalus, and another, Gisquakarn, which carried the personal property of all three men. Everything suddenly went wrong. Cheadle tried to mount the grey who threw him off on his head. The boy stopped and Gisquakarn, "rightly named the Fool", plunged into the river and swam off followed by Bucephalus. Once they were in the river the current carried the two horses swiftly down-stream. The Iroquois guide, Assiniboine, the boy and Cheadle hurried along the bank and saw both horses on a tiny sand bar a mile down-stream. Bucephalus at last tried to swim to shore but was carried on and both horses were soon swimming again. It was Assiniboine who achieved a partial rescue. At the head of a rapid he rushed into the water and reached Bucephalus, "carried off his legs and under the belly of the horse, but clung to him desperately and succeeded in bringing him to shallow water by the side; but the horse was too exhausted to come out until Assiniboine had pitched off the bags into the water; they were of course a tremendous weight now."

He could see that Gisquakarn had landed on the oppo-site bank but at a place far too steep for him to climb out. "We were much astonished with the bravery of the Assini-boine in facing such a current and rocks as he did, and we promised him £5 on the spot." The contents of Bucephalus's pack—clothing and the medicine chest—were soaked but could be salvaged. The guide went to find several Shuswap Indians to help him secure the other horse but though they searched all day Gisquakarn was never found. They had lost all their good clothing, letters and papers, watches, sextant, powder and caps, tea and tobacco. O'Byrne lost his tea-kettle but as he philo-sophically remarked, now that the tea was gone it did not matter.

The Indians told them, as though to reconcile them to the loss, that the last party of five miners who had gone down this part of the Fraser in two canoes had all been drowned.

The next day O'Byrne and the woman were at the

rear driving the little black horse. After crossing a very bad swamp, O'Byrne came running after Dr. Cheadle calling, " 'Doctor, Doctor! you had better go back directly, something's happened; don't you hear someone shouting for assistance? I expect it is Mrs. Assiniboine with one of the horses fast in the bog.' Running back I found the black down and fast enough in the quagmire, the woman having taken off the packs and trying to whack him into sufficient exertion to get out again. I set to work and helped her but, had not Assiniboine fortunately come up in the nick of time, it was all the three of us could do to haul him out. I walked back and found others already camped at the present Tête Jaune Cache. I blew up O'Byrne handsomely for leaving the woman in the lurch, and told him he would have to cry out a long time before any one came to help him now."

All evening they dried wet pemmican and clothing. "We are supposed now to be on the other side of the mountains; but we see nothing but their snowy tops on every side still."

In the country near Tête Jaune Cache they met Indians of the Shuswap, a west coast tribe, who lived on wild goats and marmots and wore robes of marmot skin. The Shuswaps could furnish no guides for their men had gone with a Yankee party. Milton bargained for two marmot robes and as they inquired the way, an old woman who said she had come over the mountains from Kamloops when she was a girl made them a rough map and assured them that they could reach the fort in eight days. The Iroquois guide had turned back the day before and with him O'Byrne's horse had mysteriously vanished. In the confusions of the last few days the two good axes had been lost and only one small one remained.

This was especially unfortunate now that a raft had to be made to cross the high and swift-running Canoe River. Assiniboine and Cheadle chopped down trees by turns with the one little axe, and dragged them to the water, where the indefatigable Assiniboine tied them together into a strong raft. The current was so powerful that they had trouble in getting everyone on board before the raft whirled down-stream "at a fearful pace, it appearing certain that we must run foul of a tree overhanging the bank on the side we started from. Very vigorous poling, urged on by the frantic shouts of Assiniboine, we just succeeded in escaping it; but the current setting in strong for the other side from this point, before we knew it we were on the far side of the river, straight for a little rapid which we passed over like an arrow, and then to what seemed certain destruction, a large pine closely overhanging the water and through the branches of which the water was rushing and boiling like a mill-stream at the wheel. Assiniboine shouted 'Land with the rope', jumping himself with one up to the shoulders in the stream, and catching a small tree round which he whipped the rope like lightning; but it snapped like a thread, and the other, which I had leaped ashore with as the raft neared the land for an instant before rushing under the pine, was dragged out of my hand in a moment. The raft rushed under the tree, I saw only O'Byrne struggling in the branches,

179

everything and everybody seeming to be swept off like flies."

An instant later Cheadle saw O'Byrne still on the raft, heard a gurgling shout from the tree and saw Milton and the woman clinging to it. Cheadle pulled himself onto a branch of the tree and reached Milton who said, "Help the woman first." This was not easy to do as she was farther out. Cheadle pulled Milton up and they tried to reach the woman but could not pull her up. O'Byrne now came along the bank and in answer to Cheadle's frantic cries, only held up his hands in despair. The boy, terrified at his mother's danger, ran for his father who had reached the raft, now cast ashore, and was frantically trying to untie a rope. Meanwhile Milton held up the woman's head which frequently disappeared under the water, and Cheadle held her by her belt and arm. "After what seemed an age," Cheadle wrote that evening, "though really very quickly, I suppose, Assiniboine came with the cord, and with his assistance we soon landed the woman all safe though fearfully numb and cold, the water being like ice."

Recriminations at once followed. Assiniboine was in a fury against O'Byrne. He said he had called to the old man as he neared land to throw him the rope which he was holding in his hand but he had continued to shake his head and cry, "No, no, no," and when the raft ran ashore, he had jumped off and run away at full speed. O'Byrne said with undoubted truth that he remembered nothing whatever from the moment when the raft went under the tree. Assiniboine's bags had been lost so that he and his family were quite destitute and the matches were gone. Cheadle gave the woman and Milton such dry clothes as he could find and the party moved inland to camp, "O'Byrne being quite miserable until out of hearing of the sound of the river."

# VI

THE CANOE RIVER accident was a kind of crisis which shook the confidence of the whole party. Things had not gone so very well before it occurred but afterward they rapidly became worse. Food ran low, the horses began to fail, and everyone was hungry and tired and as a result irritable and quarrelsome. The lack of tea they felt far more than any other lack. Milton sometimes made kinnikinnick out of the inner bark of the dogwood to smoke instead of tobacco. The horses, beside extremely hard going and the heavy packs they carried, rarely had anything to eat but twigs and mare's tail.

O'Byrne was horrified to find the men cutting down trees to make a raft to cross the Thompson River. He woke Dr. Cheadle early and took him aside. "'In the first place, Doctor, I hope that you and Assiniboine will be very careful indeed in crossing the river, for you know I think you managed very badly indeed last time, I may say disgracefully so. It was a mercy that we were not all drowned; look what an escape *I* had! Now, if you will take my advice, you will keep perfectly cool and collected

—*animosus et fortis appare*—but *aequo animo*, you know; not shout at one another as you did before; Assiniboine quite frightened me with his strong language. But I have a very particular favour to ask, and that is, that you and Lord Milton will agree to postpone crossing the river until to-morrow, for I am oppressed with a most fearful presentiment that if we make the attempt to-day we shall all be lost—every one of us drowned, Doctor. Think of the responsibility before it is too late; you and his lordship are answerable for our lives.' " Food was so short that they dared not waste a day and in spite of O'Byrne's presentiments they made the crossing safely.

But now a fresh and even more serious difficulty arose. They had been following the tenuous vestige of trail left by the emigrant party of the year before and though it was in places quite undiscernible, still it gave guidance of a kind. Here and there they had come upon signs cut on trees or upon old camp sites and been heartened to know that other men had made a way through this difficult country before them. But now the trail, faint as it was, came to an end. "We came upon a great number of trees cut down, a number of pack saddles and harness. It now became quite plain that many of the American party at any rate had become weary of the difficulties of the road and had made canoes and rafts to go down the river. They had also killed up their oxen and dried the meat. . . . On a tree written Slaughter Camp, Sept. 22, 1862 and 4 names, and they had spent some days here, by the beaten ground and tracks about." The whole party must have embarked and Cheadle and his companions had now the prospect of cutting their own road to Kamloops through untouched forest with two axe-men and one small axe. If they could have known the suffering of their predecessors on the trail the summer before they would scarcely have been encouraged.

Cheadle's party had also planned to push west to Cariboo to visit the gold-fields and Lord Milton had clung tenaciously to that idea. As the horses failed and provisions vanished it became obvious that Cariboo was much too far away and that Fort Kamloops must be their objective. They could get there either by cutting a track through the forest, an almost impossible undertaking, or by making a raft and launching themselves on the Thompson river. This they saw that the emigrants must have done but with what success they had no way of knowing. The Shuswap Indians had warned them against the Thompson as impossibly dangerous for rafts and canoes; it ran swollen and rapid before their eyes, and they remembered too plainly their disasters in the Canoe River crossing. They discussed the possibilities for a long time over pipes of kinnikinnick and O'Byrne advised them all to prepare to meet a miserable end. The tireless Assiniboine remained calm and cheerful. He would, he said, look for a route by which they could cut their way; indeed they had no other choice.

Assiniboine went off and returned three or four hours later with the body of a small black bear on his shoulders. He thought it might be possible to get through though it would be slow and heavy work. From the top of the hill he had seen "far to the south, mountains crowded be-

184

hind mountains, the everlasting pine forest extending in every direction, without a sign of open country; the only favourable circumstance which he observed being that the hills appeared to become lower, and fewer of them were capped with snow."

They all set to work eagerly to skin and cut up the bear and enjoy their first fresh meat since Jasper House. The only drawback was the lack of salt. Assiniboine spoke up, "bravely exhorting us not to be down, for we would get out of the mess. We had many jokes about eating horse. . . . All went to sleep in good spirits except O'Byrne."

Before and after Assiniboine's bear they had only a little pemmican and flour to eat, without salt or grease. For some time the staple of their diet had been rubaboo, made by boiling a piece of pemmican the size of a fist with a great deal of water and a handful of flour. It had at least the virtue of being adaptable. If they killed a partridge or a skunk it made a much appreciated addition to the rubaboo, as did a few blueberries. But on many days in this part of the journey the rubaboo was a watery mixture indeed. The Earl of Southesk had disliked rubaboo intensely and refused to touch it; Cheadle and Milton were only concerned to find something to put in it.

They could still admire the views which occasionally opened before them. "A magnificent mountain covered with glaciers appears to shut in the valley before us." The map given them by the Indian woman did not at all agree with the route they had taken thus far. On the first of August Cheadle wrote bitterly, "Perhaps this mountain to the right may be one which the woman (wretched old impostor!) said was not very far from the Fort. I don't expect to reach the Fort for above a week yet. The rest more sanguine." It had been a very bad day. "Fallen timber up and down mountain sides, ground all as rotten as the timber and abounding in bogs, quagmires and concealed springs. . . . Horses very slow and hesitating in consequence not knowing where to put their feet. Sometimes up to the hocks in soft ground, about the roots of trees, which thus makes a hole to let the hoof in and they have to struggle tremendously to get loose again.—Horses to be beaten all day long. Jump, crash, stumble, rush, tumble; refuse to go on."

Also for the first time that day they did not stop for dinner. Food was so scarce by this time that they could have a meal only morning and evening.

They were heartened to see that the valley was widening and when they camped at a long marsh there was good feeding for the horses and a feeling of space and lightness for the men. "The effect upon me was like coming out of a darkened room into broad sunlight. The gloom of the forest being so great Milton and I, upon my strong representation agreed not to discuss disagreeable subjects, or squabble any more and got on very well during the day." There were blueberries and raspberries as luscious, Cheadle thought, as English garden fruits, and tall slender bracken and fern, too, made him think of England.

On August 4, a dull morning, Cheadle described their little procession, as in the heart of the mountains South-

esk, too, had described his party. "Our procession,"
Cheadle wrote, "goes thus: Assiniboine leads with axe;
wife follows leading horse with cord; then young one
driving two horses; then Milton on horseback to give
rest lead; then I with three horses and on foot; last
O'Byrne with little black. Trousers all torn and in rags,
moccasins etc. a sorry turnout. We shall go into the
Fort nearly naked."

Assiniboine had done the greater part of the work
of chopping out a track and now his hand was so badly
lacerated by thorns that he could not use the axe. Cheadle,
accordingly, had to go ahead and hack out a path. They
crossed a flooded river with a very strong current and here
O'Byrne found a solution for the dreaded ordeal of river-
crossing. They had all started across on horseback except
O'Byrne who had resolved not to ride under any circumstances. The river was too deep and rapid to ford on
foot and after futile discussion the Indians crossed and
Milton and Cheadle started after them. But as Dr.
Cheadle's horse entered the water, O'Byrne dashed madly
in, seized the horse's tail with both hands and was easily
towed across. He never afterward felt concerned about
crossing a river. Of the crossing against such a powerful
current Cheadle wrote, "should have thought it dangerous
at one time."

On the next day, August 8, occurred the strangest of
their encounters. When the *North-West Passage* was
published several years later many readers rejected this
incident, along with the character of O'Byrne, as a fabri-
cation.

For a week the party had been lost in the sense that they struggled and blundered on with no idea whether they were moving in the right direction. They had stopped for a day so that Assiniboine could hunt, for their pemmican was gone and they had for days been constantly hungry. Milton insisted that they must kill a horse that day if they found no game. The woman mended moccasins and O'Byrne read his Paley. "The party was not a lively one, for there had been no breakfast that morning." Assiniboine came back unsuccessful from his hunt saying that he had found a dead Indian only a short distance from the camp and the others went to look for themselves. The body was "in a sitting posture, crouching with hands over knees over an old fire, . . . skin dried into parchment over back and shoulders; rest of bones nearly bare; clothes entire." But the head was gone. "In vain we searched the grass and bushes around. What could have become of it? We could find no explanation. For any animal that would have eaten the head would have meddled with the rest. Assiniboine suggested that he had met with foul play; probably from some Americans, who of course having such a bad name are accused at once if any crime is suspected. But this seems impossible from the quiet crouching posture of the body."

Close by lay a small axe, fire bag, kettle and two birchbark baskets, one containing a net and fish hooks, the other a few onions, still green and growing. Behind was a heap of bones broken into very small pieces which appeared to be from a horse's head. "The onions told us that it was spring when he died, as well as the state of decomposition of the body. The broken bones told of probable starvation and want, and the fire of small sticks, of illness and weakness. He had probably killed his horse long ago."

They went back to camp where the woman had made a paste of blueberries and a little flour, good but not very satisfying. Milton insisted that the horse must be killed for food at once, Cheadle and Assiniboine urged that it would be better to wait a day or two and try to kill partridges. At last Milton forced them to agree to kill the little black horse in the morning but no one would consent to do the killing. "We went to bed with the point unsettled. And in rather poor spirits from what we had to do next morning as well as from the effect of the sight of the dead Indian who had been in a very similar but worse position than ourselves in this very place."

The little black was shot—by Assiniboine—meat was quickly cooked and eaten ravenously by everyone but Milton who swore he could not swallow it "but during the day managed to pick a good deal." The rest of the meat was cut into thin slices and dried; there was not much of it for the horses had been starving too. The day was very hot and even Cheadle felt languid and weak. Next day they packed and taking the dead Indian's little axe with them, set out again. They shot at ducks and partridges but the powder had been damp so often that it was of little use.

Weak as they now were, the hard cutting went more and more slowly. Cheadle caught a couple of trout and gave them to Milton who refused to eat horse meat.

It was very hot and with the heavy chopping, Assiniboine began to break down. "Assiniboine very démonté yesterday. Said he could not understand why we came this pass in preference to the other. Found it strange that we did not bring a proper number of men and horses and do the thing in style if we were 'bourgeois' as we said we were. I explained as well as I could."

Assiniboine shot a porcupine and everyone enjoyed its rich delicious flesh. But "it is disheartening work cutting through thick wood for nearly a month, and I could not help contrasting my luncheon of a scrap of dried horse flesh and water therewith to the many good feeds I have had on the moors on bygone twelfths of August. Again hard work all day up and down acclivities, cutting through timber. The ground is now merely large rocks covered with moss and trees. The difficulties may be imagined by the fact that three horses fell amongst rocks and timber in such places and positions that they had to be unpacked, timber cut away, and then hauled out; pack cords cut etc. We see nothing before us but the continuation of this rapid through its narrow gorge—no other hills or indication of opening out. We went on until dusk, and then coming to a place apparently impassable, viz. an abrupt descent into the river, beset with rocks and timber, we were again obliged to camp without pasturage for the horses, poor things. I hope this will not last long for our sakes as well as theirs."

Assiniboine was in low spirits but "works like a man and the wife too who took my place ahead yesterday and cut away much better than I can." Here they had to

climb the extremely steep side of a mountain, leading
the horses with ropes, go along a few hundred yards and
then down again. Cheadle wrote, "when I got my horse
over the worst position, I looked back for O'Byrne, the
only one behind me, but he was not in sight, and after
waiting some little time I went back to look after him
and he presently hove in sight panting up the hill. 'Where
is the horse?' said I. 'Oh he's dead gone, tumbled over
the precipice; he fell headlong and must be smashed to
pieces.' 'Good heavens,' said I, 'let us go at any rate and
look for him,' and turned him back with me. The place
where he had slipped and fallen was at the height of the
ascent and when I saw what a cropper he must have gone,
I gave him up as killed. . . . I descended to the edge of
the river and there found Bucephalus on his legs astride
of a large tree which lay across a hollow; he had fallen
a hundred feet, nearly perpendicularly, over huge trees,
and finally with a grand plump over a rock some twenty
feet high on to the tree. It was the most extraordinary
escape possible. O'Byrne and I unpacked him, and rolled
him off the tree, and I found a place to lead him round
up the ascent again. Then I had to carry the bags up the
steep, very killing work, for I felt weak enough; pack
him again and off."

A few minutes later the grey horse fell over the precipice in the same way but he too was not hurt and was
rescued in the same manner. The bodies of the horses
were "mere frames of bone covered with skin, their flanks
hollow, their backs raw, their legs battered, swollen and

bleeding—a band for the knacker's yard—they were painful to look upon."

That day also they saw what Assiniboine called La Porte d'Enfer. "The river continued to narrow until making a sudden turn between two huge rocks about 60 feet high through a narrow opening boiling along. . . . Very like the Strid at Bolton Abbey, a little larger, but then a much larger river also. Certain destruction for raft or even canoe I should think."

The whole party were so low-spirited that Cheadle gave them an energetic talking-to, stating his conviction that perhaps there were no open plains such as they had been hoping to see, perhaps the mountains ran like this to the very walls of the fort which could not be very far off now. This cheered everyone and Cheadle was even able to praise O'Byrne who, he said, "bears up like a brick and I find he improves on being tried hard. We consumed our last morsel of flour in a rubaboo of two partridges, dried meat, and berries which was a great luxury, and everybody went to bed comparatively happy. Come 4 or 5 miles only. Assiniboine cut his foot badly and can hardly walk."

The next evening they ate their last bit of dried meat. Cheadle went out early to look at his lines and found one small trout. "To my surprise found the woman cutting up dry meat. She had hid some from us all and we now found the value of it. This with the shakings of the flour bag which had been wet, and which the woman scraped diligently, we made a handsome rubaboo, but this is really the last except two fish; and it must be another horse tomorrow." Unfortunately, "dried lean horse meat goes fast, and is very poor stuff to work on we find."

As they crossed a small river a horse fell and soaked the blankets, already wetted in the heavy rain. The red horse, which they killed next, tasted much better than the black had done, probably because they were all hungrier. "Milton ate it now with avidity." Killing a horse meant stopping for a day to dry the meat. "Camped on a tiny dry spot in the middle of a muskeg, water all around, dank high fern and red willow; huge pines and cedars overhead. And then one cannot help speculating about the Fort, how far it is, when we shall get there if ever; if there is a road on the other side of the river." They smoked kinnikinnick, mended their moccasins once again and wondered. Milton was irritable, insisting that they must go on by raft, while Cheadle, thinking of the rapids they had just seen, considered the river far too dangerous. In spite of himself he kept thinking of home and its comforts, of the food he would eat there, of tobacco and a long clay pipe. "But I cannot stand this, I must change my thoughts and resort to gnawing the shoulder blade of a horse. And horse is really very good meat if one had only something to it, and could get out of this cursed forest; 2½ months now without daylight."

He had developed a large boil on his knee which made walking all but impossible. There were raspberries now, large and well-flavoured but watery. The men were all so hungry and so tired that tempers were constantly on edge; Milton and O'Byrne squabbled over the raspberries like small children. Milton and the boy had an alarming quarrel. Milton asked the boy a question about the road which he answered but Milton, not understanding, repeated his question in an angry voice and the young one, as Cheadle called him, did not reply. Milton began to swear at him with some violence and the young one snatched up his gun. Cheadle, as usual, ran up, seized the gun and scolded both the boy and Lord Milton.

Feeling himself responsible for Milton's welfare, Cheadle worried a good deal about his condition. "I have no fear for myself but for him (Milton) on account of his being unable to walk or endure prolonged fatigue in case of emergency, and in addition always finding fault and quarrelling about small things of no consequence and causing Assiniboine to threaten to desert us, and I knowing that it would not require much provocation to make him do so if things became much worse. Altogether a weary time. General peacemaker. Oh! for the Fort. Have finished our fresh meat."

O'Byrne too disturbed him. He had worked hard during the last few weeks but now he seemed sunk in despair. "He confided to us that he loathed Paley, whom he looked upon as a special pleader; that his faith was sapped to its foundations, and—*curis ingentibus aeger*— he was rapidly becoming insane, adding that he should have lost his wits long ago but for his book." He had lately become very silent in company and often muttered to himself as he walked. However it was noticeable that whenever he had a meal of fresh meat he became cheerful, took a more orthodox view of things and went back to reading Paley with the old absorption. Assiniboine too was morose, talked often of leaving the party, and camped some distance from the others, holding long private discussions with his wife and son.

On August 21 they camped beside a marsh which had not only many bilberries and raspberries but, much better, definite signs that someone had passed that way. There were horse tracks, a camp site and on a tree a notice which they could not read but which nevertheless heartened them all. There seemed to be a track ahead marked by blazed trees. To Cheadle's amazement, Milton, of his own accord, got up early next morning. They made a good journey, camped on a little prairie and shot eight partridges. Expect, Cheadle wrote, "to sleep near Fort day after tomorrow, perhaps starving a bit, but no more horses to kill."

Suddenly like Robinson Crusoe, who in his picture he a good deal resembles, Cheadle saw the print of a moccasin in the sand and a canoe drawn close to the bank. There was a rustle in the bushes and he saw a Shuswap and his wife with a baby on her back. They had seen no other human being since Tête Jaune Cache and rushed forward to astonish the Indian with eager handshakes, laughter and questions he could not understand. The word Kamloops he knew and they gathered that the fort was very near. Cheadle wrote, "May reach Fort tonight. Peg along. Beautiful country. . . . I find myself very weak. No sign of Fort near." He was fortunately unaware that another week's travel lay between them and Kamloops.

Next day they met a camp of Shuswaps and asked

them how far it was to the fort. Four days they seemed to say but there was no question about the delights to be found there. Flour, one of the men said in English, sugar, tobacco, tea, and best of all, whisky. "They brought a rabbit and wanted a shirt for it, Milton giving them an old one he had on. Then O'Byrne came out and bought two more for one of his shirts. Presently the man we had met yesterday appeared quite done up; he had followed us in all haste, having some potatoes to sell! We gave him a bag and he went off and shortly returned with a few in the bottom, just dug up; these we bought with another old shirt of Assiniboine's, and with a partridge we had shot made a very good dinner." One of the men paddled them across the river and was given a buffalo robe. Cheadle wrote "I gave him my trousers and told him he must give me fish and potatoes for them."

The next day was less cheerful. Early in the morning they passed the bodies of two Indians, a man and a woman, with all their goods arranged about them, dead of either starvation or smallpox. The road led through heavy underbrush, very bad going, the mosquitoes killing. They ate quantities of berries which made Cheadle so violently ill that for the rest of the day he could not walk, could scarcely sit his horse and "cared little whether I and the horse fell or not." For the road went up high above the river, one of the horses fell into the water and Assiniboine went back on foot to get the help of the Shuswaps in their canoe. "High in the air we had to go, on a slippery sharp path, with descent of many hundred feet into river, the canoes waiting in the river below, anxiously watching our passage. Here we drove the horses along one by one."

Cheadle had hardly reached level ground when he heard the angry voices of Assiniboine and O'Byrne. When he caught up with the others he asked where O'Byrne was and Assiniboine answered sullenly that he had gone off. Assiniboine had asked him to take two horses but he had refused, "upon which he (Assiniboine) being very hot and out of temper at the time from contending with the horses, in his anger struck him a blow of his fist, and that he had gone off at a run, although they had called to him to stop." It was nearly dark and Cheadle felt so weak and ill that they decided to camp and went to bed without supper. "What has become of O'Byrne? Knowing his propensity for losing the way I was unhappy about him."

In the morning they were off early, Cheadle somewhat recovered and at the camp of two Indians they found O'Byrne, very glum. Milton gave his saddle in return for a kettle full of potatoes and they halted to eat some of them and dry their few clothes. O'Byrne had a dramatic story to recount. " 'My lord, I accuse the Assiniboine of attempting to murder me. We had some trouble with the horses, and as I stood by, not knowing how to help, he came up to me with the most fiendish expression, and deliberately hit me a tremendous blow on the head with the back of his axe. I was stunned, but managed to run off into the woods—hardly recollect anything more—wandering about bewildered until I caught sight of the fire, and found you here. You know, my lord, I warned

you and the Doctor at Edmonton of the dangerous character you were trusting yourselves with. He is a most
wicked man. I shall go on to Kamloops as soon as it is
light, and get out a warrant for the apprehension of the
Assiniboine immediately on his arrival.' "

Milton could not help laughing at his earnestness and
terror and Cheadle began by an examination of the old
man's head. It showed a very slight swelling not even
discoloured, which hardly suggested a blow with the
back of an axe. Assiniboine admitted that he had struck
O'Byrne with his fist but "not with all his might" and
that he had perhaps threatened him with the axe. "I blew
up Assiniboine, sympathized with O'Byrne, but laughed
at his notion of murderous assault, and succeeded in putting things nearly square again."

On this day the going was better though they had
nothing but a few potatoes to eat and the mosquitoes prevented sleep. Two Shuswaps they met the next day gave
them a little strong rope tobacco which after their long
abstinence made them momentarily dizzy. These Indians
took them to their camp where they washed all the
clothing they could spare and ate "a good mess of potatoes, and some dishes of weak coffee well sugared;
which I found the greatest treat I had yet had." Going
on, at dusk they found another Indian camp near the
river where they were given a little flour and fish and
more potatoes in return for shot, handkerchiefs, a waistcoat and whatever odds and ends they could find among
the meagre remnant of their possessions. Best of all they
met a half-breed who spoke French and English and said

198

that it was about "17 miles from Fort and good road. All kinds of good things there; newspapers; Yankee war yet unfinished, South the best of it. Hurrah! Hurrah! Went to bed happy."

The next day, though hope buoyed them up, was not an easy one. It must have seemed, though help was so near, one of the longest of the long days of the journey. "Fearfully hot and dusty, and a wearisome tramp I found it, being very footsore and rather weak, and the great heat making one languid in the extreme, added to this dyspepsia from potato diet. After 7 or 8 miles all glad to pull up at a stream and rest in the shade; cook a few more potatoes. Assiniboine and wife wash and put on clean things. Milton makes kinnikinnick in expectation of tobacco tonight." A little later Milton bought some tobacco from some Indians who passed and "who assured us it was quite close. I had some distrust of the state-ment from former experience of proximity of forts and walked on quickly pipe in mouth, enjoying my first smoke of pure tobacco for some six weeks; after a mile or so the rest overtook me, the sun was already set; no signs of the Fort. Assiniboine proposed that I should take his chestnut horse, and ride ahead with Milton, trying at any rate to get ourselves in, and get canoes ready to cross the rest. I gladly agreed, being very done with over 20 miles in the hot sun, and my feet very sore, and we cantered away as well as our tired horses would go; and a deal of whacking they took. To our amusement O'Byrne ap-peared tearing after us, being I suppose afraid to be left in the rear with Assiniboine!"

It was rapidly growing dark as they entered a wide plain and crossing it found a long shanty and several people sitting on the ground eating, with pots and kettles over a fire near by. An old Indian met them announcing in mixed French, Indian and English, " 'A dollar each. Camp here.' A dollar each! All right, we must eat if it costs £50 a piece, and straight let loose our horses and sat down to the remains of the repast which consisted of a greasy soup of bacon, cabbage and pease in a tin dish, beautiful white galette, and tea and sugar. Milton and I did wonders! Fat bacon, cabbage and pease and the greasy liquid went down fast, and galette after galette called for. . . . After eating all we could get hold of with perfect ferocity we desisted, telling them to prepare for three more to arrive shortly."

The old man said that he was Captain St. Paul, of whom they would certainly have heard. He gave them a room in "a kind of out-house with two broken-down bedsteads in it and fowls roosting on the beams," and announced that a dance would be held there that night at which all the world would assemble. Assiniboine and his family straggled into the clearing worn out and were given a meal. Soon afterward guests began to arrive, Indian and half-breed men and women, all gaily dressed, in bright-coloured shirts and shawls with a Spanish or Mexican air, Cheadle thought, about their hats and the silk handkerchiefs tied around their heads. The Indian men appeared smaller than Indians on the eastern side of the mountains, more civilized and better dressed. The chief trader at Fort Kamloops was away but Mr. Martin, who was in charge, welcomed Lord Milton and his party and invited them to come to the fort next day.

They were surprised to meet with such ready hospitality. "Our ragged appearance and gaunt looks greatly against us. . . . Our clothes in tatters, the legs of Milton's trousers torn off above the knees, and Cheadle's in ribbons; our feet covered only by shreds of moccasins; our faces gaunt, haggard, and unshaven; our hair long, unkempt, and matted; and we had no means of proving our identity where our appearance was so little calculated to inspire confidence or liking. But our story was believed at once, and our troubles were over at last—at last!"

"All anxious to know who we were, where from, whether intending to mine or seek employment, and seemed rather incredulous when informed that we were a mere party of *pleasure.*"

Cheadle was too tired to go to the dance, Milton danced for a short time. They went to bed but were "continually disturbed by noise and thumping on floor of dancers in next room. At last toward morning peace and rest." Next day the skeleton horses were put out to grass and the men crossed the river to the fort. "We then purchased trousers and shirts in the store, towels and soap and Burgess showing us a good bathing place, we went down to the river and had a regular scrub-down and swim afterwards; put on our new apparel and felt really comfortable once more. . . . Then—Ah! then—dinner! *Mutton chops, potatoes, fresh butter, delicious galette, rice pudding!* Never shall I forget that delightful meal. *Strong* tea and plenty of sugar. Talk of intellectual enjoyment! pooh! pooh! Your stomach is the door of true delight. No use in describing how we ate and drank."

While they ate, and it seemed to them that they could never eat enough, they heard that the North had taken Vicksburg, that the French had taken Mexico, that the Prince of Wales had married Princess Alexandra of Denmark. Nearer at hand, three hundred Indians had died of smallpox that winter and quiet had prevailed in the Cariboo since Governor Douglas had undertaken to preserve order, only two murders having been committed that year.

"Rest, eat, smoke and talk," Cheadle wrote next day, "still as ravenous as ever. I was astonished at my gaunt appearance and meagre, hatchet face." In the next three weeks he gained forty-one pounds.

O'Byrne presented the problem of the moment. They had all admired the energy he could summon up in a crisis but now that the crisis was over, his less appealing characteristics were again evident. "Sickens everybody by his talk of this great person and another in one country or another, trying to fix himself on to someone on strength of mutual acquaintanceship with third party." Since he appeared to be certain that he could go on with Cheadle and Milton, they confided their dilemma to Mr. Martin, who agreed to help them. He asked O'Byrne what he meant to do and "hinted that he fancied we did not expect his company any further, and that there was now a good road forward, and houses at which he might sleep all along. . . . In the evening he (O'Byrne) called me aside and asked me if I could supply him with a pair of socks, a silk necktie, some tea and sugar, a little bread and money enough for the steamer from Yale to Victoria. I said I would talk with Milton on the matter and also about a letter to certify that the letter of introduction from Archdeacon Collian to the Governor was lost in the Fraser. Milton kindly wrote O'Byrne's letter and supplied him with tea, tobacco and matches for his journey; Martin with cakes and bacon. . . . He then called me aside and said, 'Look here, I've got no money for the road,' in the coolest manner." When Cheadle hesitated and began to remonstrate—"this rather put my back up"—O'Byrne repeated his complaints against Assiniboine and suggested that it was Cheadle's fault that his horse had been stolen on the road. "I told him that seeing both Milton and myself had subscribed for the horse, and had brought him over here without a farthing of cost to himself, I thought it was a most disgusting and ungrateful speech for him to make, and that perhaps the conversation had better end, walking away indignant. He bid us good-bye coolly and set out, pack on back, saying we should probably never meet again, and he bore us no ill-will!"

# VII

FROM THE DAY, September 1, 1863, when Viscount Milton, Dr. Cheadle, Assiniboine and his wife and son were resting and eating enormously at Fort Kamloops the narrative of their adventures changes key. They had been in a real sense explorers in their desperate journey from Tête Jaune Cache. After Fort Kamloops they were tourists, sightseers, and though much of their further travel was arduous and even dangerous they were proceeding over well marked roads and often in public conveyances. Their journey had been one of pioneering and discovery; now it became an observation trip.

They were anxious to reach Victoria to get their letters, and Mr. McKay, the factor, when he returned, loaned them horses and arranged for them to cash their cheques in New Westminster or Victoria. Mr. McKay who was going down on business accompanied them. They took three horses for the Assiniboine family and one to carry baggage, in addition to those they rode, for they planned to camp out by the way. "Enormous appetite still," Cheadle wrote. They camped one night near a company of engineers who were at work on the new road to the gold diggings, the famous Cariboo Road, and saw a number of men, "blanket on back, halting and footsore", unsuccessful miners coming down from the mines before winter. They saw flourishing gardens of potatoes, cabbages, beans and cucumbers but British Columbia, Cheadle thought, would never be a great farming country. The thing that most impressed Assiniboine and his family was the road. "The boy became quite excited, exclaiming, whenever any person appeared in sight, 'There's another fellow!' "

They saw, as they travelled, the terraced benches of the Fraser river which had yielded less gold than the fabled Cariboo, and Boston Bar where Chinamen were working, the sight of whom greatly amazed Assiniboine. Hell's Gate on the Fraser impressed them less than the Hell's Gate they had known so intimately on the North Thompson. They reached Yale and sailed on the *Reliance* for New Westminster, passing Hope, no longer active as a mining town, and Fort Langley, the old Hudson's Bay Company post. New Westminster, the capital of British Columbia, "stands on rising ground above the river, amidst the densest forest, which has cost fortunes to clear away, averaging $3 a stump. It is finely placed and will be a pretty place in time. A deep bay of river forms a suitable harbour and the town is extremely well laid out by Col. Moody. Engineer's camp about ½ mile along river. Substantial buildings, Church and barrack rooms etc. Col. Moody's house very prettily situated. All the low land along the lower Fraser is said to be rich soil but overflowed in summer, and covered with enormous timber, a great drawback to cultivation here where labour is so dear."

Crossing at once to Victoria they were refused a hotel room by the proprietor because of their disreputable appearance, but hearing who they were he ran after them to urge them to stay. They met Colonel Moody, commander of the Royal Engineers, British Columbia, who told at great length the history of the colony, got themselves fitted out with proper clothing and dined with Governor Douglas. But one of their chief pleasures was in entertaining the Assiniboine family who had never seen a larger town than Fort Garry. "We had driven a buggy and pair of dashing horses down in the morning, I driving with Milton on the box and Assiniboine and family inside, to their immense satisfaction, and they compared this style of travelling to our wearisome march through the woods, a short time ago. In the evening we took them to the theatre, a great surprise for them. Everyone knew 'Our Indians' and they had numerous visitors in the old cabin they lived in by permission of the Hudson's Bay Company."

Cheadle did not record what Assiniboine thought of the performance of the March Troupe, girls of 18, "many of them dressed as small girls of 12 which did not at all agree with their womanly development."

In Victoria they saw O'Byrne for the last time. In the safety of civilization he shook hands with Assiniboine and forgave him everything. Later they heard that he had moved on to San Francisco and then to Melbourne,

Australia, happy, Cheadle supposed, "in any country free from wolves, grizzly bears and Assiniboines."

Here too the photograph was taken which appears as frontispiece to his book. It shows Milton and Cheadle and the Indian family all neatly dressed, seated in a row on a buffalo robe under a tree. The men hold their guns and on the grass before them lie what looks like a shot bag and a small axe, perhaps the one taken from the Headless Indian.

The Indian family was sorry to leave Victoria and especially "the delicacies provided for them by the pastry cook." They returned to Kamloops where Assiniboine was employed as a shepherd at the fort and went back the next summer by the Kootenay Pass to Fort Pitt.

It was the beginning of October but the two men, now alone, were determined to see the Cariboo gold-fields and so returned to New Westminster. So alluring were the descriptions of the capital's future that Lord Milton, in one of his fits of enthusiasm, bought seven lots of from three to nine acres at £20 to £32 each. They went to look at the new property "about ½ mile at the back of the town, but the forest was so thick and the marks so indistinct that we could not make them out."

From Douglas they went on horseback to Lillooet and there took the stage, an open wagon drawn by five horses, which carried three passengers and a ton of freight. They charged up and down hills, not even slackening at the awe-inspiring "rattlesnake grade" up Pavilion Mountain. "After ascending still higher, commence descent of Pavilion by 'rattlesnake grade', the most dangerous

207

carriage road I ever saw; the road turns 6 times, is very narrow except at the turns, the mountain side terrifically steep. We rattled down at a fearful pace, a wheel coming off, the brake giving way, or a restive horse being almost instant death. . . . Passed a magnificent camel; one of the two brought out, first tried in California and then here; failures in both countries."

Accommodation at night they found so bad that they thought longingly of their camp-fire nights in the mountains. In the wayside houses, built every few miles for the use of miners, men lay on the bar counter and on the floor. "Awful night last night; wind blowing thro' cracks in walls and floor; only one blanket apiece; 20 men in room; one afflicted with cramp in leg which brought him on his feet swearing every ½ hour. Milton and another talking in their sleep; rest snoring." Sometimes a few men went on drinking and gambling all night long. In a wayside house they met one of the men who had come overland the year before and who gave an account of the fearful raft journey down the Fraser.

At Soda Creek they took the steamer to Quesnel, from Quesnel they set out on foot for Williams Creek. The frozen ground was covered with half-melted snow and walking in their heavy jack-boots blistered their feet unbearably. Along the road they each picked up a pair of rubber boots—gum-boots—which made walking in mud and snow much easier. "By the roadside lay the dead bodies of horses and mules, some standing as they had died, still stuck fast in the deep, tenacious mud." The steeply rising, heavily-wooded trail reminded them that they were in the same forest and mountain region they had known so well on the North Thompson. The three towns Richfield, Barkerville and Cameron Town extended one after another along the fabulous Williams Creek. That spring Cameron Town had consisted of three or four houses; now six months later there were sixty or seventy houses in each of the towns. Sore and stiff, Milton and Cheadle stopped at last at Mr. Cusheon's hotel.

Next day they saw the mining operations of the Cameron Company which had passed far beyond the simple activity of the miner rocking his wooden cradle or even inspecting his flume. They went down a shaft thirty feet deep to bed-rock and saw other shafts well-timbered and roofed. Nuggets could be seen in the gravel loosened by the pick and Cheadle and Milton were allowed to wash out two pans which yielded $21. "Steele showed me about $1000 of gold in a bag."

They visited other workings along the creek, among them the rich Raby claim where they saw bits of gold in the face of the cutting. "The appearance of Williams Creek," Cheadle wrote, "is merely a narrow valley shut in by pine-clad hills, the edges and bottom partially cleared and covered with wooden huts, flumes, water-wheels, windlasses, shafts, ditches and tunnels." In the evenings they went from one house to another to look at specimens, "like the most perfectly frosted jeweller's gold and of fantastic shape. I am already beginning to hate the name," he added, after an evening of specimen-viewing but he and Milton bought several as souvenirs.

Milton also found time to gratify a negro barber from Tennessee who "said he should die happy if he could only shave a real live lord." Mine visiting after a week began to pall. "Milton went down another shaft of the *Caledonia*, and I, sick of going down in buckets and crouching along drifts, walked on to Richfield and had a pipe with the Judge." This was Judge Matthew Begbie, famous in British Columbia lore as the "Hanging Judge".

Everywhere they had noticed the predominance of American brashness and vigour, Yankee drinking before meals, Yankee expressions such as "bully for you", "played out", "a big strike", "you bet your life", "you bet your bottom dollar". Cheadle wrote, "American manners and customs rule in the mines." One man told them that though he hated Yankees he had to admire their energy for Yankees, mostly Southerners, had opened up the Cariboo in 1858 and 1859.

It was the end of October, the snow was deep, it was time for them to go. Milton and Cheadle after their ten days at Williams Creek, walked back to Quesnel Mouth in three days and were dismayed to find that the steamer for Soda Creek had stopped running for the winter. However an open boat would start next day and in this they embarked with forty passengers "packed close as negroes in a slaver." It snowed hard, all the passengers were soon wet and when the boat could not get through a riffle, a number of them had to get out and wade ashore to lighten the load. They could not reach Soda Creek that night and camped on shore, waking up covered with snow to continue their journey breakfastless. From

Soda Creek they walked on to Williams Lake where there was a fine farm with prosperous looking cattle.

The express wagon carried them on; it was heavy going for the road was a sheet of ice covered with snow, the horses often fell and the passengers had to get out and help push the wagon uphill. After five days' driving they reached the terrifying road between Lytton and Yale. It was supposed to be twelve feet wide but was "in many parts really much less from sliding down of the steep sides above the road partially blocking it; the pole was loose, spring broken, waggon generally very loose, traces continually coming off, no brake, heavy load (170 lbs. gold, 4 passengers and luggage), 2 small horses very tired; road very steep up to point of bluff, and then ditto down about width of waggon, sheer descent of 600 or 700 feet into rocky bed of Thompson, perpendicular side of mountain above." Some miles above Yale the wagon broke down completely, "iron stanchions giving way and pole and cross bars tumbling to ground; on level road; wonderful luck; if this had happened on a precipice we should probably have been lost." Another wagon was found with fresh horses and off they went to Yale, to the boat for New Westminster and then to Victoria.

Conclusions about the western colony were forming in Cheadle's mind and with these a year later he was to close his book. In British Columbia, over much of which he had travelled, he reported abundant mineral wealth, splendid trees, great quantities of excellent fish, especially salmon. There was grazing land but it was dry and would require very large extents of pasturage for every herd. Agricultural land he found very limited in amount. Near the south end of Lake Okanagan and in a few other places he reported good land but the delta of the Fraser was entirely covered with dense forest and subject to flooding. Agriculture was so scanty that the two colonies of British Columbia and Vancouver Island had to get their provisions from California.

No colony, Cheadle thought, had been more misrepresented than British Columbia. While it was under the control of the Hudson's Bay Company it had been reported as "little better than a waste and howling wilderness, wherein half-famished beasts of prey waged eternal war with a sparse population of half-starved savages; where the cold was more than Arctic, and the drouth more than Saharan."

But the first immigrants hastening into the country to find gold painted a very different picture. Now it was described in most glowing terms as a farmers' paradise but farmers who had gone there had been sharply disappointed. Truth, as usual, lay between the two exaggerated accounts. British Columbia had little farm land but the belt of the Saskatchewan river had rich prairies, ready for the plough and luxuriant grass lands which would support domestic cattle as well as buffalo. "Yet this glorious country, estimated at 65,000 square miles, and forty millions of acres of the richest soil, capable of supporting twenty millions of people, is, from its isolated position, and the difficulties put in the way of settlement, by the governing power, hitherto left utterly neglected and useless, except for the support of a few Indians and the employees of the Hudson's Bay Company. And this rich agricultural country lies but a step as it were from the gold-fields."

This sharp antithesis between the two views of the entire west of British North America is illustrated in two statements made in a single year. In 1862 John Mc-Dougall could write, "Why every mile we came is abundantly fit for settlement, and the day will come when it will be taken up and developed," and the Governor of the Hudson's Bay Company, "Beyond the Red River to the base of the Rocky Mountains, the line will pass through a vast desert, in some places without wood or water, exposed to the incursions of roving bands of Indians and entirely destitute of any means of subsistence for emigrants. With regard to a telegraphic communication it is scarcely necessary to point at the prairie fires, the depredation of the natives and the general chapter of accidents as presenting almost insurmountable obstacles."

Cheadle stated that communication was needed between east and west but here the Americans had shown the way. They had already built a road and a telegraph line to California and had started a Pacific railway. The real obstacle to a line of communication across British territory in America was the region between Lake Superior and Fort Garry, this land of swamp and forest, but Professor Hind's report had indicated that the difficulties were not insurmountable. "If a railway were constructed from Halifax to some point in British Columbia, the whole distance from Southampton would be accomplished in thirty-six days." Search for a practicable North-West Passage by sea had failed but "the North-West Passage by land is the real highway to the Pacific."

213

Milton and Cheadle in Victoria were now on the way home but in no particular hurry to get there. They saw *Camille*, "overdone by Mrs. Dean Hayne", shopped, hired full evening dress from the tailor and attended the St. Andrew's dinner. Social life in Victoria was very active with dinners, calls upon the ladies, visits to the shop of a tea importer, to Nanaimo to see the coal outcrop of "the future Newcastle of the Pacific"; they played whist, Cheadle read *Lady Audley's Secret* and they saw *The Taming of the Shrew*, "acted with great spirit."

Christmas Day they spent on the steamer *Pacific* and arrived next day at San Francisco. Two single young gentlemen, one of them a viscount, had not long to wait for social acceptance. They dined, they went to a grand ball which they were surprised to find "very well bred. The dresses of the ladies were on the whole in very good taste, of silk, or muslin, expensive and the jewellery costly. White silk with rose coloured bodice etc. Two very handsome women appeared in powder, effect not pleasing." Cheadle, comparing the young ladies of San Francisco with those at home, granted the former very pretty faces and delicate complexions, "but nearly all with the usual failing of the woman of this continent, rather too flat chested and without that lovely roundness of form and limb so characteristic of *our* girls at home." They were friendly and well-informed, he found, and without affectation. And they were great walkers; one lady told him that she knew girls who could walk five miles. Cheadle unchivalrously assured her that his own sisters could easily walk twenty.

On January 23 they were off on the *Golden City* for

Panama. They saw men from a whaling vessel chase and harpoon a whale and took on board bales of cotton at Manzanita. As it grew warmer the passengers appeared in linen jackets and straw hats, Milton creating a sensation with his pith helmet. At Acapulco they went ashore and saw for the first time pelicans flapping lazily on the rocks, piles of coconuts, oranges and mangoes. Cheadle and the captain argued furiously over the abolitionist views of Henry Ward Beecher. After the short railway journey across the Isthmus of Panama, they went on board the *Ariel*, a much smaller ship, and a week later were in New York. There they skated in Central Park, had supper at Delmonico's, and made a rapid trip to Washington, where they saw *The Taming of the Shrew* again, this time with Edwin Booth. There was little talk of the war but in the streets and public places they noticed that half the men and women were wearing mourning. On March 5 they reached Liverpool after an absence of twenty-one months.

Dr. Cheadle must have set very promptly to work to rewrite his lively journal into the more staid *North-West Passage by Land* for it was published the next year, 1865. In that year also he was elected a member of the Royal College of Surgeons and later became a distinguished London physician. He specialized to some extent in diseases of children and was one of the few doctors to support the right of women to practise medicine. In his championship of their cause, he was among the first professors to lecture at the London School of Medicine for Women. In 1884 he visited Canada with the British Association and at a banquet in Winnipeg expressed to

Dr. George Bryce, later the historian of the Hudson's Bay Company, his surprise that "the former state of scarcity of food even in Red River had been so changed into the evident plenty which Manitoba now enjoys."

Lord Milton married in 1867 and came to Canada with his wife in 1872. It seemed to him that the air of the western plains improved his feeble health and he and his wife settled in what was later described as a shack at Point de Meuron on the banks of the Kamanistiquia river, about six miles west of Fort William. A son was born there that summer. In the middle of the next winter the little house burned to the ground and the family barely escaped alive. Presumably they returned to England where in 1877 Viscount Milton died, during the life of his father, Earl Fitzwilliam. The title passed to the grandson who had been born in the shack at Point de Meuron on the banks of the Kaministiquia.

# IV. A HOME FOR MILLIONS

# I

A GREAT DEAL had happened in the decade between the start of Milton and Cheadle's journey and the start of Fleming and Grant's. Canadians had been too busy building railroads between their own towns to find time to extend them beyond their immediate borders. Joseph Howe, indeed, had prophesied in 1851 that men then living would hear the steam-whistle of the locomotive in the valleys of the Rocky Mountains. Earlier still, in Toronto, one Sir John Smythe had produced a lithographed map indicating a railroad to the Pacific by a strong black line ruled straight across the continent from Fort William to the mouth of the Columbia. It was his purpose to provide, in case of war with the United States, a means of steam communication from England to China. "I propose this," he wrote, "to run in the rear of Lake Huron and in the rear of Lake Superior, twenty miles in the interior of the country of the Lake aforesaid, to unite with the railroad from Lake Superior to Winnipeg at the south-west main trading post of the North West Company," and the statement was signed, Sir John

219

Smythe, Baronet and Royal Engineer, Canadian Poet, LL.D. and Moral Philosopher.

In general, however, little thought had been devoted to the great plains of the west until Confederation gave them paramount importance. Strong opinions were advanced on both sides of the railway question. Palliser considered a railway through British American territory impossible. "The knowledge of the country as a whole, would never lead me to advise a line of communication from Canada, across the continent to the Pacific, exclusively through British territory. The time has forever gone by for effecting such an object; and the unfortunate choice of an astronomical boundary line has completely isolated the Central American possessions of Great Britain from Canada in the east, and also almost debarred them from any eligible access from the Pacific coast on the west."

On the other hand, Hind insisted, "It is a physical reality of the highest importance to the interests of British North America that a continuous belt, rich in water, woods and pasturage can be settled and cultivated from a few miles west of the Lake of the Woods, to the Passes of the Rocky Mountains; and any line of communication, whether by waggon road or railroad, passing through it, will eventually enjoy the great advantage of being fed by an agricultural population, from one extremity to the other."

But Confederation made the west a part of Canada and its terms transformed the idea of a railway from a dream, a far-off possibility, to an immediate necessity. Surveying was going forward across the continent; on the day when British Columbia entered the Dominion, July 20, 1871, surveying parties left Victoria for the Rocky Mountains and Ottawa for the west.

By 1871, fewer well-to-do young men were travelling for sport and pleasure. The west, now that the buffalo herds were nearly gone, now that it was a part of Canada, received travellers of a different kind. Engineers and surveyors had already begun their inspection of the so far little-known plains. Practical men, traders, men of business, were to come, and before and after them the great company of settlers, farmers, who were to make the prairies in fact what Grant envisioned—a home for millions. A very few years after Grant's journey it was recorded that one met on the streets of Prince Albert, a town less than fifteen years old, "many strangers, well-dressed, watch-wearing, cigar-smoking men of the east." Of this rapid influx, Grant's expedition was a forerunner.

In 1872 Sandford Fleming set out to find a way across the western plains for the new railroad. Fleming was a Scot by birth who had come to Canada as a very young man and become chief engineer of the Intercolonial Railway. When the Parliament buildings in Montreal were burned by rioting mobs in 1849, the young Fleming rushed inside and rescued the portrait of Queen Victoria. Having superintended the construction of the Intercolonial he was a natural choice as engineer-in-chief of the projected Canadian Pacific Railway. In that capacity he stated that he "considered it necessary to travel overland to see the main features of the country with his own eyes."

To this end he journeyed through Nova Scotia and

New Brunswick along the line of the Intercolonial, which was still under construction, to its junction with the Grand Trunk at Quebec and on to Toronto. There he met his friend the Reverend George Grant who was the secretary of the expedition and who became its historian.

At the time of the journey the Reverend George Grant was pastor of St. Matthew's Church in Halifax. He had been born in Pictou County, Nova Scotia, of a family of Scots Presbyterians, had studied at Glasgow University but had returned to make his home in Nova Scotia. Though he had lost his right hand in an accident when he was a small boy, Grant was strong and active, a man of great practical capacity. At this time he was thirty-seven years old. He was a devoted believer in Confederation when opposition to it in Nova Scotia was most bitter, and the future greatness of Canada was a subject which enlisted all his ardent enthusiasm.

His close friend, Sandford Fleming, had awakened his interest in the Red River several years before he had any idea of going there. When the crops of the little settlement were destroyed by grasshoppers in 1868, Fleming had written to Grant asking him to make a collection for the starving settlers. Grant had raised and sent three thousand dollars but he wrote, "I could have collected the money quite as easily and the givers would have given quite as intelligently, had the sufferers been in Central Abyssinia." Though Grant had strongly supported Confederation, before and after its consummation he had known nothing whatever of the North-West and near the end of his life he confessed, "This journey resolved the uneasy doubt in my mind as to whether or not Canada had a future; for from the day we left Collingwood till we reached Victoria, the great possibilities of our great North-West impressed us." For "the North-West was to the average man of that day a sub-arctic region, the prey of hailstorms, hostile Indians, and grasshoppers, British Columbia a sea of mountains, New Ontario a barren wilderness effectually separating Eastern from Western Canada."

"Travel a thousand miles up a great river; more than another thousand along great lakes and a succession of smaller lakes; a thousand miles across rolling prairies; and another thousand through woods and over three great ranges of mountains, and you have travelled from Ocean to Ocean through Canada."

With these memorable words Grant began the book, *Ocean to Ocean*, which he wrote from the diary he kept on the journey with Sandford Fleming to the Pacific coast. Unlike Southesk, Milton or Cheadle, Grant was a Canadian and he went west not as a visitor seeing with interest a picturesque colony, not to collect buffalo heads and the horns of mountain sheep, or for health or excitement. The railroad motivated the journey; settlement was continuously in his thoughts. He looked everywhere for possible farming land and likely town sites, attacking the west with the energy and vigour which marked his whole life.

He kept his diary with care; "notes had to be taken, sometimes in the bottom of a canoe and sometimes leaning against a stump of a tree; on horseback in fine weather, under a cart when it was raining or when the sun's rays

223

were fierce; at night, in the tent, by the light of the camp-fire in front; in a crowded wayside inn, or on the deck of a steamer in motion. And they were written out in the first few weeks after our return."

The expedition had a specific mission and a rigid time-table. Indeed the journey from Lake Superior to the Pacific was covered in the fastest time ever made up to that day with no stopping to hunt or to pan for gold or to seek adventure. The trip was well organized, the party well equipped and supplied.

At the Queen's Hotel in Toronto on July 15 the party met and was photographed; Sandford Fleming and Dr. Moren, big men with bushy beards, Grant slender and lightly bearded, Frank, Fleming's son, much the youngest of the party. The next day they took the train for Collingwood.

"Collingwood is an instance of what a railway terminus does for a place. Before the Northern Railway was built, an unbroken forest occupied its site, and the red deer came down through the woods to drink at the shore. Now, there is a thriving town of two or three thousand people, with steam saw-mills, and huge rafts from the North that almost fill up its little harbour, with a grain elevator which lifts out of steam barges the corn from Chicago, weighs it, and pours it into railway freight-waggons to be hurried down to Toronto, and there turned into bread or whiskey, without a hand touching it in all its transportations or transformations."

The train arrived there at noon and the steamer *Frances Smith* was to start at two for Fort William.

Porters rushed back and forth with the luggage in such haste that the gangplank was knocked askew and one of the porters fell head first into the water. "That's the second time he's tumbled in," cried somebody cheerfully, "and he can't swim." The man rose to the surface, struck his head on a heavy float in the space between the pier and the steamer's side, sank and did not rise again. While the watchers looked about for ropes and did nothing, a young man suddenly ran through the crowd, jumped into the water and with some difficulty rescued the drowning man. A bystander said that he was a fisherman who the summer before had jumped into Lake Superior from the deck of a steamer to save a child who had fallen overboard. "Nobody seemed to notice him or to think that he deserved a word of praise." This was too much for Grant who hurried after him to offer thanks and a small reward. But the young man refused; he was a good swimmer, he said, and his clothes were not hurt.

The start was successively delayed; from two o'clock it was postponed to six, from six to midnight and at last the *Frances Smith* left Collingwood at five-thirty next morning. But then she steamed only as far as Owen Sound where five hours passed in argument between the Captain and the government inspector, with Fleming urging speed upon both. When they left Owen Sound in the evening it was to go only as far as Leith, six miles off, to take on wood. Ten cords were to be loaded and two or three men set to work, each carrying a few sticks at a leisurely pace. Fleming again approached the captain who was dancing with passengers in the cabin. It would take all night, the captain assured him, for the men to get the wood on board. At once half a dozen passengers began to carry sticks and the steamer sailed at two a.m. "An inauspicious beginning to our journey this! Aided all the way by steam, we were not much more than one hundred miles in a direct line from Toronto, forty-four hours after starting. At this rate, when would we reach the Rocky Mountains?"

As they passed Manitoulin Island next day one of the passengers exclaimed, "Why, there's quite a scenery here!"

At Bruce Copper Mines they saw the shanties of three or four hundred men who worked the mines, and then at Sault Ste. Marie passed through the canal on the United States side. He could travel, Grant wrote, from ocean to ocean, four thousand miles on Canadian territory but for this half mile at the Sault it was necessary to use the American canal; Canada ought surely to build a canal of her own. As a matter of fact around 1800 the North West Company had had locks there to take up loaded canoes for the needs of the fur trade.

Fleming had met among the passengers a man whom he asked to accompany the expedition. "At whatever point the steamer touched, the first man on shore was the Botanist, scrambling over the rocks or diving into the woods, vasculum in hand, stuffing it full of mosses, ferns, lichens, liverworts, sedges, grasses and flowers till recalled by the whistle that the captain always obligingly sounded for him. Of course such an enthusiast became known to all on board, especially to the sailors, who designated him as the haymaker. They regarded him,

because of his scientific failing, with the respectful toler-
ance with which fools are regarded in eastern countries,
and would wait an extra minute for him, or help him
on board, if the steamer were cast loose from the pier
before he could scramble up the side." This was Professor Macoun, referred to in Grant's record always as "the
Botanist."

He had taken the voyage on Lake Superior probably
as a holiday tour but his encounter with Sandford Fleming was to change the direction of his life. John Macoun,
born in Ireland, had come to Canada in 1850 to farm and
had picked up a knowledge of botany and geology. In
1868 he had been appointed professor of these subjects
at Albert College, Belleville. His enthusiasm attracted
Fleming's attention and his discoveries on this expedition
led to others. In 1879 he was appointed explorer for the
Canadian government in the North-West Territories and
soon afterwards botanist to the geological survey. He
became assistant director to the survey and continued in
that capacity to the end of his long life. He published
catalogues of Canadian plants and birds and a vast descrip-
tive volume on the North-West which he knew thoroughly.

His eagerness carried him far ahead of the others.
When the ship carrying the Fleming party entered the
harbour of Gargantua, his friends saw, as soon as the
steamer docked, the figure of the Botanist climbing on
the highest hill along the shore. Here a number of fishermen had made their summer camp to catch white-fish
and trout. The whole party was rowed ashore to swim,

scramble up the hills or walk along the beach covered with blossoming wild pea vine. The Botanist brought back to the steamer with him specimens of rare mosses and ferns and accounts of the view northward over rugged, tree-covered hills.

In the harbour of Michipicoten Island, the *Frances Smith* tried to pull off the S. S. *Manitoulin* which had run aground several days before. While these attempts were being made, unsuccessfully, some of the passengers, infected with the Botanist's zeal, offered to help him collect plants. "He led them a rare chase over rocks and through woods, being always on the lookout for the places that promised the rarest kinds, quite indifferent to the toil or danger. The sight of a perpendicular face of rock, either dry or dripping with moisture, drew him like a magnet, and with yells of triumph, he would summon the others to come and behold the treasure he had lit upon. Scrambling, puffing, rubbing their shins against rocks, and half breaking their necks, they toiled painfully after him, only to find him on his knees before some 'thing of beauty' that seemed to them little different from what they had passed by with indifference thousands of times."

"The scenery of Nipigon bay," Grant wrote, "is of the grandest description; there is nothing like it in Ontario. . . . The time will come when the wealthy men of our great North-West will have their summer residences on these hills and shores." There was an old Hudson's Bay Company station at Nipigon river and also the headquarters of several Canadian Pacific Railway surveying parties. While Fleming consulted with the surveyors, Doctor Moren attended one of the engineers who was ill. Within an hour the steamer was off to navigate the narrow western channel before darkness fell.

"The most wonderful vein of silver in the world has been struck here." They were at Silver Island at one o'clock in the morning, the rocky islet from which the year before thirty men had taken silver valued at $1,200,000. "In all probability the mine is worth millions." An American company was working the mine and the exciting find had naturally "stimulated search in every other direction around Lake Superior." "Those rocky shores," Grant wrote with his usual enthusiasm, "may turn out to be the richest part of the whole Dominion."

That morning they reached Thunder Bay—from Toronto "by rail ninety-four miles, by steamboat 530 miles." None of the party had ever travelled west before and they looked eagerly from the deck of their steamer at Prince Arthur's Landing which is now Port Arthur.

They were about to launch upon the new Canadian route from Lake Superior to Red River. The great Sir George Simpson, taking with him the Earl of Southesk, had travelled for the first time in 1859 to Fort Garry by way of the United States and from that time the American route had been used for Hudson's Bay Company supplies. The long and round-about route by St. Paul and St. Cloud, with its many changes of vehicle, had been traversed by Lord Milton and Dr. Cheadle and, in the ten years since their journey, by many others, both travellers for pleasure and emigrants.

During these years, argument for and against a possible all-Canadian route had swung forward and back. It was claimed that the region between Lake Superior and Red River was impenetrable for emigrants with baggage. No, it was argued, a route could be determined upon and made passable. This discussion might have gone on for years longer but rebellion threatening in Red River, acted, like the discovery of gold, as a stimulant, a galvanic agent, to stir up rapid and vigorous response. The Dawson route had been opened as a military necessity in 1870, and over it, Colonel Wolseley's force had taken three months to cover the distance from Thunder Bay to Fort Garry. It was imagined that emigrants bound with all their goods for Red River would follow this route with its equipment of boats and rest houses in the charge of station masters. Fleming and his party were now to test the practicability of this new and promising road to the interior.

# II

Prince Arthur's Landing, named after Queen Victoria's son, who had visited there in 1866, had a hundred shanties and stores, for silver had been found in the neighbourhood and, as California and the Cariboo had abundantly shown, no magnet could draw population like the hope of treasure. Like Sir George Simpson, Fleming could command transport. A wagon took the party's baggage after breakfast and somewhat later Fleming and Dr. Moren started in a buggy, the rest of the small party in another wagon for Shebandowan Lake, forty-five miles away. It was late July, wild berries flourished, the road was good. A perfect place for farmers to settle, Grant wrote, with the mines providing a market for farm produce.

Three hours' driving brought them to the fifteen-mile shanty where they had the best dinner they had eaten since they left Toronto—broth, beefsteak, bread and tea. They went on again, finding the soil rich and, fortunately, a bridge thrown across the Kaministiquia River. At the Matawan River, bridged too, they met a Mr. Aitken who had recently come from Glengarry. What did he think of the new country? Settlement was in the minds of all the party for the new railroad would depend upon settlement and they plied Aitken with questions.

"He had arrived exactly two months ago, on the 22nd of May, and he had now oats and barley up, potatoes in blossom, turnips, lettuce, parsnips, cucumbers etc., all looking healthy, and all growing in land that, sixty days before, had been in part covered with undergrowth, stumps and tall trees, through which fires had run the year previous. Mr. Aitken was in love with the country and, what was of more consequence, so was Mrs. Aitken, though she confessed to a longing for some neighbours. They intended to make it their future home, and said that they had never seen land so well suited for farming. Everything was prospering with them. The very hens seemed to do better here than elsewhere. One was pointed out with a brood of twenty strong healthy chickens around her; Guinea hens and turkeys looked thriving."

The men were not a little amazed at all they saw. "Our former ideas concerning it (the North-West) had been that it was a barren desert; that there was only a horse-trail, and not always that, to travel by; that the mosquitoes were as big as grasshoppers, and bit through everything." On the contrary the land was fertile, the road good, the mosquitoes, so far, no more vicious than those at home.

However they had been in the new country only half a day, and the late afternoon and evening proved less encouraging. From Matawan to Shebandowan the tim-

ber was poor, the road very bad "varying between corduroy, deep sand, and rutty and rooty stretches, over which the waggon jolted frightfully." At Shebandowan they spent the night and in the morning gathered at the wharf. The next three hundred and eighty miles through the chain of lakes was to be covered in canoes. Fleming looked at the mountains of baggage, then at the canoes and proposed that a large part of the baggage should be left behind and that from Fort Garry on each person's possessions should be severely limited.

The selected luggage was stowed in place, the men seated themselves, the Indians paddled out into the lake where—shades of the North-West voyageurs!—they hooked their canoes onto a small steam tug "kept on the lake for towing purposes." Off went the tug at a rate of seven knots, drawing after it a big barge loaded with emigrants, then a large canoe with three of Fleming's party and seven Indians, next two more large canoes each with members of the party and six Indians, and last the canoe of the inevitable two young men travelling for pleasure. They glided easily along past the dark, fire-ruined shores of the lake where silver had been found and where "prospecting parties are now searching all accessible spots."

The Indians were Iroquois, for two centuries the chosen canoemen of explorers and travellers who could command their services, as well as the canoemen *par excellence* of the fur trade. Their leader, Ignace, had been a guide for Sir George Simpson for fifteen years while one of the steersmen had been a cook on Sir

George's expeditions "and looked every inch the butler of a respectable English family." Ignace had been a famous runner who had beaten all competitors from towns near his native Caughnawaga on the St. Lawrence. Another Indian had gone down the Mackenzie River to the Arctic with one of the parties searching for Sir John Franklin.

Three hours carried them to the west end of the lake where a large camp of Ojibways had assembled to make treaty with the Indian Commissioner. Here for the first time the party saw a portage made. The distance to Lake Kashaboye was three-quarters of a mile. "The Indians emptied the canoes in a trice; two shouldered a canoe, weighing probably three hundred pounds, and made off at a rapid trot across the portage. The others loaded the wagon of the station with the luggage, and carried on their backs by a strap passed over their foreheads, what the wagon could not take. This portage-strap is three or four inches broad in the middle, where it is adjusted to the forehead; its great advantage to the voyageur is that it leaves him the free use of his arms in going through the woods."

The steam tug on Lake Kashaboye was—authentic touch of the machine age—out of order, and the Indians paddled across the lake. The next portage to Lac des Mille Lacs was the Height of Land "where water begins to run north and west instead of east and south. The lakes, after this, empty at their west ends."

When they reached the lovely Lac des Mille Lacs the steam launch was found to be at its farther end, and the

235

Indians paddled the canoes out to meet it. Here the shores had not been burned over and the Botanist rejoiced. " 'This expedition,' he said, 'is going to give me a lift that will put me at the head of the whole brigade;' but, as we drew near our third portage for the day, his face clouded. 'Look at the ground, burnt again.' One asked if it was the great waste of wood he referred to. 'It's not that, but they have burned the very spot for botanizing over.' "

There was no steamer on the next lake, Baril, and the Indians paddled its length to the next portage. Here there was "a comfortable tent pitched for the emigrants, strewn with fragrant pine and spruce branches."

Grant was delighted with the Indians. "Their canoes were attended to, as well as the baggage, in half the time that ordinary servants would have taken. They would carry as heavy a load as a Constantinople porter, at a rapid trot across the portage, run back for another load without a minute's halt, and so on till all the luggage was portaged, and everything in readiness for starting on the next lake." "Our Ojibways had silver rings on their fingers, broad gaudy sashes and bedraggled feathers bound round their felt hats. The Iroquois dressed as simply and neatly as blue-jackets."

The whole party sat around the camp-fire to enjoy the first gypsy meal of fried ham and tea and fell asleep in their tent very quickly after the four lakes and portages of the day's travel.

When they woke next morning the Botanist was already out searching for specimens. A cold mist clung

236

to the ground and the surface of the water as they launched on Lake Windigoostigwan. The next portage was two miles long and took three hours to cross because "the wagon had to make two trips from lake to lake, over a new road with our luggage." This portage was in the charge of a Glengarry man who had lived there all winter and who said that he preferred the winter weather to that of Ontario. The winter days had been clear and sunny, the snow powder-dry and very soon after it melted in May, spring had begun in earnest. Beyond another Ojibway encampment, where Grant was shocked by the appearance of the women, "dirty, joyless-looking and prematurely old", they came to Lake Kaogassikok.

As they paddled down this lake, the party looked at the well-wooded shores and reflected that "when the country is opened up, all this timber will be very valuable, as sleepers and ties for the Pacific Railway, and lumber fit for building purposes can be obtained here in abundance, if nowhere nearer the plains. The trees can be cut at the water's edge, rafted, and sent by water to Winnipeg." Beyond Kaogassikok there were two portages on Pine and Deux rivers with only two miles of water between them and here the quantities of baggage caused long delays. They had not reached the farther side of the next lake when the guides suggested camping though the sun had not set. They landed at the foot of a hill, pitched their tents, and went for a swim while Louis laid supper "on a clean tablecloth on the sward. The country ahead broke into knolls, looking in many parts like cultivated parks; around us the white tents and the ruddy

237

fires, with Indians flitting between, or busy about the canoes, gave animation to the scene."

Watching the Indians at work, and these highly-skilled and long experienced guides, the élite of their craft, were well worth watching, Grant wrote, "The Indians never halt without at once turning their canoes upside down, and examining them. The seams and crevices in the birch-bark yield at any extra strain, and scratches are made by submerged brushwood in some of the channels or the shallow parts of the lakes. These crevices they carefully daub over with resin, which is obtained from the red pine, till the bottom of an old canoe becomes almost covered with a black resinous coat."

Next morning at four o'clock they set out in such vigour that the three canoes began to race. Ignace's hair was grey, he was much older than the others but still a master paddler. "Doggedly, and with averted head, he dug his paddle deeper in the water, and pegged away with his sure steady stroke, and though the others, by spurting, forced themselves half a canoe length ahead at times, they had not the stay of the older man, and every race ended with Ignace leading."

After the halt for breakfast it began to rain with violence. Waterproofs which covered their baggage were not proof against this water and only constant bailing kept the canoes from filling. They passed into the Maligne River and shot their first rapids. "To shoot the rapids in a canoe is a pleasure that comparatively few Englishmen have ever enjoyed. . . . The excitement is greater than when on board a steamer, because you are so much nearer the seething water, and the canoe seems such a fragile thing to contend with the mad forces, into the very thick of which it has to be steered. Where the stream begins to descend, the water is an inclined plane, smooth and shining as glare ice. Beyond that it breaks into curling, gleaming rolls which end off in white, boiling cauldrons, where the water has broken on the rocks beneath. On the brink of the inclined plane, the motion is so quiet that you think the canoe pauses for an instant. The captain is at the bow—a broader, stronger paddle than usual in his hand—his eye kindling with enthusiasm, and every nerve and fibre in his body at its utmost tension. The steersman is at his post, and every man is ready. They know that a false stroke, or too weak a turn of the captain's wrist, at the critical moment, means death. A push with the paddles, and, straight and swift as an arrow, the canoe shoots right down into the mad vortex; now into a cross current that would twist her broadside round, but that every man fights against it; then she steers right for a rock, to which she is being resistlessly sucked, and on which it seems as if she would be dashed to pieces; but a rapid turn of the captain's paddle at the right moment, and she rushes past the black mass, riding gallantly as a race horse. The waves boil up at the side threatening to engulf her, but except a dash of spray or the cap of a wave, nothing gets in, and as she speeds into the calm reach beyond, all draw long breaths and hope that another rapid is near."

Toward noon they reached Island Portage and dined there on tea and fat pork under the shelter of an upturned canoe for it was raining hard. There was a steam launch on the next lake—Lake Nequaquon—which towed them its twenty-four miles to Loon Portage. Then a short paddle and Mud Portage "worthy of its name", a short paddle and American Portage. Here they pitched tents and hung their wet clothing to dry before the fires. "Tired enough all hands were, and ready for sleep, for these portages are killing work." The Botanist's valise had been soaked but while the rest sorted out and dried their possessions, he searched eagerly for new plants between the trees and along the edge of the marsh.

At three next morning they were up and off between low, wet shores into Lake Nameukan, glad to have the sun come out at last and shine, toward noon, with real summer heat. Before breakfast they paddled twelve miles and after it the canoes entered another paddling race. Proud old Ignace could not be beaten but two younger men cut off several turns of the river by slipping through a passage among the reeds and came out ahead of him, a manoeuvre of which Ignace took no notice. About noon, after two more short portages, they came to Rainy Lake and a steam launch. The engineer promised to bring them to Fort Frances before sundown but just then across the portage came "a band of eighteen emigrants, men, women and children, who had left Thunder Bay five days before us, and whom we had passed this fore-noon, when we took our short cut. They had a great deal of baggage, and were terribly tired. One old woman, eighty-five years of age, complained of being sick, and the doctor attended to her. As we had soup for dinner, he sent some over to her, and the prescription had a good effect. While waiting here we took our half-dried clothes out of the bags, and by hanging them on lines under the warm sun, got them pretty well dried before starting."

At three o'clock they set out, the launch towing two big barges carrying the emigrants and their belongings, and four canoes. "In half an hour every Indian was asleep in the bottom of his canoe." The afternoon was warm, the scenery monotonous, the steamer small and overtaxed. By evening it was clear that Fort Frances could not possibly be reached that night and they landed on a sandy shore near two empty log huts. The weary emigrants occupied the huts while Fleming and his party camped on the beach and the Botanist, fearing an early morning start, ranged through the darkness holding up a lighted pine torch to catch at least a glimpse of the plant life along the shore.

Soon after four next morning they were off again, shooting the rapid over which the lake pours into Rainy River. The emigrants on their barges had to wait till men could be sent from the fort to help them through the rapid.

The Hudson's Bay Company post made up the whole of Fort Frances together with the houses of its employees within their ten-foot stockade. The post overlooked Chaudière Falls, the obstacle to canoemen which dictated the post's situation, and stood on a grassy plain which yielded wheat, barley and potatoes. But on the potato leaves Grant saw "the Colorado bug, that frightful pest which seems to be moving further east every year." A few cattle grazed on the open plain but beyond its level acres stretched marshland and beyond that the rock appeared.

A few Ojibways were still in their wigwams near the fort but scores of bare tent poles showed where a thousand of the tribe had gathered a week or two earlier to meet the Indian Commissioner. The meeting had been planned for the drawing up of terms as to passage of the emigrants through the country and settlement there but no agreement had been reached. Indeed the Ojibways were a scattered tribe and had no chiefs empowered to speak for them all, so that a large gathering was very difficult to deal with. The Ojibways, Grant thought, were much less strong and capable than his Iroquois canoemen. It was not easy to persuade a few Ojibways to join the party to take the place of those who had agreed to come only as far as Fort Frances. Many of the men wore brass or silver wire plaited in their long hair or streamers of gay ribbon and all had some good clothing for they had been employed to work on the road, to widen the portages or to hunt and fish for the engineers. Also at Fort Frances two steamers were being built, each a hundred feet long, to be used on Rainy River and Lake of the Woods and some of the Indians had been hired to cut and carry timber for the carpenters.

From here the party followed Rainy River which formed the boundary between the United States and Canada, running the Manitou rapids and then the Sault. The rich vegetation—for the Botanist found wild pea and vetch vines growing eight feet long—moved Grant to one of his eager, optimistic prophecies. "The time will come when every acre of these banks of Rainy River will be waving with grain, or producing rich heavy grass, for countless herds of cattle. . . . Every mile (along Rainy River) seemed well adapted for cultivation and the dwellings of men." They pressed on till after midnight to reach Hungry Hall, the Hudson's Bay Company post. So many wigwams were crowded around the fort that the party paddled a mile farther on, pitched the tents "over luxuriant masses of wild flowers heavy with dew, and in a few minutes were all sound asleep."

The next day was Sunday and the steamer did not start until ten o'clock. While the camp was enjoying the luxury of a leisurely breakfast, a dignified old Indian chief appeared on the bank. Only one man attended him but two or three canoes full of Indian families paddled close to shore to watch and listen. Exclaiming "B'jou, B'jou," he shook hands with everyone and then, holding in his two hands the symbols of war and peace, a knife and a pipe, he began a long speech. Its burden was that of the speech made to Milton and Cheadle and to every traveller across the plains in those years. "Pointing, with outstretched arms, north, south, east and west, he told us that all the land had been his people's, and that he now, in their name, asked for some return for our passage through it. The bearing and speech were those of a born orator. . . . It was astonishing with what dignity and force, long, rolling, musical sentences poured from the lips of one who would be carelessly classed by most people as a savage." When he had finished he sat down at a distance and began to smoke his pipe.

While some kind of reply was being formulated, the chief was given breakfast. A plate of fried pork was placed before him with a huge, thick pancake and a large pannikin of tea. After a dignified pause he began to eat and presently signed to his attendant to eat also. When he had finished, he was told that the party "would bring his views to the notice of the Government and that his tribe would certainly receive justice. . . . He at once assented, though whether he would have done so with equal blandness had we given him no breakfast is questionable."

When the steamer came, their canoes were hitched on and drawn through sedges and spreading marsh into the Lake of the Woods. Here such a violent thunder storm came up—"first we had the wind and rain on our backs, then on the left, then in our faces, and then on the right"— that the steamer made for the shelter of a small sandy island and its fires were put out until the storm should pass. Since there was not enough wood on the island to supply all the camp-fires, Fleming's party paddled on to another island, this one well-wooded, where the Botanist found twenty-four kinds of wild flowers which he had not seen before during the trip and eight kinds which he could not recognize. The regular dinner of pork, biscuit and tea was elaborated, because it was Sunday, with soup, sausage, mustard and marmalade. After dinner Grant conducted a short religious service using the form of worship compiled for surveying parties, and the Indians sang "Veni Creator" in Iroquois.

244

Next morning the lake was very rough and when the little steamer arrived, the Indians were unwilling to be towed by her. "They said that it would be safer to trust to the paddles, that the waves in the middle of the traverse would be heavy, and that, if the canoes were forced through them, the bow or side would be broken in." One wonders whether the Indians did not often regard with some misgiving the little steamers shuttling up and down these successive lakes, noisy, undependable and constantly agape for wood. But they were not slow to enjoy the advantages the steamer offered and when they had been urged into the usual flotilla, they all lay down in their canoes and slept. The flotilla, on this windy day, was not arranged as formerly in a long single line. The canoes were drawn up two abreast and tied to the big barge carrying the emigrants' luggage, so that the barge broke the waves and the canoes rode safely behind it.

Fires had so often swept the shores of the Lake of the Woods that in many places little timber remained and the low rocks lay bare and blackened. The barge put up a sail and between sail and steam reached seven or eight miles an hour, though the tug had to stop twice to wood up. This was the last lap of the water portion of the journey. Through wide stretches of weeds and scrubby woodland they approached the North-West Angle. From here a road had been made to Fort Garry to escape "the terrible portages of the Winnipeg River and the roundabout way by Lake Winnipeg." The land levelled; they were nearing the prairies, the long middle stretch of the journey.

245

The Angle, as it was called, looked very animated with fifty or sixty Indians "crowded about the landing place, and the babble and bustle was to us like a return to the world." The Indians greeted the Ojibway canoemen boisterously and took them off to a dance, leaving the party to camp in a very dirty, mosquito-infested spot.

The next day, July 30, was the hardest of the journey thus far and one that even in the mountains the travellers remembered as painfully long and exhausting. They left the Angle in wagons at four in the morning and ended the day at two the next morning, having covered a distance of eighty miles. The country was monotonous, at first marshy with an abundance of raspberries and wild currants and flocks of wild pigeons "resting calmly on the branches of dead trees by the roadside, as if no shot had ever been fired in their hearing." The road had been hard to make, "corduroyed and covered over with clay and sand or gravel."

When the marshy region was past, light sandy soil followed, a feast for the Botanist. "He counted over four hundred different species in this one day's ride. Great was the astonishment of our teamsters, when they saw him make a bound from his seat on the waggon to the ground, and rush to plain, wood, or marsh. At first, they all hauled up to see what was the matter. It must be gold or silver he had found; but when he came back triumphantly waving a flower or bunch of grass, and exclaiming, 'Did you ever see the like of that?' 'No, I never,' was the general response from every disgusted teamster."

One of these was a Scot who "had come to the Angle

this spring, and was getting thirty dollars a month and his board as a common teamster. He was saving four-fifths of his wages, and intended in a few months to buy a good farm on the Red River among his countrymen, and settle down as a Laird for the rest of his life. How many ten thousands more of Scotch lads would follow his example if they only knew how easy it would be for them!"

At White Birch River, having covered thirty miles, they stopped to eat bologna sausage and bread baked by the station-keeper. He too was a Scot, he had once been a soldier and now he was busily learning the Cree and Ojibway languages. He suggested that the failure of the negotiations for a treaty with the Ojibways was due to pressure from Indians in the United States, urging the Ojibways in Canada to make unreasonable demands. It was found, in general, that Indian treaties were quite easy to arrive at everywhere except along the United States border.

Another seventeen miles and at White Mud River they had dinner—the usual menu with the addition of tomato soup and a gift of bread and blueberry jam from the wife of the station keeper.

Oak Point, the next stage, was thirty-three miles away over a very bad road. In the course of this lap of the journey they crossed the boundary into the new province of Manitoba. "Clouds gathered, and as the jaded horses toiled heavily on, the rain poured down furiously and made the roads worse. It was so dark that the teamsters couldn't see the horses; and, as neither of them had been over this part of the road before, they had to give the horses free rein to go where they pleased, and—as they were dead beat—at the rate they pleased. The black flies worried us, and we were all heavy with sleep. The hours dragged miserably on, and the night seemed endless; but, at length emerging from the wooded country into the prairie, we saw the light of the station two miles ahead. Arriving there, wearied and soaked through, we came to what appeared to be the only building—a half-finished store of the Hudson's Bay Company;—entering the open door, barricaded with paint pots, blocks of wood, tools, etc. we climbed up a shaky ladder to the second floor, threw ourselves down on the floor, and slept heavily beside a crowd of teamsters whom no amount of kicking could awake."

The voice of the irrepressible Botanist woke them next morning. " 'Thirty-two new species already; it's a perfect floral garden.' We looked out and beheld a sea of green sprinkled with yellow, red, lilac and white. None of us had ever seen a prairie before and, behold, the half had not been told us! As you cannot know what the Ocean is without seeing it, neither can you in imagination picture the prairie." From Oak Point "after a good breakfast of mutton chops and tea, prepared by the half-breed cook at the Station, we started in our wagons for Fort Garry across the prairie. Tall, bright yellow French marigolds, scattered in clumps over the vast expanse, gave a golden hue to the scene; and red, pink and white roses, tansy, asters, blue-bells, goldenrods and an immense variety of compositae thickly bedded among the green grass, made up a bright and beautiful carpet. Farther on, the flowers were fewer; but everywhere the herbage was luxuriant, admirable for pasturage, and, in the hollows, tall enough for hay."

In the afternoon they crossed the Red River in a scow, reached the village of Winnipeg and went on to Fort Garry and Government House. "Thus we finished our journey from Lake Superior to Red River, by that Dawson Road, of which all had previously heard much, in terms of praise or disparagement. The total distance is about five hundred and thirty miles; forty-five at the beginning and a hundred and ten at the end by land; and three hundred and eighty miles between, made up of a chain of some twenty lakes, lakelets and lacustrine rivers, separated from each other by spits, ridges, or short traverses of land or granite rocks, that have to be portaged across."

"The mode of travelling," Grant wrote, "whether the canoes are paddled or tugged, (is) novel and delightful; and if a tourist can afford a crew of Indians and three or four weeks' time, he is certain to enjoy himself, the necessity of roughing it adding zest to the pleasure."

"But as a route for trade," he went on very moderately, "for ordinary travel or for emigrants to go west, the Dawson road, as it now exists, is far from satisfactory. . . . This year about seventy emigrants have gone by the road in the six weeks between June 20 and August 1. The station-masters and other agents on the road, as a rule, do their very utmost; they have been well selected, and are spirited and intelligent men; but the task given them to do is greater than the means will permit. The road is composed of fifteen or twenty independent pieces; is it any wonder if these often do not fit, especially as there cannot be unity of understanding and of plan, for there is no telegraph along the route and it would be extremely difficult to construct one?"

The fourteen hundred men of the Red River Expedition—British regulars and Canadian militia—with the seven hundred voyageurs sent to help them forward had in 1870 crossed forty-seven portages in all. Sent off in relays to avoid congestion at the portages, the troops at times had been spread over one hundred and fifty miles of the route.

The exigencies of the Dawson road and the effectiveness of his men in opening it as they went along, so impressed Colonel Wolseley that when in 1884 as Lord Wolseley he led an expedition to relieve General Gordon at Khartoum, he sent for some of his Canadian voyageurs to help him convey his troops up the Nile. As a result four hundred Canadians went from the lakes and portages of the Dawson route to see service in Egypt.

The route had been opened to emigrants the year after its use by the expedition and even before it was declared available four hundred settlers had gone over it. Arduous as it was, it had demonstrated that the western prairie could be reached by a route entirely on Canadian soil.

But the route was not really new. Dawson had rediscovered not discovered it. For this was the old French canoe route to the North-West, retraced and modernized with steam tugs and station shanties. In 1731 La Jemeraye had sent furs down to Montreal over this route in charge of one of the sons of La Vérendrye, and for many years it had seen the annual passage of loaded North-West canoes through the seemingly endless chain of lakes and sedgy rivers.

Even with continued improvement the route was too difficult. In 1874 the longer land stretches were provided with passenger stages and freight wagons but still the constant shifts of passengers and baggage from land to water and from water to land were too irritating, too wasteful and exhausting. One is not surprised to find that it was abandoned as an emigrant route in 1876. Today the Canadian National Railway follows this path struck out by La Jemeraye before 1731.

Manitoba, the fifth province of Canada, in these years
before its territorial extension north and west, was the
smallest of all the provinces. Two thousand white people
and thirteen thousand Indians and half-breeds lived there,
and though settlers were coming in, the rigours of the
Dawson route as yet restricted their numbers. Because
of the recent Fenian troubles a battalion of Canadian
militia was stationed along the Red River as a guarantee
of peace. The farms were flourishing but it would be
another four years before that historic first shipment of
857 bushels of wheat was carried from Winnipeg through
the United States to Toronto.

John McDougall, making his first excited journey
across the plains in 1860, saw one house on the spot where
Winnipeg would later stand; two years later he saw five or
six houses. James Hargrave wrote that a store was built
about 1860 at the place where the Assiniboine and Red
River trails met, close to the boundary of the Hudson's
Bay Company land reserve. The land was so low and
swampy, he said, that no one had been willing to build
there but it was the meeting place of the road to the

grain country on the Red River and the road to the fur country of the west along the Assiniboine. The store stood alone in this desolate place and then a house was built near it and then several log cabins and then another store which at once involved the first one in litigation.

By 1867 Hargrave described Winnipeg as consisting of a cluster of houses and the George Hotel, equipped with a billiard saloon. It had even a theatre fitted up in a room above the store with a small stage, a curtain and footlights. The first performance which everyone in town attended was a pantomime depicting with raucous vigour the humours and disasters of life in the George Hotel. The George, far from resenting the unsparing portrayal, set a lighted candle in every one of its windows to celebrate the occasion. Tragedy threatened when one of the candles set fire to a curtain, but a passer-by saw it and put out the flames before much damage was done.

The ladies of Winnipeg held a Christmas bazaar and the Burns Club gave a dinner on St. Andrew's Day. There was as yet no church but the Archdeacon preached in the improvised theatre. Church services were held regularly, a little later, in the court room, the Wesleyan on Sunday morning, Presbyterian in the afternoon and Church of England in the evening.

The next year, 1868, Professor Sand, "World Renowned Magician and Ventriloquist", gave three performances in the course of which he thrust a carving knife into his right arm and walked up and down so that everyone could see. Then he withdrew the knife and healed the wound before the eyes of the audience.

253

In 1868 Winnipeg had fifty houses and six stores, a church had been built and St. John's College and School soon had forty-two students. Winnipeg also had saloons; Grant wrote, "the drunkenness of Winnipeg is notorious." He visited the town ten years after its first building had stood alone at the cross-roads between the wheat country and the fur country. It had been then and was still at the time of his visit a small village of little importance beside the busy Company post at Fort Garry. Yet only ten years later still Upper Fort Garry was sold to Winnipeg by the Hudson's Bay Company and only its north gate remained as a relic of what had been for a time the centre of the fur empire.

Already the great influx of settlers had begun. John McDougall in that same summer of 1872, returning from a visit to Ontario with the young second wife he had married there, found the steamship for Fort Garry so crowded that he could with difficulty persuade the captain to let his party come aboard. "This," he wrote, "was the beginning of the rush to Manitoba." The steamer *International* also was "crowded from the main to the hurricane deck with men and women seeking their fortune in this great free country. They were of all classes— tradesmen of all sorts; also nondescripts who had come to the west thinking that perhaps this strange land might locate them, for thus far in life they had found it impossible to locate themselves." In Winnipeg, McDougall saw "west and east slowly coming together. The iron-less cart and flashy buggy were standing or rolling side by side."

Grant and his party made their calls in and about Fort Garry during those first days of August. They saw the United States consul, the Land Commissioner, the officers of the Battalion. They went to Kildonan, the Scottish settlement, to call on the Reverend Mr. Black, they talked to Archdeacon McLean who was on his way to England to lecture on the Canadian North-West as a home for emigrants. Archbishop Taché insisted that the Saskatchewan valley was not good for grain-growing but praised the region around Lac la Biche, still farther north.

In two days the party was ready to leave, for all arrangements had been most briskly and efficiently made. Emilien was to be head guide as far as Fort Carlton. The caravan seemed to Grant very long and the quantity of supplies far too generous "but before many days we found that everything was needed." There were six Red River carts carrying tents, baggage and provisions, two buck-boards, drivers, and two young men to look after the eighteen horses.

Emilien left the fort with the carts and the band of horses and several hours later the men followed, looking with interest at farms along the way. There was no doubt of the richness of the soil; only, as everyone said, a market was lacking. Here they passed the farm of a man named Morgan who had bought it several years before for £50 "and this year he had already been offered £450 for the potatoes growing on it." In the sunny afternoon they drove through "a fine farming but unfarmed country", the road very good, the air warm and pleasant. "Far away stretched the level prairie, dotted with islets of aspens; and the sun, in his going down, dipped beneath it as he does beneath the sea."

When they camped for the night on Long Lake with dry wood for the fires and grazing for the horses, they were joined by that veteran traveller of prairie trails, the Reverend Mr. George McDougall. George McDougall appears through the eyes of his admiring son as a legendary and yet extremely active figure. He had none of his son's love of physical exertion and was never fond of dog-driving yet in Grant's words he "had been nine times over the plains, and evidently knew the country better than our guides." He had learned Cree but never attempted to preach in that language, finding the use of an interpreter more effective. He commanded great respect from Indians, half-breeds and traders; he was tireless and without fear.

He had been attending in Winnipeg the first Missionary Conference held west of Lake Superior at which missionary work in the west had been reviewed and plans made for the future. Most important to Mr. McDougall was the fact that his son John, who had already served as a missionary in the west for twelve years, had been ordained as a minister and appointed to open a new mission at the foot of the Rocky Mountains.

Mr. McDougall was at this time stationed at Edmonton and was returning home with his Cree servant Joseph or Souzie as he was called in his own tongue. The two of them joined Fleming's party for the journey west.

Souzie had a dramatic story of his own. In 1870, the year of the terrible smallpox epidemic, John McDougall

256

went with a large party to hunt buffalo and get provision for the winter. His father urged him as he set out to allow no strangers to enter his camp for the epidemic was spreading rapidly and had already caused hundreds of deaths. John was with some difficulty able to keep travellers away but he made one exception when a friend of his appeared near the camp. "He was attired in old-time mourning, a filthy robe belted around the waist, moccasins and breech-cloth." His wife, children and friends had all died of smallpox. Souzie was alone and had nothing but his pony. John could not reject this forlorn figure. He found a pair of trousers, a shirt, blanket and a cake of soft soap. Beside the lake he made Souzie strip and wash very thoroughly, his horse and gun as well as himself, and then swim his horse into deep water while John made a fire and burned the robe, saddle and every article of Souzie's clothing. Then, hoping that infection had been effectively prevented, he took Souzie into his own tent. "He in turn became hunter and scout and guard and servant and friend" to all the McDougalls.

Next morning as the Fleming party travelled toward the village of Portage la Prairie—"when the railway is built," Grant wrote, "a large town must spring up"— they passed three encampments of Sioux, each of about twenty wigwams. These Sioux had fled to Canada after the Minnesota massacre of ten years before, which Lord Milton and Dr. Cheadle had missed by a margin of two days. The massacre, like most massacres, had not been entirely unprovoked. The Sioux claimed that the United States government had not paid them their full allow-

257

ances and that the agents kept them waiting sometimes
for weeks. Before the terrible massacre of 1862 a large
part of the tribe had gathered to receive allowances and
had been kept waiting for the agent more than six weeks.
Starved and outraged the warriors had at last flung themselves upon the white settlers, killing and burning with
ferocity. As a result, the route by St. Paul was closed for
a time and parties of Sioux, fleeing from American re-
prisals, began to appear in the British west. Bands followed one another until many hundreds of Sioux had
come north from Minnesota, asking for protection. They
had in the intervening years done no actual damage but
they presented a constant problem, now threatening the
settlers, now destitute and begging for and receiving relief.
Grant's party was told that the Sioux encampment they
passed had always been very quiet though "one amiable-
looking old woman was pointed out as having roasted
and eaten ten or twelve children."

Soon after they left the Hudson's Bay post at Rat Creek
they saw sullen dark clouds gathering, lightning flared
and "with the suddenness of a tornado the wind struck—
at first without rain—but so fierce that the horses were
forced again and again off the track. And now, with
the wind came rain—thick and furious; and then hail—
hail mixed with angular lumps of ice from half an inch
to an inch across, a blow on the head from one of which
was stunning. Our long line of horses and carts was
broken, some of the poor creatures clung to the road,
fighting desperately, others driven into the prairie and,
turning their backs to the storm, stood still or moved

sideways, with cowering heads, their manes and long tails floating wildly." Violent as the storm was, it was soon over and the sun shone out in a sky without a cloud. They camped that night near the large house of a man named Grant from Nova Scotia, "now the farthest west settler." They were at last "on the confines of the Great Lone Land."

There were already settlers along Rat Creek, for that day fifty people assembled in Mr. Grant's house for a service led by Mr. McDougall. The farms were doing well. Mr. Grant had been there for three years and had 120 acres in wheat, barley and potatoes. "There is no limit to the amount they may break up except the limit imposed by the lack of capital or their own moderation. This prairie land is the place for steam ploughs, reaping, mowing and threshing machines. With such machinery one family can do the work of a dozen men."

As they rode forward suddenly a body of sixty or eighty Sioux "came sweeping across the prairie in all the glory of paint, feathers, and Indian warlike magnificence. . . . Some of them rode horses, others were in light baggage-carts or on foot. All had guns and adornment of one kind or another. A handsome brave came first with a painted tin horse a foot long hanging from his neck down on his naked breast, skunk fur round his ankles, hawk's feathers on his head, and a great bunch of sweet-smelling lilac bergamot flowers on one arm to set him off the more." The chief came forward wearing a necklace of bear's claws and moccasins striped with a pattern of porcupine quills dyed vivid gold and behind him loomed the medicine man, six foot three in height, gaunt and haggard, wrapped in a single blanket. They wanted a powwow with tea and tobacco but the party, pressed as usual for time, could only shake hands all round and ride on.

The next day they left the new province of Manitoba behind them and Grant summed up in his diary its great advantages as a place of settlement. Rich soil, level land, no trees or stones. Rumour had it that Indians were hostile and mosquitoes and locusts a plague but such rumours were easily traced to their source. Settlers who had come to the country by way of St. Paul told them that "they were repeatedly warned not to impoverish their families by going to a cold, locust-devoured, barren land, where there was no market and no freedom, but to settle in Minnesota." Even in Winnipeg, American agents and sympathizers had cried down Manitoba and urged the superiority of the American west. But Indians had never given the settlers trouble, mosquitoes were no worse than in Ontario or Nova Scotia and locusts "have proved a plague only two or three times in half a century." Even the fears of severe winter cold and deep snow had proved illusory. Snows were not heavy, the cold was dry, the winter sky clear and bright.

The railroad would soon open markets; Winnipeg would soon become a population centre. "This little village is becoming a town; houses are springing up in all directions with a rapidity known only in the history of western towns; and the demand for provisions, stock, farm implements, and everything on which labour is expended, is so much greater than the supply, that prices are enormously high. The intending settler, therefore, should bring in with him as much of what he may require as he possibly can." Homesteading offered land to the settler on most generous terms and the system of reserves would settle the Indian population. In a word "there seems nothing lacking in this country but good industrious settlers."

A single doubt, however, clouded Grant's perfect confidence in the prairie as the ideal home for settlers. The party came upon the ominously named Salt Lake where the water, brackish to the taste, had left a white crust on the dried-up portion of the lake bed. Already the question had occurred to him for there were few rivers and the creeks they crossed were very small. A farmer on Rat Creek had told him "that a beautiful stretch of prairie, immediately to the west of his location, which had been taken up by a friend of his, had been abandoned because no water could be got." A few days later they found water "hard and brackish, scarcely drinkable, and not good even to wash with. It gave an unpleasant taste to the tea." Grant suggested that the government should sink test wells where the adequacy of the water supply was in question and where there were saline lakes, artesian wells might be bored to try to reach fresh water at a lower level. The problem of water supply continued to occupy his mind as they launched upon the ocean of grass.

Often now the Doctor went shooting in the early morning, and brought back plover, ducks and pigeons which Terry, the cook, prepared for breakfast. Their horses were doing forty or forty-five miles a day quite easily. The 215 miles from Fort Garry to Fort Ellice was covered in less than six days but the whole party to avoid delay did not go to the fort. While the main body continued their course north of the fort, Fleming himself and two others went to get supplies and some government horses which had been wintered there. By night they caught up with the rest of the party, bringing flour, pemmican, salt and dried meat.

The whole technique of camping was of great interest to Grant. The requirements of a good camping place, he wrote, were "woods, water and feed for the horses, . . . if [one] can get a hilly spot where there are few mosquitoes, and a sheet of water large enough to bathe in, and a resort of game, so much the better." Two men slept in each tent, with a waterproof and a blanket on the ground for each man and another blanket to cover him. At night the harness was taken off the horses and they were turned loose, with hobbles of buffalo raw hide, or shaganappi, on the leaders or the individuals most likely to stray.

Mr. McDougall who with his Cree man, Souzie, had gone on a side journey, now caught up with the party. Souzie had "never been east before" and he had been dazzled by the sights of Winnipeg—the Red River steamboat, the free-flowing rum. He had been taken to hear a sermon and "when the plate came round at the church, Souzie rejoiced, and was going to help himself, but, noticing his neighbours put money in, he was so puzzled that he let it pass. He chuckled for many a day at the simplicity of the Winnipeggers: 'Who ever before saw a plate handed round except to take something from it?' And when he saw the review of the militia, its orderly drill amazed him. 'Wonderful!' he exclaimed, 'I have seen a hundred men turned into one.'"

They crossed the Assiniboine river where the water was only three feet deep but the bottom was of shifting sand so that the horses could not be allowed to stand still. From the Qu'Appelle River they turned north though they would have liked to continue along the river bank where a half-breed named Mackay told them that "the buffalo were in swarms." "Mackay was on his way back to Fort Garry with the spoils of the hunt. He had left home with his wife and seven children and six carts, late in May, joined a party at Fort Ellice and gone up to the high plains, where the source of the Qu'Appelle is, near the elbow of the South Saskatchewan, and obtained his food for the year in the way most pleasing to a half-breed. They had all lived sumptuously while near the buffalo, and when they had dried enough meat to fill their carts, at the rate of ten buffalo to a cart, they parted company; and he and his wife, with the meat and skins, turned homewards, to do little for the rest of the year but enjoy themselves. This is all very well when the buffalo are plenty; but as they get scarcer or move farther away, what is to be done?"

The next day they met another half-breed with buffalo skins and dried meat in his cart bound for Fort Garry. He told the party that there was buffalo hunting among the Touchwood Hills only two days farther on, which "excited our men to the highest pitch, for the buffalo had

263

not come on this route for many years, and eager hopes were exchanged that we might see and get a shot at them. Wonderful stories were told of the buffalo hunts in former days, and men, hitherto taciturn, perhaps because they know little English . . . began explaining volubly—eking out their meaning with expressive gesticulation—the nature of a buffalo hunt." Later, in the Touchwood Hills region, "Marchaud rode in advance, gun slung across his shoulders, but although he scanned every corner of the horizon eagerly, and galloped ahead or on either side to any overhanging lip of the plateau, no herd or solitary bull came within his view. They were not far off, for fresh tracks were seen. The tracks of former times are indented in the ground like old furrows and run in parallel lines to the salt lakes, as if in those days the prairie had been covered with wood, and the beasts had made their way through in long files of thousands."

The temperature fell sharply now at night; the men rose shivering for their early start and looked forward to the hot mug of tea by the camp-fire. More blankets were given out and three now slept in each tent instead of two.

Beyond the new province of Manitoba they were in what Grant called No Man's Land. He and the others were concerned by the constant evidence of prairie fires. "The rich grass is destroyed by the autumn fires which a spark kindles, and which destroy also the wood, which formerly was of larger size and much more abundant than now. This destruction of wood seriously affects the water supply. Lakes that once had water all the year round are now dry, except in the spring time. But when settlers come in, all this shall be changed. The grass will be cut at the proper time, and stacked for the cattle, and then there shall not be the wide spreading dried fuel to feed the fires, and give them ever increasing force. Fields of ploughed land, interspersed here and there, shall set bounds to the flames, and tourists and travellers will be less likely to leave their camp-fires burning, when they know that there are settlers near."

Also the destruction of the trees by fire was one cause of early frosts. Settlers would plant trees and protect them "but settlers will not come, till there is a railroad to bring them in." The Hudson's Bay Company, concerned about the damage done by fires, had required each of its parties to carry a spade with which to throw earth over the camp-fire to make sure that it was put out. "But since miners, traders, tourists and others have entered the country, there has been a very different state of affairs. Some of the spring traders set fire to the grass round their camps, that it may grow up the better and be fresh on their return in autumn. . . . And the Indians and the Hudson's Bay parties seeing this, have become nearly as reckless."

The party's routine was to drink a mug of hot tea and then travel a spell before halting for breakfast. On August 9 they travelled thirteen miles before breakfast and sixteen miles through beautiful lightly-wooded country before dinner. Ten miles farther on they had expected to camp but the ponds were dry and they pushed on toward a lone tree which they reached at sunset and near which they found water enough for themselves and their horses. The day's travel amounted to about forty-two miles.

Emilien, the head guide, had at first objected to the customary Sunday halt and insisted on making at least a short journey on that day but now he too was tired and agreed willingly to a Sunday rest. Quite apart from the short services which Indians and half-breeds attended of their own accord, the Sunday rest was necessary. "All through the week there has been a rush; the camp begins to be astir at three in the morning, and from that hour till nine or ten at night, there is constant high pressure. At the halting places meals have to be cooked, baggage arranged and re-arranged, horses looked to, harness mended, clothes washed or dried, observations and notes taken, specimens collected, and everything kept clean and trim; rest is therefore impossible. From four to six hours of sleep are all that can be snatched. The excitement keeps a mere tourist up, so that on Saturday night he feels able to go ahead, but if he insists on pushing on, the strain soon becomes too much, and he loses all the benefit to his health that he has gained; and as the men have none of the excitement of novelty, they need the periodic rest all the more."

Apart from plovers, prairie hens and ducks there was almost no game but one day they suddenly saw a brown bear on a small hillock. "Had the horsemen and guns been in front as usual, he could have been shot at once, but before they came up, he was off, at a shambling but rapid gait among the thickets, and there was not time

266

to give chase. This was a disappointment, for all of us would have relished a bear-steak."

They had seen no Indians since Rat Creek but now they came upon two buffalo-skin tents of Ojibways who had been buffalo hunting. Their carts were piled with skins "and the women were engaged at the door of a tent chopping up the fat and meat to make pemmican. Marchaud, our guide, at once struck a trade with them, a few handfuls of tea for several pieces of dried buffalo meat. The men seemed willing that he should take as much as he liked, but the oldest squaw haggled pertinaciously over each piece, and chuckled and grinned horribly when she succeeded in snatching away from him the last piece he was carrying off."

The road was here so bad that an axle broke and the cart had to be abandoned since time could not be spared for making repairs. Only Red River carts could have endured the constant jolting. "When any part broke before, a thong of shaganappi—or buffalo raw hide—had united the pieces. Shaganappi in this part of the world does all that leather, cloth, rope, nails, glue, straps, cord, tape, and a number of other articles are used for elsewhere. Without it the Red River cart, which is simply a clumsy looking, but really light, box cart with wheels six or seven feet in diameter, and not a bit of iron about the whole concern, would be an impossibility. These small-bodied, high-wheeled carts cross the miry creeks, borne up by the grass roots, and on the ordinary trail, the horses jog along with them at a steady trot of four or five miles an hour. Ordinary carts would stick hopelessly in the mud at the crossings of the creeks and marshes and travel slowly on a good trail."

When they came out upon an open plain they saw weather-bleached buffalo skulls on the ground; all the other bones had been chopped and boiled by the Indian women for the oil in them. Fleming picked up several of the most perfect skulls to send back to Ottawa. "Great was Souzie's amazement at such an act. He had been amused at the Botanist gathering flowers and grasses; but the idea of the great O-ghe-ma coming hundreds of miles, to carry home bones without any marrow in them, was inexplicable. He went up to Frank and explained by gestures that they were quite useless, and urged him to throw them out of the buck-board, and when Frank shook his head he appealed to Mr. McDougall to argue with us. All his efforts failing, he gave it up; but whenever his eyes caught sight of the skulls it was too much for even Indian gravity, and off he would go into fits of laughing at the folly of the white men."

Farther on they passed again into a region of rolling hills, woods and little lakes and toward the north "a prairie fire, kindled probably by embers that had been left carelessly behind at a camp. . . . Masses of fiery smoke rose from the burning grass and willows." Fortunately, rain threatened. "The speed with which our arrangements for the night were made astonished ourselves. Everyone did what he could; and in five minutes the horses were unharnessed, the tents pitched, the saddles and all perishable articles covered with waterproofs."

Since they were in buffalo country, though they had

not seen a single buffalo "we met or passed a great many teams and 'brigades' today; traders going west, and half-breeds returning east with carts well-laden with buffalo skins and dried meat." The great Red River Spring and Fall Buffalo Hunts still persisted as they had done for so many years though now herds were smaller and harder every year to find.

The Council of the North West Territories was obliged to make stringent rules to protect the buffalo though, as usual with such rules, the difficulty lay in carrying them out. Buffalo were never to be hunted from January first to the first of June, buffalo pounds involving wholesale slaughter were not to be used, no buffalo under two years old was to be killed and so on. The failure of these and other protective efforts is apparent in the fact that less than twenty years later Indians passed through railway trains as they crossed the prairie offering buffalo horns for sale as souvenirs.

On the last ridge before the South Saskatchewan River, Grant and his companions looked across lovely and empty country. "Where hundreds of homesteads shall yet be, there is not one. . . . The intense saltness of many of the lakes was to us the only doubtful feature in the landscape. One at our feet several miles long had a shore of brightest red, sure sign of how it would taste. All at the foot of the ridge with one exception are saline; after going on a few miles and mounting a slope, they are fresh." The sun set, clouds threatened rain, another axle broke, but the party was impatient to see the great river. "Never were buck-boards tested more severely, and no carts but those of Red River could have stood for ten minutes the bumps from hillock to hillock, over boulders, roots and holes, at a break-neck rate. The last mile was down hill. The Doctor and the Chief dashed on at a gallop and only drew rein when, right beneath, they saw the shining waters of the river. The rest of us were scarcely a minute behind, and three rousing cheers sent back the news to the carts. In twelve working days, we had travelled five hundred and six miles, doing, on this last, forty-six; and the horses looked as fresh as at the beginning of the journey; a fact that establishes the nutritious properties of the grasses, their only food on the way, as well as the strength and hardihood of the breed."

"A month from Toronto and we were on the Saskatchewan."

# IV

Now ONLY the river and eighteen miles of country lay between them and Fort Carlton; while the horses swam, they crossed the Saskatchewan on the Hudson's Bay Company scow. Some of the horses "were very reluctant to go into the water, but they were forced on by the men who waded after them—shouting and throwing stones— to the very brink of the channel. Once there they had to swim. . . . The river for a few minutes looked alive with horses' heads."

Fort Carlton which had stood since 1787 on the south bank of the North Saskatchewan was still a transport centre and the half-way house between Edmonton and Fort Garry. A few years after this time, however, in the troubles of 1885, it was raided by Indians and abandoned.

Mr. Clark, the Hudson's Bay Company agent, received them with a dinner of pemmican, "a strong but savoury dish", which Grant liked. However he was assured that this particular sample was pemmican of better than average quality. There was no farm at Fort Carlton, Mr.

Clark explained, because the Indians who came "to trade and to see what they could get, would, without the slightest intention of stealing, use the fences for firewood, dig up potatoes and turnips, and let their horses get into the grain fields. He had therefore established a farm at the Prince Albert Mission, fifty miles down the river. With regard to crops, barley and potatoes were always sure, wheat generally a success, though threatened by frosts or early drought, and never a total failure. This year he expected two thousand bushels of wheat from a sowing of a hundred."

No pause could be made in this expeditious journey and after eating dinner and writing letters to be sent back, the party left their old guides behind and with fresh horses and supplies crossed the North Saskatchewan that afternoon. Mr. McDougall still accompanied them and also the Mr. Macaulay who had been stationed at Jasper House nine years before when he had provided Lord Milton and Dr. Cheadle with a dinner of mutton and white-fish near Tête Jaune Cache. They had about three hundred and eighty miles farther to travel up the North Saskatchewan to reach Edmonton.

When the party prepared to cross the Jackfish River running out of Jackfish Lake, the water was found to be too high and they went on to find a ford. But suddenly their Indian helper, Little Bird, pointed back. The independent Souzie had driven calmly into the water in his light wagon and the horses and carts were following him. It was decided that the buck-boards and big wagon should follow too for only Greasy's cart had stuck in the mud.

"The big wagon, with the Chief and the Doctor mounted on the highest pinnacle, followed; but, when near the other side, its iron wheels sank in the black muddy bottom, and the horses while struggling to extricate them, broke the whippletree and parts of the harness, leaving the wagon and contents in the middle of the stream. Maxime and Keasis rushed to the rescue and untackled the horses. The Chief and the Doctor, stripping from waist to feet jumped down into the water, and putting their shoulders to the wheels while the other two pulled, amid cheers from the rest of us on the other side and countless bites from the mosquitoes, shoved the big thing to the bank. The buck-boards followed, and then Greasy, who had been left all the time in the middle of the stream, cudgelling his horse, and yelling 'Ho Rouge! Ho Rouge!' supplicated help, as his arm and throat had quite given out. He was told to help himself and to our great satisfaction, the old fellow had to jump down into the water and shove his cart out. . . . We camped at once on the bank, for it was after sunset, though the mosquitoes, that always haunt woods and streams, tormented our horses so much that the poor brutes could not eat, but crowded round the smoke of our fires, making the place look even more like a gypsy encampment than usual."

From Carlton they had brought new men—Legrace, old and dried up, a hunch-backed young Indian named Keasis or Little Bird, and Greasy who stirred up his red horse with constant shouts of "Ho Rouge! Ho Rouge!" Terry, the Irish cook, assumed that this must be the usual way of rousing slow horses in the west and began to shout "Haroosh! Haroosh!" as he whipped his white horse.

Pemmican was now the substance of every meal; "though none of us cared for it raw at first, we all liked it hot. Cooked for a few minutes in a frying pan with a little water and flour, and a dust of pepper and salt, onions added if you have any, it is called 'réchaud' and a capital dish it is."

They came to the Bears' Paddling Lake; "the lake is very shallow but has a firm sandy bottom, and the Indians have often seen bears about its shores, enjoying themselves in the water." This lake was a landmark, mentioned by many travellers. A day or two later they "halted on the road for breakfast; but after having unharnessed the horses, found, to our disgust, that the water was salt. A breakfast of dry bread and dry pemmican was hurriedly made; and we found that on the plains, any meal without tea, is as poor an affair as bacon and beans without the bacon."

Legrace who "boasted in a dignified way that in his time he had killed two Blackfeet" was a great taleteller. When they halted in sight of Horse Hill he told them that it had been named for a fight between the Crees and the Blackfeet, forty years before. "The Crees were encamped near a thicket at the foot of the hill, and a party of Blackfeet, that had made a successful raid far from their own borders, discovered them and charged. But the Crees were prepared, and a still larger body of them on the slope of the hill hidden by a ravine, swept round and drove their enemies into it; and though many of the

Blackfeet escaped, all their spoil was retaken and forty horses were killed, an extraordinary number, for the aim is always to capture the horses."

The Blackfeet had suffered again in a raid only a few years earlier. They "discovered a Cree camp among the hills and rushed on it; but when they entered the pass, a second and a third camp appeared on each side. Their only hope was escape, and they dashed straight on, to find that they had rushed into a deep hollow, the opposite rim of which was topped high with snow-banks curling over in folds, so that there was no possibilty of mounting it. The Crees closed round with yells of triumph, and for once they had their will on their enemies. It was not a fight but a massacre. Seventy were killed in a few minutes, and then the Crees in a fit of generosity, or because they were glutted with blood, opened out and let the rest go."

Legrace told of a chief named the Swan, who was still not an old man, though he was dying of consumption. "Dressing himself one day in all his bravery, he mounted his fleet horse and rode straight for the Cree camp. A hundred warriors were scattered about the tents, and in the centre of the encampment two noted braves sat gambling. Right up to them the Swan rode, scarcely challenged, as he was alone, clapped his musket to the head of one and blew his brains out. In an instant the camp was up; dozens of strong arms caught at the reckless foe, dozens of shots were fired, while others rushed for their horses. But he knew his horse, and, dashing through the encampment like a bolt, made good

275

his escape, though chased by every man that could mount."

The party came to the English River named because an Englishman had been drowned while crossing it in a spring flood, just as Frenchman's Knoll was so called because a Frenchman had once been killed there. Suddenly at sight of a certain hill, Souzie cried to Mr. McDougall, "I know now where I am!" "He went up to Frank and formally shook hands with him, to indicate that he welcomed him to his country." He had attached himself particularly to young Frank Fleming, teaching him Cree words and telling him long stories by means of gestures.

Little Bird who had been half starved when he joined the party ate far too much pemmican and when they camped, he lay down before the fire with his head wrapped in his blanket. "The Doctor prescribed castor oil, and Terry put the dose to his mouth. As the Little Bird took the first taste, he looked up and noticing the comical look about Terry's countenance, thought that a practical joke was being played at his expense, and with a gleam of fire in his eyes spit it out on him. The Doctor had now to come up and with his most impressive chief-medicine-man air, intimate that the dose must be taken. The Little Bird submitted, drank it as if it were hemlock, and rolled himself up in his blanket to die. But in the morning he was all right again though weak; and gratefully testified that castor oil was the most wonderful medicine in the world."

Fort Pitt lay out of their direct route and so they were

not to visit it but the party halted at the Pitt horse guard where three hundred horses, more than at any other post, grazed on the thick, short prairie grass. "Not one in ten of those horses had ever got a feed from a man. They cropped all their own food; and sleek and fat as they are now, they are equally so in midwinter; pawing off the dry snow they find the grasses abundant and succulent beneath. Better witnesses to the suitableness of this country for stock raising on an extensive scale, than those three hundred horses, could not be desired. . . . At the guard, only one Indian is in charge of the whole herd. The horses keep together and do not stray, so gregarious are they. The chief difficulty in obtaining some for a journey is to detach them from the pack." The chief work of the Indian keeper "seems to be making little inclosures of green logs or sticks, and building fires of green wood inside to smoke off the mosquitoes. Round these fires the horses often stand in groups, enjoying the smoke." The keeper's lodge, a large one made of fourteen buffalo skins, had a fire in the centre and the family slept round it in a constant smoke which kept out mosquitoes but also dried the skin and made the eyes sore.

While they looked at the horses, Mr. Sinclair, the Hudson's Bay agent at Fort Pitt, came to the guard to meet them bringing with him "a huge shoulder of fresh buffalo meat, some tongues and a bag of new potatoes. Terry was at once set to work on the fresh meat with orders to cook enough for twenty. None of us had ever tasted fresh buffalo before, nor fresh meat of any kind since leaving Red River. . . . Falling to with prairie appetites, each man disposed of his three portions with ease. The prairie wolves were yelping not far off, but nobody paid any attention to them. Tender buffalo steak, and new potatoes in delicious gravy, absorbed every one's attention. The delights of the table when you are in the best of health and keen-set are certainly wonderful." After the dinner had been eaten, the guides were still grouped around the cook's fire, eating, laughing and joking. Greasy or Haroosh "sat on a hillock, holding tit-bits to the fire on a little wooden spit, for Terry's frying pan could not keep up to him, and his greasy face shone in the ruddy light. So they continued till we went to bed. That they were at it all night cannot be positively affirmed, but in the morning the first sight that met our eyes was Haroosh in the same place and attitude, cooking and eating in a semi-comatose state."

They set off that morning, August 22, from the Pitt horse guard with three new guides and fresh horses on what turned out to be one of the best days of the whole journey. In perfect weather they rode through country "of varied beauty, rich in soil, grasses, flowers, wood and water." From low hills they could see "clumps and groves of tall white spruce in the gullies and valleys, and along lake sides, branching poplars with occasional white birch and tamarack, mingled with the still prevailing aspen. . . . Last but not the least important item, Terry had in his cart new potatoes and buffalo steak, good as any porter-house or London rump steak, enough even for our appetites."

In the afternoon they met their first Crees in a camp

of five or six tents. "Two broad-backed healthy young
squaws met us first, coming up from a lake with half a
dozen dogs. One squaw had a bag filled with ducks, on
her neck, and the other had tied her game round the
back of a dog. Some of the men came to shake hands
all round and to receive the plug of tobacco they looked
for. Others lounged round in dignified indifference,
with blanket or buffalo robe folded gracefully about
them—evidently knowing or hoping that every attitude
was noticed. Not a man was doing a single hand's turn,
and not a woman was idle."

Farther on two chiefs rode up, Rolling Mud and
Walker with Out-Turned Feet. They shook hands and
Fleming gave them a meal of tea and pemmican which
they preferred to fresh buffalo meat.

That afternoon the big wagon broke down when
"the iron bolt, connecting the two fore wheels with the
shaft, broke in two. Shaganappi had been sufficient for
every mishap hitherto, but this seemed too serious a case
for it; but, with the ready help of Mr. McDougall, shaganappi triumphed, and we were delayed only an hour.
No one ever seems non-plussed on the plains. When an
axle broke, the men would haul out a piece of white
birch, shape it into something like the right thing, stick
it in, tie it with shaganappi, and be jogging on at the
old rate before a professional carriage builder would
make up his mind what was best to be done."

At night they camped close to the Saskatchewan on
the bank of Moose Creek. "Then a mighty supper of
buffalo steak for us, and limitless pemmican for our Cree

visitors, rounded off one of the pleasantest days of the expedition."

Next day they passed a "large brigade of Hudson's Bay Company carts, that had left Carlton for Edmonton a week before us, heavily laden with stores. They were driven by several of Mr. McDougall's people, half-breeds and Crees, from Victoria, an united family of husband, wife and half a dozen young children being at the head of the brigade. The expense of bringing anything into or sending anything out of the country by this old-fashioned way is enormous. The prime cost of the articles is a bagatelle. Transport swallows up everything. No wonder that the price of a pound of tea, sugar or salt is here exactly the same. They weigh the same and cost the same for carriage."

The party was now little more than a hundred miles from Edmonton and one of the men rode forward to order pack-saddles and make arrangements for the mountain journey. With him went Mr. Macaulay who was returning from a year's visit to Scotland and was anxious to see his wife and family. "The country now became more hilly, the hillsides covered with heavy wood, and the hollows with marshes or lakelets. Vegetation everywhere was wonderfully luxuriant. Flowers re-appeared, but the general colour was blue in place of the former yellow or lilac; mint, blue bells, a beautiful tall larkspur, but principally light blue and dark blue asters. Our Botanist was disappointed to find that, amid such wealth of vegetation, there were but few new species. The same plants have kept by us for a thousand miles. Mint and a saxifragaceous plant had accompanied us from Rainy Lake; gentians, asters, castilia, anemones, and goldenrods from the eastern verge of the prairie."

The approach of a thunder storm drove them rapidly toward the shelter of the settlement of Victoria, Mr. McDougall's old mission. The houses and the Hudson's Bay store were on the river bank out of sight of a traveller passing on the trail. Men were making hay in the valley, hurrying too before the threat of rain, and the party camped at a spring near them. The storm passed quickly, the sky cleared and Mr. McDougall rode to the fort for supplies. "Mr. Tait, the Hudson's Bay agent, had no fresh meat; but, hearing of our arrival, he with oriental hospitality had ordered a young ox to be killed and a quarter sent over for our use."

Next day they walked across the ridge to hold a Sunday service at Victoria where there were three principal buildings, the church, which also served as a school, the mission house and the fort. "The log-houses of the half-breeds (English and Scotch) intermingled with the tents of the Crees, extended in a line from this west end along the bank of the river, each man having a frontage on the river, and his grain planted in a little hollow that runs behind the houses, beneath the main rise of the ridge. Most of their hay they cut in the valley, on the other side of the ridge where we had camped. . . . The settlement is seven years old, and consists now of between twenty and thirty families of half-breeds and from ten to a hundred tents of Crees, according to the time of year, each tent housing on an average seven or eight souls."

The Reverend George McDougall had founded the settlement there because it was a place of resort of the Crees and because the location had good soil, "river, lakes abounding in fish and wild fowl, and nearness to the plains where the buffalo are always found."

He had left his son John there with Mr. Thomas Woolsey and one or two hired men to create a mission. "One small house," John wrote, "and a roofless stable were the only improvements." It was here that Mr. O'Byrne had spent the winter before his fortunate meeting with Dr. Cheadle and Lord Milton. While Mr. Woolsey "was kept busy holding meetings, attending councils, visiting the sick, acting as doctor and surgeon, magistrate and judge," John, then twenty, and the hired men were "fencing and planting a field, whip-sawing lumber, taking out timber up the river and rafting it down to the mission, also building a house." With all the other work they had to keep a constant watch and conceal the horses for "the southern Indians were coming north and the northern Indians going south," and there were constant rumours of horse-stealing and scalp-taking.

From its first year the new mission was called on to feed and shelter starving Indians and all travellers for there was no Hudson's Bay post nearer than Edmonton, about ninety miles away. Stables and other out-buildings and a small church were built. In the second year of the mission the McDougall family came from Norway House to settle there. A new house was built and no one could have been as glad to see its completion as Mrs. McDougall, John's mother, who for seven months had lived in "the crowded conditions of our one-roomed log building. Thirteen of us called it home, ate there when we were at the mission and nearly all slept there. All the cooking and washing was done in this little place."

From this time John no longer lived regularly with his parents and brothers and sisters at Victoria but travelled almost constantly, following the buffalo herds to get food, visiting Indian encampments, setting up a new mission at Pigeon Lake to which he took his young half-breed wife. When he went to Fort Garry for supplies for the missions, to his delight he was given bread for the first time in two years, and even pancakes and maple syrup—after many years "still sweet to my taste."

But he often had occasion to visit Victoria and reported that Indians were coming in such numbers that the Hudson's Bay Company opened a post there in 1864. Soon afterward a school was started for the McDougall children, the children of Mr. Steinhauer, the missionary at Whitefish Lake, and a few Indian children. The garden yielded potatoes and some barley but meat was of course still the chief food. By 1865 about twenty-five English half-breed families had settled near the mission and the next winter was full of activity. "Religious services and literary entertainments occupied the evenings," John wrote, "and out-door games, such as football, snowshoe and dog-train races and foot races, for the day." When the buffalo hunt went well the mission community feasted; at other times food might become very scarce. John found his family "making meal after meal on wild duck eggs. Mother had neither tea nor coffee, the sugar was all gone, neither bread nor vegetables were forth-coming."

Victoria along with the entire Saskatchewan country had in 1870 suffered a terrible epidemic of smallpox. John was for most of the time encamped with a hunting party; it was there that he disinfected Souzie and took him into his service. He wrote harrowing accounts of the disease among the Indians who were at the same time disturbed and sullen because of rumours of the rebellion at Red River.

One of John's patients was Thomas Woolsey who died of the smallpox under the fluttering willow leaves of a little brush hut. In the valley of the Bow River, Indians in many camps sickened and died. One Stony said later to John McDougall, "it was a graveyard, and the crying went up both day and night."

Near the bend of the Battle River, John came upon a Sarcee or Blackfoot camp of about forty lodges in which all the inmates were dead of smallpox. The few sur-vivors had taken the horses and escaped. Close to the camp they saw "flights of carrion birds and met troops of wolves." They were still near this "death camp", as John called it, when he heard news from Victoria that two of his sisters had died of the smallpox and that his father had quarantined himself with his family and would allow no one to come near the house. John hurried toward home, meeting on the way an Indian who said that another of the McDougall sisters was dead and that his father was dying. As he approached, John met his brother-in-law, Richard Hardisty. This famous member of a famous fur-trading family had married John's oldest sister, Eliza, several years before. Hardisty reported that the senior McDougall was recovering.

John walked alone to the mission stockade that night and heard his father's feeble voice ask, "Is it you, John?" and then command, "Come no nearer." They talked for a few minutes through the stockade and the father showed where his three daughters had just been buried. Then John was obliged to go away knowing that one of his own baby daughters was in the quarantined house. The rest of the family survived the smallpox though John's young first wife died soon afterward.

All this must have passed through the mind of George McDougall as he visited again his old home at Victoria, though apparently Grant and the other visitors knew nothing of what had happened to their companion so short a time before.

For years the Reverend George McDougall had acted as chaplain to the fort at Edmonton and in 1871 the Wesleyans decided to establish a mission there. The senior McDougall had been sent to take charge of it and John had been left in charge of the mission at Victoria which was now well established and the centre of a growing community. This mission had recently passed to the care of Mr. Campbell who had not yet returned from the Wesleyan Conference at Winnipeg. After his ordination there a month or two before, John McDougall had been directed to open still another new mission in the region of the Bow River valley.

Grant was much interested in the mission at Victoria.

"When we arrived at the church it was almost filled with about eighty whites, half-breeds and Crees. The men sat on one side, the women on the other, and the children in a little gallery or loft with the schoolmaster and monitors. The service was in English, but some Cree hymns were sung, and Mr. McDougall announced that there would be a service in Cree in the evening, through the medium of an interpreter. The conduct of all present from first to last was most devout, notwithstanding that many present understood but imperfectly what was said. The children led the singing, and though there was a lack of bass voices on account of the absence of the principal members of the choir, it was singularly sweet and correct."

Mr. Snyder, the schoolmaster, was present, a man who had notably adapted his style of teaching to the problems presented by his pupils' way of life. "Mr. Snyder had eighty Cree children at his school. When the Indians moved out to the plains to hunt buffalo, the master would pack up his spelling-books and slates, and go off with them, setting up his establishment wherever they halted. He spent from two to six months of the year teaching in this rotary style—hunting half the day, teaching the other half."

So far north there were often light frosts in July and August so that farming was an experiment. It seemed promising, however, for wheat, sowed for the last seven years, had failed only once because of a local drought. Several half-breed families had not gone to the plains for buffalo in the last few years but had settled down to raise wheat, barley and potatoes.

286

Fleming and his party invited Mr. Tait, Mr. Snyder, the schoolmaster and Mrs. Campbell, the wife of the missionary, to have supper with them. Mrs. Campbell was the first lady to visit their camp; "her presence lifted up everything and had a very appreciable effect on our style of passing things round the table; everyone was as anxious to help her to something as if she had been Her Majesty in person; Terry, naturally and nationally the soul of politeness, was especially attentive. Rather than let her put preserved peaches on the plate beefsteak had been on, he removed the plate and whipping out his pocket handkerchief, that had not been washed since he left Fort Garry, proceeded to clean it. Luckily the Doctor noticed him in time."

Wherever they stopped the Doctor was in as great demand as Dr. Cheadle had been on the same route nine years before. "He visited and prescribed for all the sick in the settlement and, finding in the fort a medicine chest that had been sent out as a present by Dr. Rae but had never been used, he explained to Mr. Tait how and when to give different medicines, and wrote out general directions that could be easily understood and acted upon."

The next day they crossed Sucker, Vermilion and Deep Creeks, among others, Grant reflecting on the lack of originality shown in choosing names for natural features. "In the North-West there are half a dozen 'Red Deers', 'White Muds', 'Vermilions'; next in popularity to these come the names of members of the Royal Family."

The following day about noon they reached Edmonton; "the first great half of our journey from Fort Garry, the prairie as distinguished from the mountain part, was over." At this transition point where other parties, among them Southesk's and Dr. Cheadle's, had spent days in interviewing guides, examining horses, hearing the news, exchanging stories of grizzlies and Blackfeet, Fleming's party spent no time at all. Arrangements were so quickly made that they could start again on the very next day. In their camp near the new church Mr. McDougall was building, the party was photographed—"tents, carts, buckboards, with Terry seated on his pots and pans mending his pants and smoking the inevitable cutty, in the foreground."

Fort Edmonton standing some distance east of the present city had been twice destroyed and rebuilt, once on the river flats and later on the bluff above the river. The windmill at Fort Edmonton had long been a landmark but by the time of Grant's visit a horse-power mill was in operation. John McDougall was one of a party of visitors to the mission and farm at Whitefish Lake, at about this time, when the Chief Factor presented the mission with a plough and "offered to grind their grain at the Hudson's Bay mill at Edmonton (only one hundred and fifty miles distant) for little cost." Fort Edmonton itself was removed in 1915 to make way for the Parliament Buildings of the province of Alberta.

Grant's party said good-bye to their travelling companion, Reverend Mr. McDougall, whom they were not to see again. Three years later, in January 1876, the food supply was low at Morley, John's new Bow River mission, near the present city of Calgary. Father and son set out, accordingly, to look for buffalo. They killed six and were bringing home a large supply of meat when at night they became separated. After days of anguished search, the son found his father frozen to death on the prairie he knew better than most guides.

John McDougall, the son, lived well into the years of the new, settled, agricultural west which he and his father had so long foreseen. "All day long," he had written of a journey across the empty prairie, "as I rode in advance of my boys and carts, I was locating homes, and selecting sites for village corners, and erecting school-houses and lifting church spires, and engineering railway routes, and hoping I might live to see some of this come to pass, for come it would." He did indeed see much of it come to pass as he wrote his reminiscences, retiring in 1906 and living on in Calgary until 1917. Coming to the west in 1860 he had served the government in both North-West rebellions through his intimate knowledge of the Indians; and he had seen, as he said, "thousands of prosperous homes dot these plains and fill these valleys."

The Fleming party, hurried as they were, found time to make the inevitable investigation of the coal outcrop on the river bank. In the smithy "it burnt well and gave a good heat when the bellows was applied, but it would be very difficult to kindle without the bellows." It seemed to Grant even dirtier than Pictou coal which, as a friend of his said, yielded "at the rate of two tons of ashes to one of coal."

And again, like Southesk and Cheadle before him, Grant met miners at Edmonton. They had come from

Peace River and their "reports of the Ominica gold mines were not very encouraging. The men who wash the Saskatchewan sand bars for gold make on an average four dollars per day, but that does not satisfy them; five dollars a day is called wages. This year there are only fifteen miners on the Saskatchewan."

The large farm at the fort had "raised wheat for thirty years and it has failed only two or three times; barley and potatoes and turnips are sure crops." As at Carlton, Indians would sometimes burn the fences for fuel and let their horses get into the fields but "a thousand bushels of wheat are usually stored from a sowing of a hundred; and last year, two hundred and fifty kegs of potatoes (eight gallon kegs) were planted, and about five thousand were dug. The same land has been used for the farm for thirty years, without any manure worth speaking of being put on it."

In all the vast, rich, open country they had crossed, the only large settlement was at Red River, the only farms were there and at the Hudson's Bay posts. Half-breed farming was conducted on peculiar lines. "They are farmers, hunters, fishermen, voyageurs all in one; the soil is scratched, three inches deep, early in May, some seed thrown in, and then the whole household go off to hunt the buffalo. They get back about the first of August, spend the month haying and harvesting, and are off to the fall hunt early in September. Some are now so devoted to farming that they only go to one hunt in the year. It is astonishing that, though knowing so well how not to do it, they raise some wheat and a great deal of barley, oats and potatoes."

Water was one difficulty and test wells must be sunk, Grant thought, to discover where it might be found. Wood was not plentiful but coal could take its place. "By river or rail, coal can be carried in all directions for every purpose; and it is highly probable that we have the most extensive coal-fields in the world." With farms laid out and fewer prairie fires, trees would have a chance to grow. Summer frosts remained as a danger; the remedy was to sow wheat very early, perhaps to grow other crops and to concentrate on stock raising. In spite of these apparent difficulties, Grant found it "impossible to avoid the conclusion that we have a great and fertile North-West, a thousand miles long and from one to four hundred miles broad, capable of containing a population of millions. It is a fair land; rich in furs and fish, in treasures of the forest, the field and the mine; seamed by navigable rivers, interlaced by numerous creeks, and beautiful with a thousand lakes; broken by swelling uplands, wooded hillsides, and bold ridges; and protected on its exposed sides by a great desert or by giant mountains. The air is pure, dry and bracing all the year round; giving promise of health and strength of body and length of days. Here we have a home for our own surplus population and for the stream of emigration that runs from northern and central Europe to America. Let it be opened up to the world by rail and steamboat, and in an incredibly short time the present gap between Manitoba and British Columbia will be filled up, and a continuous line of loyal Provinces extend from the Atlantic to the Pacific."

# V

DEPARTURE FROM Edmonton, slow as it proved to be for even the best equipped party, was hastened on August 28 by a rumour "that quickened everyone's movements." It was the old standard rumour once more. They heard that "Crees and Blackfeet were fighting on the other side of the river, a report based, as we afterwards learned, on no other ground than that 'some one' had heard shots fired, at wild ducks probably enough." They took leave of their guides and of the ardent Botanist who was sent to report on the plants of the Peace River district. Souzie was particularly sorry to part with young Frank Fleming. "Souzie mounted his horse and waited patiently at the gate of the Fort for two hours, without our knowledge. When Frank came out he rode on with him for a mile to the height of a long slope; then he drew up and putting one hand on his heart, with a sorrowful look held out the other; and, without a word, turned his horse and rode slowly away." They kept Terry the cook with them and took in addition a guide and two packers.

Mr. Hardisty, the factor, rode with them as far as the

horse guard at St. Albert. There they changed their horses and later visited Bishop Grandin and his church. The priests and sisters were nearly all French Canadians. St. Albert had been settled nine years before and had had a population of nearly a thousand half-breeds until the terrible smallpox epidemic of 1870. At St. Albert 300 had died, many had moved away in terror and the settlement was only now recovering. Like the people at Victoria, these spent "half the year at home, the other half on the plains. The children are sent to school only when they have no buffalo to hunt, no pemmican to make, or no work of greater importance than education to set them at." Grain crops grew fairly well and "turnips, beets, carrots and suchlike vegetables grow to an enormous size. A serious drawback to the people is that they have no grist-mill; the Fathers could not get them to give up the buffalo for a summer and build one on the Sturgeon. They would begin it in the fall and finish it in the spring; but the floods swept it away half-finished, and the Fathers have no funds to try anything on a solid and extensive scale."

The Doctor as usual went to see those who were sick while the others looked at the church, which represented enormous labour, "when it is considered that there is not a sawmill in the country and that every plank had to be made with a whip or hand-saw. . . . The sacristy behind, was the original log church and is still used for service in the winter."

They had crossed the Sturgeon River twice that day and when they had crossed it three more times the next day they reached St. Ann's, the real setting-off place. "From St. Ann's," Grant wrote, "the road is only a horse trail through the woods, so often lost in marshes or hidden by windfalls that a guide is required." Valad was the guide, Brown and Beaupré the packers, and they set to work to transfer all baggage from carts to pack-saddles.

Mrs. Adams, wife of the Hudson's Bay man at Lake St. Ann's, gave them a dinner with those half-forgotten delicacies cream and butter, and the delicious St. Ann's white-fish, so long a staple of the fur trade in that part of the country. "It provides for all demands up to Edmonton. Last year thirty thousand, averaging over three pounds each, were taken out and frozen for winter use." Here summer frosts were serious, the barley had been nipped several times and a field of potatoes "cut down to the ground."

Grant watched with great interest as Brown and Beaupré arranged the heavy wooden pack-saddles. "Wooden pads suited to the shape of the horse's back, with two or three piles of buffalo robe or blanket underneath, prevent the cross legs and packs from hurting the horse. All the baggage, blankets, provisions and utensils are made up into portable bundles as nearly equal in size and weight as possible. Each of the packers seizing a bundle places it on the side of the saddle, another bundle is put on the top between the two, and then the triangular-shaped load is bound in one by folds of shaganappi twisted firmly but without a knot, after a regular fashion called the diamond hitch. . . . As our object was speed we dispensed with tent, extra clothing, tinned meat, books etc. and thus reduced the loads at the outset to a hundred or a hundred and thirty pounds per horse. . . . There was now before us a journey of five or six hundred miles, through woods and marshes, torrents and mountain passes; for we could not depend on getting supplies of any kind or fresh horses on this side of Kamloops; though there were probabilities of our meeting with parties of engineers between Jasper House and Yellow Head Pass."

Eight packed horses, eight saddled and one spare, set out early in the afternoon. "Valad rode first, two pack-horses followed, Brown next, and so on till the Chief or some other of the party brought up the rear of the long line on the seventeenth horse. If any of the pack-horses deviated from the road into the bush, the man immediately behind had to bring him back. The loud calls to the obstinately lazy or straying 'Rouge', 'Brun', 'Sangri', 'Billy', 'Bischo', varied with whacks almost as loud on their backs, were the only sounds that broke the stillness of the forest; for conversation is impossible with a man on horseback in front of or behind you, and there is little game in these woods except an occasional partridge. After the first day, the horses gave little trouble as they all got accustomed to the style of travelling, and recognized the wisdom of keeping to the road. Two or three old hands at the work always aimed at getting one of their companions between them and a driver, so that their companions might receive all the occasional whacks, and they share the benefit only of the loud calls and objurgations; but the new ones soon got up to the trick, and their contentions for precedence and place were as keen as between a number of old dowagers before going in to dinner. These old hands carried their burdens with a swinging, waddling motion that eased their backs, and saved them many a rude jar."

The first five miles were easy but then "crashing through windfalls or steering amid thick woods round them, leading our horses across yielding morasses or stumbling over roots and into holes, with all our freshness we scarcely made two miles an hour, and that with an expenditure of wind and limb that would soon have exhausted horse and man."

At night a lean-to took the place of the tents they had left behind. "You require only a large cotton sheet in addition to what the forest supplies at any time. Two pairs of cross-poles are stuck in the ground, as far apart as you wish your lodging place for the night to be long; a ridge-pole connects these, and then half a dozen or more poles are placed slanting against the ridge-pole. Cover the sloping frame with your cotton sheet, or in its absence birch-bark and your house is made. The ends are open and so is the front, but the back is covered and that, of course, is where the wind comes from. The ventilation is perfect, and as your fire is made immediately in front, there is no lack of warmth."

The length of time needed to unpack and pack the horses made it necessary to travel only two spells a day instead of three and so the party ate breakfast before starting in the morning. When they camped for dinner, Fleming took a pick and went at once to get some coal. "Carrying a number of pieces in our hands we proceeded to make a fire and had the satisfaction of seeing them burn, and of cooking our pemmican with the mineral fuel. . . . Beaupré, who all this while had been washing sand from the river in his shovel for gold, and finding at the rate of half a cent's worth a shovelful, was amazed at our eagerness, or that there should have been any doubt about its being coal. He and his mates when mining on different rivers, had been in the habit of making fires with it whenever they wished the fire to remain in all night."

It was September and "warm as the days now were the nights were so cold, though there was no actual frost, that we usually kept our clothes on, in addition to the double blanket. Our bag or boots served for pillow, and none of us was ever troubled with wakefulness."

"Our progress was so slow, averaging only two miles an hour, that we were all dreadfully tired. The trail was not bad in itself, with the exception of a few small morasses, some of black muck, and others of a tenacious clay, but at every four or five yards a tree, or two or three branches were lying across, as firmly set by having been trodden on as if placed in position, and they prevented the horses from getting into a trot."

In the dusk before they camped the spare horse had wandered away. Beaupré went after him and tried to drive him toward camp but he plunged into the woods and disappeared. Next morning when they woke at four, Valad had already gone to look for the horse and the rest of the party went on, leaving Valad's saddle with some bread and pemmican hanging on a tree. Going was slow, the path "so heavily encumbered in places with fallen timber that no trace of it could be seen. A rough path had to be broken round the obstacle and sometimes Beaupré had difficulty in finding the trail again." Valad did not come up with them until almost night. He had found the horse; "three times he turned him but the horse always got away by dashing into the brush. Valad then went ahead and set a wooden trap on the road, but the horse avoided it, and Valad gave up the chase. On his way back, he found that the squirrels had eaten his breakfast. Shouldering his saddle, he followed our trail and rejoined us having walked forty-one miles and eaten nothing. His moccasins had been cut with the stumps and thorns; but though footsore in consequence, he made light of it and went to work with his usual promptness."

Three horses went lame and the next morning Valad extracted long splinters from the unshod hoofs of two of them. The third would allow no one near him so Valad tied a shaganappi lasso around his hind legs and around his neck, threw him down and was able to remove the splinter. It rained and "the horses, sinking almost to their bellies, floundered in the mud at a fearful rate." That day they reached the McLeod River and Fleming found, chalked in red on a large spruce tree, a message from the emigrant party who had crossed the mountains before Milton and Cheadle. Only a few words were still legible.

August 10th, 1862

East Tilbury

and
Robert Campb

for Cariboo
a hard road to travel.

Following the McLeod they found the land between the deep windings of the river "the worst part of the road, though it was all so bad that it is invidious to make comparisons. The country was either bog or barren—both bad—for the whole had recently been burned over, and every wind had blown down its share of the burnt trees. There was no regular trail. Each successive party that travelled this way, seemed to have tried to make a new one in vain efforts to escape the difficulties. Valad went ahead, axe in hand, and between natural selection and a judicious use of the axe, made a passage; but it looked so tangled and beset that the horses often thought they could do better; off they would go, with a swing, among the bare poles for about two yards before their packs got interlaced with the tough spruce. Then came the tug; if the trees would not give, the packs had to, and there was a delay of half an hour to tie them on again. . . . Wandering from the trail, the horses got mired in muskegs or stuck between trees, or when the blackened tough spruce branches bent forward by a pack-horse swung back viciously in the face of the unfortunate driver."

"The prospect too was dismal and desolate enough for Avernus or the richest coal-fields; nothing but a forest, apparently endless, of blackened poles on all sides." During the day they met two Indians, bound for Edmonton, who stopped to eat pemmican with them. They were Iroquois, "their ancestors had been in the employment of the North-West Fur Company, and on its amalgamation with the Hudson's Bay, had settled on Smoking

River, on account of the abundance of fur-bearing animals and of large game, such as buffalo, elk, brown and grizzly bears, then in that quarter."

Heavy and laborious as the going was, Grant watched with amusement the difference between Brown, the Scot, and Beaupré, the Frenchman, in struggling with the horses. "Brown continued imperturbable no matter how the horses went. Beaupré, the mildest mannered man living when things went smoothly, could not stand the sight of a horse floundering in the mud. . . . Gripping the tail with his left hand, as the brute struggled up the opposite hill . . . he whipped with his right; *sacré*-ing furiously, till he reached the top. Then feeling that he had done his part, he would let go and subside again into his mildest manners."

When the McLeod swung south in a great loop they took their way across a chord of the arc, in the middle of which, beyond the Medicine River, there was a very treacherous muskeg. Valad and Brown set out to examine the ground for a safe crossing place but "Beaupré, leading his horse by the bridle dashed in close to the swollen river, at a most unlikely spot, exclaiming, 'I'll chance it anyway.' The words were only out of his lips when he fell into a pool up to his middle; but, undismayed he scrambled out and keeping close to beds of willow and alder, actually found a way so good that all the rest followed him. Only one pack-horse sank so hopelessly deep into a hole that he had to be unpacked and lifted out, Beaupré hoisting by the tail with a mighty hoist—for the man had the strength of a giant." The week had been

300

so exhausting that they were very glad to leave the McLeod behind and to realize that it was Saturday. A hundred and twenty miles had been covered during the week and the leaving of the McLeod was celebrated by a round of toasts to the Queen, wives and sweethearts, the Dominion and the Railroad.

The Doctor, on Sunday, like Viscount Milton on another occasion, decided to make a plum pudding. They were not tired of pemmican, indeed they all liked it for it kept well and "two pounds weight with bread and tea, we found enough for the dinner of eight hungry men." For a pudding they had neither plums, suet nor a bag. "But we had berry pemmican and pemmican in its own line is equal to shaganappi. It contained buffalo fat that would do for suet, and berries that would do for plums. Only genius could have united plum-pudding and berry pemmican in one mental act. Terry contributed . . . the sugar bag, which might be used as there was very little sugar left for it to hold. Pemmican, flour and water, baking soda, sugar and salt were surely sufficient ingredients." At three the bag was put into the pot; at five they ate the first course of the dinner—pemmican, with a special treat of reindeer tongues. Then they gathered eagerly round the pot but the pudding when it came out "would not unite"; it was only boiled pemmican. The Doctor was astonished, Frank "savage in his lamentations"; Fleming calmly proposed more boiling. Half an hour later "with fear and trembling the Doctor went to the pot; anxious heads bent down with his; tenderly was the bag lifted out and slit; and a joyous shout conveyed the intelligence that it was a success, that at any rate it had the shape of a pudding. Brown, who had been scoffing, was silenced; and the Doctor conquered him completely by helping him to a double portion. How good that pudding was! . . . To have been perfect the pudding should have had more boiling; but no one dared to hint a fault, for was not the dish empty? . . . Brown was engaged on the spot to make a better if he could at the Yellow Head Pass camp."

At noon the next day "we got our first sight of the Athabasca, from a high bluff, and beyond it to the southwest, fifty miles off but seemingly close at hand, the Rocky Mountains covered with snow. . . . From the terrace above our camp, the mountains seemed immediately beyond the wood on the opposite side of the river. They towered up in a grand silver-tipped line closing the western horizon so high up, that the sun always sets here more than half an hour sooner than on the plains."

Here "while hacking with his axe at brush on the camping ground, Brown struck something metallic that blunted the edge of the axe. Feeling with his hand he drew out from near the root of a young spruce tree, an ancient sword bayonet, the brazen hilt and steel blade in excellent preservation, but the leather scabbard half eaten as if by the teeth of some animal. It seemed strange in this vast and silent forest wilderness thus to come upon a relic that told, probably, of the old days when two rival fur companies armed their agents to the teeth, and when bloody contests often took place between them. Brown

302

presented the treasure trove to the Chief, for his museum, as a memento of the Athabasca."

They rode next day in the face of the mountains "that stood in massive grandeur, thirty miles ahead." Here as Southesk and after him Dr. Cheadle had done, Grant pictured his companions. "Valad led the way, clad friar-like in blue hooded capote which he wore all regardless of the fact that the sun was shining; Brown next, in rugged miner costume half-leather, half-woollen, and Beaupré in the same with a touch of colour added; the Chief and the Doctor in their yellow moose-hide jackets; even Terry, who of late invariably brought up the rear, ceased to howl 'git up out o' that' to the unfortunate animal he sat upon, dropped his stick and put his pipe in his pocket. He had seen Vesuvius, the Himalayas and the Hill of Howth, but they were 'nauthin' to this.'"

Frank shot a beaver and "in fifteen minutes Valad had the animal skinned, boned, the whole of the meat stretched out in one piece on a brander of sticks and exposed to the fire to grill; the tail on another stick and the liver on a third." The five of the party who had never tasted beaver before pronounced "the meat tender though dry, the liver a delicious morsel, and the tail superior to the famous moose-muffle. Within an hour after that beaver had been industriously at work on his dam, he formed part of the interior economy of eight different stomachs, and scarcely a scrap was left to show what he once had been."

Next day in the Jasper valley they rounded Roche à

Perdrix and then Roche à Myette, the valley's dominant peak. Looking back at Roche à Perdrix "Valad in grave tones told the story of his old partner—an unfortunate half-breed—who when hunting big-horn on its precipitous slopes, twenty-two years ago, was carried over one of them on a snow-slide and dashed in pieces." Fleming made pencil sketches of the glorious view before them and Grant longed for a camera. "A good photographer would certainly make a name and perhaps a fortune, if he came up here and took views."

They camped on a small island, for the water of the Athabasca was high but might subside during the night. There were no poles to hold the sheet for their usual shelter so they spread their blankets on the gravel beside an aspen thicket, with a good fire at their feet. By morning the river had fallen six inches but it was still too deep for the pack-horses so the men set to work to make a raft. As they had only one axe the work took time. "Fifteen or sixteen logs bound together by three strong cross-poles, and tied each to each with folds of rope, composed the raft. Between the cross-poles a number of smaller ones were laid, to serve for a floor and keep the luggage from getting wet. The Chief and the two packers were then left to manage the raft, and the rest stripped to the middle and rode across—Centaur-like—driving before them the unsaddled pack-horses." Two more miles and they were at Jasper House—fifteen days after leaving Edmonton. The house had long been abandoned as a permanent trading centre though it was opened twice a year to receive furs.

They were now for all practical purposes without a

guide for Valad did not know the country beyond Jasper House and frequently missed the way. It rained heavily all night and in the morning Fleming announced "that the flour bag was getting so light that it might be necessary to allowance the bread rations. That struck home, though there was abundance of pemmican and tea."

They came to the torrential Snaring River with a bed of large boulders which "make the footing so precarious that if a horse falls, there is little hope for him or his rider. Valad crossed first. As the water came up to his horse's shoulder, and the horse stumbled several times, it was evidently risky. Just at this moment, Brown who had gone down-stream to look for another ford, called out that he saw footprints of men and horses. Off went the Chief, and at the same moment Valad screamed across the torrent that white men had just been there. The traces of three men and three shod horses (showing that they did not belong to Indians) were clearly made out going down in the direction of the Athabasca; but though guns were fired as a signal, no response was heard; and the word was passed to cross at the lower ford. Beaupré took some pemmican in his pocket as a precaution, in case all hands but himself were lost; notwithstanding the omen, we reached the other side safely." Did the hoof-marks show that the survey party they were expecting had missed them and gone on to Jasper? While they wondered, a Shuswap rode up, shook hands all round and handed Fleming a paper. "Hurrah! it was from Moberly, and stated that he had just struck fresh tracks and had sent back this Indian to learn who we were." Valad tried to talk to the Shuswap in Cree, Beaupré in French but he shook his head. Brown tried Chinook which Hudson's Bay agents used with the Pacific Coast Indians and the Shuswap brightened. He answered in Chinook that Moberly's camp was five or six miles back, with lots of men and horses, and " 'lots of grub, lots of good things.' ... He was offered some pemmican and took it, but said that he had never seen such food before." They sent him back with a note to Moberly and went on seven miles farther to camp "on a terrace overlooking the river and surrounded on all sides with snow-capped mountains."

As they reached the Miette River next day Moberly caught up with them. "Except the two Iroquois at the McLeod, his was the first face we had seen since leaving St. Ann's, and to meet him was like re-opening communication with the world, although we, and not he had the latest news to give." The Miette valley opened so pleasantly that they could not believe in its bad reputation and began to imagine that they might reach Yellow Head Pass before night. They were wrong. "Long swamps that reminded us of the muskegs on the McLeod, covered with an underbrush of scrub birch, and tough willows eight to ten feet high that slapped our faces, had to be floundered through. Alternating with these, intervened the face of a precipice, the rocky bed and sides of the river, or fallen timber, stumps and blackened poles, to climb, to scramble over or to dodge. No wonder that Milton and Cheadle bade adieu to the unkindly Miette with immense satisfaction. We had to cross and recross the river or parts of it seven or eight times in the course of the afternoon. . . . Four hours hard work took us over five miles, and by that time everyone was heartily sick of it, and full of longing to reach Moberly's camp. As we stumbled about on a patch recently burnt over on the south side of the river, one of his Indians that he had thoughtfully sent back, met and guided us to a desolate looking spot, the best camping ground he had been able to find. Some little grass had sprung up on the blackened soil, and no one was disposed to be particular. Supper was left in the hands of Tim—Moberly's Indian cook—and he prepared a variety of delicacies that made up for all other deficiencies; bread light as Parisian rolls, Columbia flour being as different from Red River as Tim's baking from Terry's; delicious Java coffee, sweetened with sugar from the Sandwich Islands, that now supply a great part of the Pacific coast with sugar; and crisp bacon, almost as great a luxury to us as pemmican to Moberly's men."

Next morning, crossing the Miette for the last time, they found the trail made by Moberly's men for the survey party. The camp was near the entrance to the Yellow Head Pass; "instead of contracted canyon or savage torrent raging among beetling precipices as we had half feared, the Pass is really a pleasant open meadow." Here Brown set to work to make the promised pemmican pudding but it was so large that at six o'clock it needed another hour's boiling. The survey party's cook "in ignorance of what Brown was about, had prepared at his fire a genuine old fashioned plum-pudding; and full justice was done to this, till the pemmican one was ready.

... An hour after dinner, all gathered around our tent, to try the second pudding and decide on Brown's reputation. Terry in preparing the sauce had used salt instead of sugar ... but the pudding was a decided success, though eaten under the great disadvantage of no one being very hungry."

## VI

"Moberly welcomed us into British Columbia, for we were at length out of 'No man's land', and had entered the western province of our Dominion." At the summit of the Pass "we had left the Miette flowing to the Arctic Ocean, and now came upon this, the source of the Fraser, hurrying to the Pacific." They were to meet another survey party at the west end of Moose Lake before camping that night but the distance was forty miles and the going very bad.

This day, September 16, turned out to be the worst day of the whole journey, approached only by the trip of July 30 from the North-West Angle to Oak Point. "Worse cannot be said of it." It was dark as they reached the east end of Moose Lake and the party fell into three groups; Moberly and the Doctor had ridden ahead to the survey camp to get supper ready, three or four miles behind them came the packers and pack-horses, and Fleming, Frank and Grant came far in the rear. "In the dense dark woods the moon's light was very feeble, and as the horses were done out, we walked before or behind the poor brutes, stumbling over loose boulders, tripped up by the short sharp stumps and rootlets, mired in deep moss springs, wearied with climbing the steep ascents of the lake's sides, knee-sore with jolts in descending, dizzy and stupid from sheer fatigue and want of sleep. A drizzling rain had fallen in showers most of the afternoon, and it continued at intervals through the night." Then when they reached the camp there was no feed; "our poor horses most of which had now travelled eleven hundred miles, and required rest or a different kind of work, had had a killing day of it and there was no grass for them." But a supply of beans and corned beef was ready for the men and "wrapping dry blankets round our wet clothes, and spreading waterproofs over the place where there were fewest pools of water, we went in willingly for sweet sleep."

The Doctor, however, was almost too excited to sleep, for he held in his hand the spoon and fishing line belonging to the Headless Indian made famous by Dr. Cheadle. One of the packers had found the fallen tree near the body and had given the Doctor the spoon made of horn and the fishing line of native hemp. He put them away carefully "among his choicest treasures" and made careful notes of the place where the body had been buried so that he might examine the site when the party reached it.

Since they were following so closely the route taken by Milton and Cheadle nine years before, Grant referred constantly in his diary to the events of that earlier and more difficult journey. The two accounts, he wrote, which "have discredited the whole book to many readers, are those concerning Mr. O'Byrne and the Headless Indian. Not only did we find both verified, but the accounts of the country and the tale of their own difficulties are as truthfully and simply given as it was possible for men who travelled in a strange country. . . . The pluck that made them conceive, and the vastly greater pluck that enabled them to pull through such an expedition was of the truest British kind. They were more indebted than they perhaps knew as far as 'Slaughter Camp', to the trail of the Canadians who had preceded them, on their way to the Cariboo; but from that point, down the frightful and unexplored valley of the North Thompson, the journey had to be faced on their own totally inadequate resources. Had they but known it, they were beaten as completely as by the rules of war the British troops were at Waterloo. They should have submitted to the inevitable and starved. But luckily for themselves and for their readers, they did not know it; and thanks to Mrs. Assiniboine, and their own intelligent hardihood that kept them from giving in, they succeeded where by all the laws of probabilities they ought to have disastrously failed."

From this point Fleming's party was to proceed, as Milton and Cheadle had done, to Tête Jaune Cache and then follow the North Thompson down to Kamloops, turning west from there. "We are now in the heart of the Rocky Mountains, between the first and second great ranges, nearly a day's journey on from Yellow Head Pass, with jaded horses and a trail so heavy that fresh horses cannot be expected to average more than twenty miles of travel per day." In the morning everyone felt the effect of the wearing journey of the night before and after a few hours' listless crawl it was decided to camp in an open glade where there was grass for the horses. Fleming had to receive reports from the surveying parties and give them instructions; the rest built a big fire and hung wet clothes and blankets near it to dry. The survey party had worked round the north side of Moose Lake where the bluffs were not so sheer as on the south side; Grant reflected that the labour and patience of the surveyors were such as "few who ride in Pullman cars on the road in after years will ever appreciate."

Next day as they travelled the rough trail along the Fraser, they left their horses to go down and look at the first canyon. "The rocks closed in the river for some hundred yards to a width of eight feet, so that a man could jump across. Down this narrow passage, the whole of the water of the river rushed—a resistless current, slipping in great green masses from ledge to ledge, smashing against out-jutting rocks, eddying round stony barriers till it got through the long gateway." The canyons presented, Grant wrote, "formidable obstacles to railroad construction."

When they met the main body of the survey party they exchanged their weary horses for fresh ones and took on two new packers, Valad, Brown and Beaupré going back with the horses to the survey camp. Only Terry the cook remained with them and this not from personal attachment but because "he wished to go on to Cariboo to make his fortune at the mines there." When they met the first survey party they had exchanged their pemmican for a supply of pork and this was now found to be a great mistake. The pork had not a streak of lean; Beaupré and Valad had been ill from the change, and "the Doctor was reduced practically to two meals a day, for he could not stand fat pork three times." For the last meal before the three men turned back "Brown made us a plum cake for tea, and in honour of the occasion, a tin of currant jam that had been put up to be eaten with mutton, if big-horn were shot, was produced. On being opened, it turned out to be only tomatoes, to our great disappointment, but still it was a variety from the routine fare, and relished accordingly."

They had come to the Grand Fork of the Fraser and to Tête Jaune Cache and they looked eagerly toward Mount Robson which Dr. Cheadle had seen so clearly. Gusts of wind "nearly blew away our fires and tents" and rain fell in sharp showers between which "once or twice the sun broke through, revealing the hillsides, all their autumn tints fresh and glistening after the rain, and the line of their summits near, and bold against the sky; all except Robson's peak, which showed its huge shoulders covered with masses of snow, but on whose high head clouds ever rested." The horses were fresh but the going was very heavy and they were glad to find on the Fraser a boat belonging to the railway survey. "Into it were pitched saddles and packs, and we rowed ourselves across while the horses swam."

When they reached the Canoe River, Grant remembered the terrible crossing of Milton and Cheadle. "At the crossing of the Canoe, there was a raft on the other side, but as the river had fallen two feet in the course of the day, we tried the ford and found it quite practicable, —the water not coming much higher than the horses' shoulders; so that the crossing which had so nearly cost Lord Milton and Mrs. Assiniboine their lives did not delay us ten minutes."

Jack and Joe, the new packers, were Canadians, one from New Brunswick, the other from Ontario, and both had been for a long time on the Pacific Coast. They briskly called the Doctor "Doc", talked of "Frisco" and addressed every stranger not as Captain but as "Cap".

They travelled the next day toward the North Thompson down a valley "narrow and closed in at its south-west end by the great mass of Mount Milton which fronted us the whole day. [Mount Milton] is a mass of snow-clad peaks that feed the little Albreda with scores of torrents, ice-cold and green coloured, and make it into a river of considerable magnitude before it flows into the Thompson." Grant was impressed by the enormous trees, the ferns six feet high, a water lily with leaves three feet long. "Everything on the Pacific slope is on a large scale,—the mountains, the timber, the leaves, ferns and the expectations of the people." Unable to reach the Thompson that night, they camped and set out again at 4:30 next morning. The trail was "as bad as well could be, worse than when Milton and Cheadle forced through with their one pack-horse at the rate of three miles a day; for the large Canadian party had immediately preceded them, whereas no one attempted to follow in their steps till McLellan in 1871, and in the intervening nine years much of the

314

trail had been buried out of sight, or hopelessly blocked up by masses of timber, torrents, landslides, or *debris*. Our horses, however, proved equal to the work. Even when their feet entangled in a network of fibrous roots or sank eighteen inches in a mixture of bog and clay, they would make gallant attempts at trotting; and by slipping over rocks, jumping fallen trees, breasting precipitous ascents with a rush, and recklessly dashing down the hills, the eight miles to the crossing of the Thompson were made in three hours."

"Struggling through sombre woods and heavy under-brush, every spray of which discharges its little accumulations of rain on the weary traveller as he passes on, is disheartening and exhausting work. The influence of the rain on men and horses is most depressing. The riders get as fatigued as the horses; for jumping on and off at the bogs, precipices, and boulder slides, thirty or forty times a day, is as tiresome as a circus performance must be to the actors."

They crossed the Thompson and were going on in the rain wet and exhausted when Grant noticed a blazed tree with a piece of paper pinned to it. "In V's Cache There is a box for S. Fleming or M. Smith." V's cache was a small log shanty; Jack unroofed it and jumped in. There were stores for the engineers and a box which Jack broke open with a stone. Candles, canned meats, Worcestershire sauce, jam, six bottles of Bass pale ale. The men all cheered. Part of the treasure was put back for M. Smith. "Four bottles of the ale, a can of the preserved beef, and another of peaches were opened on the spot, and Terry producing bread from the kitchen sack, an impromptu lunch was eaten round the Cache, and V's health drunk as enthusiastically as if he had been the greatest benefactor of his species." They left a note of thanks for V and rode on much more cheerfully.

A little later they heard a bell and met a man walking between two heavily loaded horses. "He turned out to be one John Glen—a miner on his way to prospect for gold on hitherto untried mountains and sand-bars. . . . John Glen calculated that there was as good gold in the mountains as had yet come out of them, and that he might strike a new bar or gulch, that would pan out as richly as Williams Creek, Cariboo; so putting blankets and bacon, flour and frying-pan, shining pickaxe and shovel on his horses, and sticking revolver and knife in his waist, off he started from Kamloops to seek 'fresh fields and pastures new'. Nothing to him was lack of company or of newspapers; short days and approach of winter; seas of mountains and grassless valleys, equally inhospitable; risk of sickness and certainty of storms; slow and exhausting travel through marsh and muskeg, across roaring mountain torrents and miles of fallen timber; lonely days and lonely nights; if he found gold he would be repaid." John Glen brought a letter for Fleming from the Hudson's Bay factor at Kamloops which said that the party's personal baggage had arrived from Toronto by way of San Francisco and would be held for them.

Darkness came early in the narrow Thompson valley and when they camped, Terry found to his horror that the tea-kettle was missing. They had only one other pot which had been used for boiling pork, porridge and everything else. Both frying-pans had lost their handles but Terry had made a stick into a handle for one of them and Joe improvised a kind of pincers to lift the other. "Supper was prepared with these extemporized utensils. The Doctor and Frank fried slap-jacks and then boiled canned goose in the one pan. Terry fried pork in the other; and boiled dried apples in the pot before making the tea in it." At breakfast next morning Jack was gone. He had turned back to look for the lost kettle and about noon he returned with it. He had found it about four miles back and "a cup of tea was at once made in it for him as a reward."

Across the river they saw "a lofty pyramid—with a twin peak a little to the south, and a great shoulder also snow-covered." This was Mount Cheadle and their march the next day showed them another view of the twin peaks "rising stately and beautiful".

"Jack rose this morning at 3 a.m. and made up the fire by kicking the embers together and piling on more wood. In a quarter of an hour after, all hands were up, folding blankets, and packing. We breakfasted by moonlight, and would have been off by five, but two of the horses had wandered and it was some time before they were found. Jack tracked them to an island in the river and had to wade across for them." None of the horses had previously strayed beyond sound of the bell. Jack and Joe had been astonished when they first joined the party to be asked why one of the horses wore a bell. "The bell is hung round the neck of the most willing horse of the

317

pack, and from that moment he takes the lead. Till he moves on, it is almost impossible to force any of the others forward. If you keep back your horse for a mile or two when on the march, and then give him the rein, he dashes on in frantic eagerness to catch up to the rest. Get hold of the bell-horse when you want to start in the morning, and ring the bell and soon all the others in the pack gather round."

The sun rose from behind Mount Cheadle but the air was cold all day and the men dismounted when they could and walked to keep warm. Toward sunset they came to the place near Goose Creek where the bones of Dr. Cheadle's Headless Indian had been found. At the site the Doctor found a board inscribed in pencil: " 'Here lie the remains of the "Headless Indian", discovered by Lord Milton and Dr. Cheadle, A.D. 1863. At this spot we found an old tin kettle, a knife, a spoon, and fishing line; and 150 yards up the bank of the river we also found the skull, which was sought for in vain by the above gentlemen. T Party, C.P.R.S. June 5th, 1872.' Scratching on the ground with his wooden spade the Doctor was soon in possession of the skull and of the rusty scalping knife, that had been thrown in beside it, and finding the old kettle near, he appropriated it too, and deposited all three with his baggage, as triumphantly as if he had rifled an Egyptian tomb."

A body of legend had grown up around the body of the Headless Indian. The men of the survey party who found the head had their own theory. "As the body could not have walked away and sat down minus the head, the explanation of the packers was that the Assiniboine on his unsuccessful hunt for game had killed and eaten the Shuswap, and turned the affair into a mystery by hiding his head. Poor Mr. O'Byrne, of whom we heard enough at Edmonton to prove that his portraiture is faithfully given in *The North-West Passage by Land*, will accept this solution of the mystery if no one else will." An article in a learned journal has apparently quite seriously suggested that Dr. Cheadle carried the head away and hid it in order to mystify the others, an effort, if this were true, in which he certainly succeeded. The Doctor on this occasion suggested "that the man's head had dropped off, and been carried to a distance by the wind or some beast." Terry, the cook, was shocked by the whole affair and could only be reconciled to the Doctor's exhumation of the skull by the plea that it might lead to the discovery of the murderers.

Next morning the whole party rose shivering at 3 a.m. to discover that the temperature was seventeen degrees— "not so very low, but we had been sleeping practically in the open air, and in a cold wind with rather light covering." Terry cooked a porcupine Frank had killed the evening before but no one cared to eat much of it. As they approached the terrifying canyon of the North Thompson which "had all but defeated Milton and Cheadle's utmost efforts", they heard a bell. Fortunately there was room for them to draw back while a long pack-train passed them. "It was on its way up to Tête Jaune Cache with supplies, and consisted of fifty-two mules led by a bell-horse, and driven by four or five men, repre-

senting as many different nationalities. This was the first
train that had ever passed through the canyon without
losing at least one animal. . . . Two months before, a mule
fell over. The packers went down to the riverside to look
for him, but as there was no trace to be seen, resumed
their march. Five days after, another train passing near
the spot heard the braying of a mule, and guided by the
noise looked, and found that he had fallen on a broad
rock half way down, where he had lain for some time
stunned. Struggling to his feet, fortunately for him the
apparaho got entangled round the rock, and held him
fast till he was relieved by the men of the train from his
razor bridge over the flood. This was a more wonderful
deliverance than that of Bucephalus when abandoned by
Mr. O'Byrne."

"For several miles, the river here is one long rapid,
dashing over hidden and half-hidden rocks scattered over
every part of its bed. The great point of danger is reached
at Hell Gate." The party had just passed that raging
tumult when they heard another bell and saw a mule-
train headed by Mr. Smith, engineer on the Pacific side
of the mountains, who was on his way to Tête Jaune
Cache to look for a pass through the Gold range. He
produced a lunch of bread and cheese and the Fleming
party who had not seen cheese for two months ate it with
great avidity. Fleming considered that it was too late
in the year to make the journey and the two parties went
together toward Kamloops. At the end of the canyon
where the river spreads calm and wide and is called Stillwater, they found the tents of two survey parties which

had finished work on their respective sections. Each of the parties was made up of sixteen or eighteen men "so that the valley was alive with men and mules, all busy packing up to start for Kamloops in the morning. . . . We heard for the first time scraps of general election news, the item of most recent interest being the election of Sir Francis Hincks as M.P. for the Vancouver district; but the one that delighted us most being the victory of the Canadian team at Wimbledon in the competition for the Rajah of Kolapore's cup against the eight picked shots of the United Kingdom."

"A mighty supper" followed, beefsteak, bacon, stuffed heart, loaves of bread and "the remains of a plum-pudding with which they had entertained Mr. Smith the day before, seasoned with blueberry jam made by themselves. There was so much to talk and hear about, such a murmur of voices, the pleasant light of so many fires, the prospect of a warm sound sleep, and of more rapid journeying hereafter, that there was nothing wanting to make our happiness complete except letters from home."

One of the packers, "an old Ontarian was diligently perusing the *Toronto Globe* of August 9th; and as it contained the latest news, he kindly presented it to the Chief. The paper was filled with electioneering items; but though we would have preferred a larger infusion of European news, very little was left unread."

As they went on the next day, "the meadow now ceased, and the valley contracted again. We could easily understand the dismay with which Milton and Cheadle beheld such a prospect." Below Mount Cheadle the valley of the Thompson had opened out and at the Great Canyon had closed in narrowly again. Then at Stillwater it had opened as though "about to emerge into an open country of farms and settlements; but again the hills closed in, and the apparently interminable narrow valley recommenced." But Fleming's party knew what to expect as Dr. Cheadle's had not; they were well fed and well mounted, the day was warm and bright. The hills, too, were lower and more broken and late in the afternoon the party came to an open space, Round Prairie, where they were to camp. That night again they read eagerly the two-months-old newspapers.

Next morning they broke camp in heavy rain. "The cotton tent weighs thrice as much as when dry. The ends of the blankets, clothes, some of the food, the shaga-nappi, etc. get wet. The packs are heavier and the horses' backs are wet; and it is always a question whether or not waterproofs do the riders any good." About noon the rain ceased and they stopped for dinner on Pea Vine Prairie where they "saw for the first time the celebrated bunch-grass, which has no superior as feed for horses or cattle; especially for the latter, as the beef that has been fed on it is peculiarly juicy and tender." They camped beside a creek and "Frank who had become quite an adept at constructing camp-fires, built up a mighty one, at which we dried wet clothes and blankets. Our camp presented a lively scene at night. Great fires before each tent lit up the dark forest, and threw gleams of light about, that made the surrounding darkness all the more intense. Through the branches of the pines the stars looked down on groups flitting from tent to tent, or cumbered about the many things that have to be cared for even in the wilderness, cooking, mending, drying, overhauling baggage, piling wood on the fire, planning for the morrow, or taking notes."

The following day brought them to the Clearwater so called because of the contrast of its waters with the clay-filled waters of the Thompson into which it empties. Here there was a survey depot with a three-ton boat in which supplies were brought down from Kamloops. "We said good-bye to Jack and Joe, and gave ourselves up to the sixth lot of men we had journeyed with since leaving Fort Garry, and the fourth variety of locomotion, the faithful Terry still cleaving to the party." The horses' packs were thrown into the boat, the horses themselves were to be brought down along the trail by the guides. Four men were to row the boat; "the oars were clumsy but the men worked with a will, and the current was so strong that the boat moved down at the rate of five or six miles an hour." Just before twilight they went ashore to camp and eat a supper composed of porridge, pork and beans, and more porridge for dessert. This, the last camp before Kamloops, was the sixtieth from the start at Lake Superior.

Except for the small tents of a few Siwash Indians they saw no houses along the river bank till nearly sunset next day when they saw "the first sign of settlers—a fence run across the intervale from the river to the mountain, to hinder the cattle from straying. Between this point and Kamloops there are ten or eleven farms—

323

'ranches' as they are called on the Pacific slope—all of them taken up since Milton and Cheadle's time. The first building was a sawmill about fifteen miles from Kamloops, the proprietor of which was busy sawing boards to roof in his own mill, to begin with. Small log cabins of the new settlers, each with an enclosure for cattle called 'the corral' close to it, next gladdened our eyes, so long unused to seeing any abodes of men."

It was very dark long before they reached Kamloops and none of the crew knew the river so that "we grounded three or four times, but as the boat was flat-bottomed, and the bed of the river hard and gravelly, she was easily shoved off." But at last they saw the waters of the South Thompson into which the north branch runs and reached Fort Kamloops a quarter of a mile below the junction of the rivers. "The agent at once came down, and with a genuine H.B., which is equivalent to a Highland welcome, invited us to take up our quarters with him. Gladly accepting the hospitable offer, we were soon seated in a comfortable room beside a glowing fire. We were at Kamloops; beside a Post Office and a waggon road; and in the adjoining room, the half-dozen heads of families resident in or near Kamloops were holding a meeting with the Provincial Superintendent of Education, to discuss the best means of establishing a school. Surely we had returned to civilization and the ways of men!"

# VII

THOUGH THEY were not as hungry as Dr. Cheadle's party had been, how much they enjoyed breakfast; "mealy potatoes, eggs and other luxuries . . . explained satisfactorily the process by which Dr. Cheadle added forty-one pounds to his weight in three weeks' stay at Kamloops." In fact all members of the Fleming party had gained weight during the two months' journey. The only flaw in their pleasure at returning to "sleep in real beds under a raftered roof" was that there was no mail waiting for them.

Going briskly forward, as usual, the party proceeded by boat and on horseback to Ashcroft to meet the Governor. The country around Ashcroft appeared very dry and, like much of the land they had seen in British Columbia, would need irrigation before it could be farmed. The Doctor was called to set a Chinaman's broken leg and that evening they met Judge O'Reilly who had so effectively kept order among the thousands who had come to the gold-mines of the Kootenay.

Next morning they set off for Lytton by the mail wagon over the remarkable wagon road which had served the Cariboo so well. Now, in 1872, the gold-rush was over though miners were still at work. "These are chiefly Siwash and Chinese, who take up abandoned claims, and wash the sand over again, being satisfied with smaller wages than what contents a white man. None of them dream of going to the wayside hotels and paying a dollar for every meal, a dollar for a bed, a dollar for a bottle of ale, or twenty cents for a drink. The Chinaman cultivates vegetables beside his claim; these and his bag of rice suffice for him, greatly to the indignation of the orthodox miners. The Siwash catches salmon in his scoop net from every eddy of the river, and his wife carries them up to the house and makes his winter's food."

Lytton was "a single row of frail unpainted sheds or log shanties, the littleness and ricketiness of which are all the more striking from the two noble rivers that meet here and the lofty hills that enclose the two valleys. Its population of perhaps a hundred souls is made up of Canadians, British, Yankees, French, Chinamen, Siwash, half-breeds." Though the town looked poor, the hotel proved comfortable and the food good. "The explanation of this contrast, huts in which the tenants live like fighting cocks—is that none of the people came here to stay. They came to make money and then return home; therefore it is not worth their while to build good houses or furnish them expensively; but they can afford to live well."

They went down the Fraser from Lytton to Boston Bar, where sand was still being washed by a few hopeful miners. At Spuzzum's Creek they came to a halt for men were building the bridge and only the stringers had been laid. They were advised to cross on foot and walk the ten miles to Yale. "Several of the huge freight waggons used in British Columbia, each drawn by twelve or sixteen oxen, and fully a hundred pack-mules had come on before us, to cross; but having been told that there was no chance, their drivers had unharnessed or unpacked them, and were idling about." Steve, the stage driver, was not willing to stop. "He offered ten dollars if the men would stop their work and place loose planks across the stringers. The bargain was struck and in an hour the job was done. Steve unharnessed his horses and walked them across, and the men dragged after him not only his waggon, but also the mail coach which by this time had caught up to us." They reached Yale, the head of navigation on the Fraser, before dark and hurried to the post office. Letters and papers were there for every member of the party except Grant, who had to content himself with newspapers lent by the others.

"October 4th. At Yale, we said good-bye to horses. Henceforth steam, the nineteenth century horse, would carry us down the river, along the coast, and across the continent homewards. Canoe and barge, buck-board and cart, saddle and pack-horse, buggy and express waggon belonged to the past of the expedition." The steamer took them to New Westminster where Grant at last got his letters. New Westminster, called Stumpville, with a population of less than a thousand, was the only town on the enormous delta of the Fraser, "a district including much land fit for agriculture, (where) the population and importance of the country and town are sure to

327

increase." But the Fraser delta, Grant wrote, was not promising as the site for a port "because the entrance is intricate on account of the tortuous channel and shifting shoals that extend out for some distance into the Gulf of Georgia. The excellent harbour of Burrard's Inlet, nine miles to the north, will therefore be generally preferred for shipping purposes. This has been already proved to a certain extent. The New Westminster proprietors of a large steam sawmill finding Burrard's Inlet the fitter port for their shipments of lumber, transferred the machinery and set up their mill on the north side of the Inlet; so that now, little or nothing is exported from New Westminster, except fish and cattle from the neighbouring settlements."

That morning they drove "nine miles across the spit of land, on one side of which is New Westminster, to Burrard's Inlet on the other side". They were crossing the site of the future city of Vancouver of which there was as yet no trace. Two years later a few houses at Granville would be granted a post office and the city would make its beginning. They admired, as they drove, the varieties of fern by the way, and then embarked on a tiny steamer to visit the saw-mill on the other side of the Inlet, the first industry to herald the future city. Thirteen million feet of lumber, all Douglas fir, had been exported from there the year before. The workmen were white, Chinese, Siwash Indians and Sandwich Islanders. One of the Indians, Big George, had worked at the mill for years and saved $2000. "Instead of putting this in a savings-bank, he had spent it all on stores for a grand

328

'Potlatch', summoning Siwash from far and near to come, eat, drink, dance, be merry, and receive gifts. Nearly a thousand assembled; the festivities lasted a week; and everyone got something, either a blanket, musket, bag of flour, box of apples, or tea and sugar. When the fun was over, Big George, now penniless, returned to the mill to carry slabs at $20 a month."

Above the beach, covered with chips and sawdust, the workmen lived in little houses perched on the rocks at the foot of the steep wooded hill. The woods were so full of deer that dogs often drove them down to the harbour; the overseer said that "he could shoot a deer any day within two hours."

That evening the party transferred to the steamer *Sir James Douglas* to explore Bute Inlet. This was one of the proposed termini of the railroad. One party urged a terminus on the mainland at New Westminster or Burrard's Inlet. But residents of Victoria, Esquimalt and Alberni argued for a terminus on Vancouver Island, the railroad to cross the Straits of Georgia to Bute Inlet by Valdes Island. Accordingly surveys were being made of both routes. On board the steamer were "the member for New Westminster, a zealous advocate of Burrard's Inlet, and the member for Victoria—a true believer in an Island terminus. To a student of human nature it was amusing to notice with what different eyes each looked at or refused to look at the difficulties of the rival routes. The former gazed exultingly on the high bluffs and unbroken line of mountains, that rose sheer from the waters of Bute Inlet. But his sarcasms were invariably met by a counter reference to the canyons of the Fraser and the Thompson."

While Grant and the others enjoyed the splendour of the scene, "rifts in the mist, as it was broken by projecting peaks, revealed mountain sides curtained with glaciers," Fleming received reports from the survey parties camped along the shore. From Bute Inlet the steamer proceeded through Seymour Narrows where the bridge between Valdes and Vancouver Islands would have to be built if an Island terminus was decided upon. Grant was surprised to find that none of the British Columbia gentlemen on board had ever before gone up Bute Inlet or through the Narrows. The province's "representative men . . . know little beyond their own neighbourhood or the line of their one waggon-road. Distances here are so great, the means of communication so limited, and the mountainous character of the country renders travelling so difficult, that the dwellers in the few towns and settlements have hitherto seen but little of the Province as a whole." This ignorance of the province probably in part accounted for the nature of some of the schemes so airily proposed.

At Nanaimo the party visited the coal-mines; the population of seven or eight hundred all depended on mining. In glorious weather they visited Esquimalt and then Victoria where "one of the first persons we met in the street was Terry. Having no further need of his services, we had parted with him last week at New Westminster. He had gone on to Victoria direct and had monopolized the lionizing intended for the whole party; had been interviewed about our marvellous North-West passage by land, with results as given in the newspapers, that spoke quite as much for Terry's imagination as for his memory. He had conjured up a canyon on the Canoe River twenty miles long, where no canyon is or ever had been; had described us as galloping down the Yellow Head Pass till arrested by the sight of quartz boulders gleaming with gold, and rocks so rich that Brown and Beaupré had deserted to go back and mine; and with many another fact or fancy equally readable, made the hearts of the reporters glad." As a result of his brief notoriety, Terry had "been plundered of every dollar. He was now looking round for work; and before we left Victoria, hired as general servant on board a ship going north." Grant recommended him as "a good servant, a good tailor, a good cobbler, and indeed anything but a good cook, the post which, unfortunately for us, he filled."

Victoria had five thousand people, "Greek fishermen, Kanaka sailors, Jewish and Scottish merchants, Chinese washermen, French, German and Yankee restaurant-keepers, English and Canadian office-holders and butchers, negro waiters and sweeps, Australian farmers."

"In a few years," Grant reflected as he left Victoria, "we shall have a railway with but one break from the Pacific coast to the extreme easterly side of Newfoundland, and thence daily steamers will cross the Atlantic in a hundred hours. Canada will be as near London as Scotland and Ireland were forty years ago. It will be easier to make the journey from Victoria to London than it was to make it from the North of Scotland at the beginning of the century."

"On Saturday morning, October 19th, we breakfasted

at the Lick House, San Francisco. On Saturday the 26th
we breakfasted at home in Ottawa."

Grant closed his account with a summary of the distances he had covered.

| | |
|---|---|
| Distance travelled by railway | 957 miles |
| Distance travelled by horses, including waggons, pack- and saddle-horses | 2,185 miles |
| Distance travelled by steamers on St. Lawrence and Pacific waters | 1,687 miles |
| Distance travelled by canoes and row-boats | 485 miles |
| From Halifax to Victoria, between July 1 and October 11 | 5,314 miles |

Grant's intense enthusiasm for the west never slackened. Some of his prophecies were in part wide of the
mark as that in a chapter of *Picturesque Canada* where
he wrote, in 1882, "Before long Winnipeg will be more
populous than Ottawa, or, its citizens would say, than
Toronto; the Saskatchewan a more important factor in
Canadian development than the St. Lawrence; and the
route from Hudson's Bay to Liverpool perhaps as well
established as the beaten path from Montreal and Quebec."

His prophecy that he "would live to see Manitoba
and the territories export twenty million bushels of wheat"
was derided; yet he lived to see them export fifty-five
million bushels of wheat, and to know that this was but
the foretaste of what a few years would bring.

In 1877 Grant became Principal of Queen's University
at Kingston. Six years later he undertook a second trip
to the west coast. The route by Yellow Head Pass explored

and recommended by Fleming had been rejected for political reasons, but it was followed later by the Canadian Northern and the Grand Trunk Pacific. Sir Sandford Fleming, as he was now, the Chancellor of Queen's University, asked the Principal to go with him on another mountain adventure. Seldom can the Chancellor and Principal of a University, both men in middle age, have embarked on a more arduous journey. They took the train to Calgary; from there the journey through Kicking Horse Pass and down the Illecillewaet was much more difficult than the journey of eleven years earlier.

They were the first party to push their way to the coast by the new route. Though the book about this journey was written not by Grant but by Fleming, Grant wrote a partial account. Of the latter part of the journey down the Illecillewaet, he said, "In all my previous journeyings, other men had been before me, and had left some memorial of their work—a railway, a macadamized or gravelled road, a lane, a trail or at least blazed trees to indicate the direction to be taken. Now we learned what it was to be without benefit of other men's work. Here there was nothing even to guide, save an occasional glimpse of the sun, and the slate-coloured, churned-up torrent, running generally west or south-west, hemmed in by canyons, from which we turned aside only to get mired in beaver dams or alder swamps, or lost in labyrinths of steep ravines, or to stumble over slides of moss-covered rocks that had fallen from over-hanging mountains. It rained almost every day. Every night the thunder rattled over the hills with terrific reverberations, and

333

fierce flashes lit up weirdly tall trees covered with wreaths of moss, and the forms of tired men sleeping by smouldering camp-fires."

Sir Sandford Fleming, who retired from government service in 1880, became a charter member of the Royal Society and one of its early presidents. He served Queen's University as Chancellor for thirty-five years. It was he who encouraged the construction of a cable system linking together the British Empire, and who invented a unified method of time reckoning throughout the world. Like Grant an ardent imperialist he had a hand in governing both the old régime and the new as a director both of the Hudson's Bay Company and the Canadian Pacific Railway.

Principal Grant, also a president of the Royal Society in its early years, was an important builder of the present Queen's University. Not his eagerness alone but all the faith and enthusiasm of a young, hopeful, expanding country illuminate the rhapsody on his journey with which he closed his book *Ocean to Ocean*.

"From the sea-pastures and coal-fields of Nova Scotia and the forests of New Brunswick, almost from historic Louisburg up the St. Lawrence to historic Quebec; through the great Province of Ontario, and on lakes that are really seas; by copper and silver mines so rich as to recall stories of the Arabian Nights, though only the rim of the land has been explored; on the chain of lakes where the Ojibway is at home in his canoe, to the great plains, where the Cree is equally at home on his horse; through the prairie Province of Manitoba, and rolling meadows

334

and park-like country, out of which a dozen Manitobas shall be carved in the next quarter of a century; along the banks of

*A full-fed river winding slow*
*By herds upon an endless plain,*

full-fed from the exhaustless glaciers of the Rocky Mountains, and watering 'the great lone land'; over illimitable coal measures and deep woods; on to the mountains, which open their gates to lead us to the Pacific; down deep gorges filled with mighty timber, and rivers whose ancient deposits are gold beds, sands like those of Pactolus, and channels choked with fish; on to the many harbours of mainland and island; over all this we have travelled, and it is all our own."

335

# INDEX

336

337

339